Hi Kev

Sorry for the late delivery! It was a pleasure meeting with you both and I hope you enjoy the book :)

All the best,
Katie Sutherland

P.S. Sorry you have to share the book but at the rate I give books away I will never make a profit!

by Katie Sutherland

authorHOUSE®

AuthorHouse™
1663 Liberty Drive, Suite 200
Bloomington, IN 47403
www.authorhouse.com
Phone: 1-800-839-8640

This book is a work of non-fiction. Unless otherwise noted, the author and the publisher make no explicit guarantees as to the accuracy of the information contained in this book and in some cases, names of people and places have been altered to protect their privacy.

First published by AuthorHouse 8/27/2008

ISBN: 978-1-4343-5668-0 (e)
ISBN: 978-1-4343-5728-1 (sc)

Library of Congress Control Number: 2008900021

Printed in the United States of America
Bloomington, Indiana

This book is printed on acid-free paper.

Now if you had met me a year ago, you would know my sentiments on middle-aged women. I have to be truthful here: my least favorite age group out there is middle-aged women. This fact alone makes this story that much more interesting. For some reason Cosmos had it in my fate for me to be on the adventure of self-discovery with this particular woman who tested my entire belief system and self.

This tale isn't pretty, fluffy, or anything you would normally chat about at the hair dressers. NO, NO, NO. This quest I embarked on was to retrieve what I hadn't realized I had lost.

Last September, if you had told me that my life would do a complete turn around, changing from its original state, I would have told you that you were mad.

I have spent the past five months of my life living in a van with a woman with whom I can only compare to Charlotte the spider. I am of course referring to the magical creature that changed a naïve pig's life into one of magic and discovery in the book *Charlotte's Web*. Through unwavering devotion and strength, the spider showed the pig that beauty is cultivated from within and that even one animal's belief in another is enough to move mountains. The following story is how one woman saved my life in more ways than I can ever describe.

I met Jude in the rainy city of Vancouver. We had both been attending a holistic workshop and felt an instant connection between the two of us. Her teachings of spirituality and living a humble life intrigued parts of my soul I had forgotten about. Within a single month, Jude had become my closest friend. After several weeks of our work shops, Jude decided she no longer wanted to participate. I was devastated. Although she told me that we would stay in touch I felt betrayed that she had left.

A few weeks later, I found myself magnetically drawn to the Vancouver Public Library. As I maneuvered my way through the rainy dark streets of Vancouver, I began contemplating my life. Here I was, a mid twenty year old girl trying to find my way. The first five years of my twenties had lead me to many dead ends and it was beginning to feel the same in Vancouver. I had finally met someone who truly understood me and she had disappeared from my life.

Jumping over a mud puddle, I found myself staring up at the grand old building containing wisdom in written form. Still unsure has to why I needed to be at the library; I rode up the elevator to the third floor and sat down to prepare to write in my journal. After five minutes of pouring my heart out, I felt the undeniable urge to look up. Tilting my head forward I found myself looking directly at Jude. GADZOOKS!!

As though in slow motion, Jude stood up from her computer station, walked towards me. Starring right into my eye, she said "Kiddo, you look terrible! What are you doing here?"

Feeling like this encounter was surreal I struggled to utter a response. Clearing my throat loudly, I finally mustered, "Oh, Jude. I don't know what I am doing anymore! I feel so lost right now, and nothing seems to be working out." Searching her face for understanding, I sat there awaiting a response.

Inhaling deeply, Jude paused before she answered "Katie, the most important rule of the universe is: you can't force anything and you must pay attention. Your meant to be working with children, but aren't doing it that is why you are feeling lost." With that she sat down at my desk.

It was at that magical moment life as it would never be the same. Destiny, faint and universal forces had all scheme together brought this wise woman back into my life. Jude and I spent the entire day together, walking the streets of Vancouver and furthering my spiritual knowledge. From that point forward, my thirst for knowledge was quenched through our precious meetings.

"If you believe you will achieve." Those were the first words Jude spoke to me while describing spirituality. She spoke about having a belief system, which is the basement of the house, and if it is strong, your structure can't be rocked by anyone except yourself, if you self-sabotage. She also so taught me to cleanse my aura nightly and encouraged the use of my sixth sense. We are all born with a predisposition to intuition, but if we don't use it, we lose it. (Basically, it can be awakened, but a strong work ethic is needed.)

The tale begins during Christmastime, a seemingly jolly time. Yet for me, life was rapidly unwinding. To mix things up, my mother had decided that Christmas was to be spent at my place in Vancouver, and that is where the beginning of my awakening took place.

My parents sailed over on the twenty-fourth of December and were greeted to one stressed out chick. Having just finished at the school, working two jobs and discovering my spiritual awareness, it's a fair bet to say I was one tired, stressed-out lady.

Mom's idealistic and somewhat delusional ideas about "the perfect family Christmas" (can anyone say oxymoron?) dissipated as my extremely cranky mood shifted around us like silent toxic gasses from your best friend's little brother. Christmas day brought with it yet more tension. Sleeplessness left me feeling grumpy, irritable, and not very jolly. Humbug indeed!

Around 10:00 a.m. I went to pick up Jude from her place. Seeing how she had became such an icon in my world, I really wanted my mom and Dad to meet her and perhaps enjoy some of her truthful ways. The minute she walked in the door, the energy in the room shifted. My mom eyed her wearily as Jude waltzed into the room, ready to share the day with us. It felt like two different worlds colliding as I witnessed the interaction between the three most important people in my world.

The interaction was surreal as my extremely quiet parents met my very verbal friend Jude. Although I don't regret this day, it remains with me as a turning point, for it was a day of so much clarity. As I silently surveyed the scene, it finally dawned on me that the relationship my parents had for twenty-six years was living in delusion, not admitting to certain truths, and most of all, just existing together. I asked myself how they lost their togetherness. I accredited my clarity to Jude's teaching of self-love and spirituality before entering into a relationship.

What I saw that morning devastated me as I watched my mom and dad interact like I had seen too many times before. But this

3

time I was able to feel my dad's sadness and suppression of emotion from years of not properly communicating. Glancing at my mom, I saw her silent control over the scene and was bewildered by her controlling behavior.

Later on that afternoon, Jude and my parents went for a walk while I stayed at home, dwelling on the reality of my parents' relationship. It really saddened me and my feelings of unhappiness deepened.

Once the troops arrived back from their walk, I drove Jude home and we discussed her first impressions of my parents. Jude explained to me that they both felt very proud of me but also wondered why I moved around so much.

Arriving back home to my apartment, I walked in to find a typical mom-and-dad scenario. They both were reading silently. I'm not sure if it was my sadness, burnout, or a combination of the two, but I felt terrible and retreated back to my room to read about fairies.

Halfway to my room, I heard my mom calling out that my mood had destroyed the day and saying that they were leaving. *Fabulous news,* I thought, as my mood sunk to an all-time low. Sitting down on my bed, I began to cry. Because my dad and I are so close he wandered over to see if I was all right. The instant he gave me a hug, my tears wouldn't stop as I felt guilt for having ruined a day my mother had so greatly anticipated. True to form, Mom stayed in the living room, while my dad was the one to pick up the pieces. As my dad left to get some fresh air, my mom sat in stony silence in the living room. As more tears flowed from me, I made my way to the bathroom to wash some clean water over my tearstained face, "Do you want a hug?" my mom called out from the living room. These were words I had heard my entire life. But all of a sudden it felt as though I was hearing them for the first time. Since when does a mother have to ask a child's permission to give it the purest form of love? As I turned down her offer, my anger again mounted as I asked my mom why she had asked me when actions were more what I needed and wanted. **ALL I WANTED WAS JUST A HUG WITHOUT A THOUGHT PROCESS!** I felt huge walls up between the two of us and retreated back to my room.

That day remains significant for it was the day I finally saw my parents for what they were: my equals, with issues of their own who needed help and compassion. How were they to realize they were perpetuating the vicious cycle of predisposed genetic behaviors? By remaining silent and not properly communicating with each other, they were buying into what had been taught to them years ago by their parents. All too often I have used the excuse that my parents operate in a certain manner and therefore I did too, until I met Jude!

One of her teachings is that we all have choices in our lives and we can either buy into what is dictated to us or choose to change behaviors we don't like in ourselves or family members. For me this is called **breaking the mold**. By choosing to change our behavior patterns, we in turn break that nasty genetic cycle that tells us we will end up exactly like our parents. Jude says that if the learner has learned, then the teacher has taught.

On a spiritual level, I can explain that information as such: When our souls return back to physical form, we choose the families we are born into and continue on with lessons we didn't learn in previous lifetimes. Hence our souls remain the same but our minds and behavior patterns are shaped through our families and loved ones. To simplify, at any given point, we all have the freedom to decide whether to listen and live through our souls or ignore our essence and allow circumstances we were born into to dictate our future.

Several days after Christmas, I grew lonely after, yet again, another attempt at dating went down the toilet. Repeating old patterns, I began reminiscing about my first love, Stephen, and our relationship in the past.

It had been two and a half years since we had been together, but I had placed the relationship on such a pedestal that I was sabotaging any other opportunities that came my way. I spent five days daydreaming about Stephen while he was traveling in South America. Instead of communicating my feelings towards him, I decided to internalize them out of fear of ruining his trip. I knew he was on a spiritual quest himself, and disclosing my undying love for him would most definitely change his course.

It was December 31, when I received an e-mail exclaiming his gratitude that we were friends. Although the email was sent as a friendly gesture, I read between the lines and sensed that he had moved on from our hot and cold relationship. I felt as though someone had taken the world's biggest hammer and smashed it down on my heart, leaving pieces everywhere.

The New Year brought with it the crabbiest of hermits as I went further into myself. During this dark time, I began reading more on spirituality and came across a book that spoke of light workers. Light workers are extra sensitive people who feel they have been placed on earth to serve humanity on a global level. As I fumbled through the pages of the book, bumps instantly appeared all over my body. This book sounded like me! I felt my spirits lift as I read more and came to the understanding that I wasn't the only person who grieved deeply for the world. Now I had come to understand that I needed to save me, not the world. My dark mood in January had been a physical manifestation of years of suppressing my words and denying my own emotions.

A week after my insight into light workers, questions popped into my head as I stewed over my next move along my spiritual path.

conversations with the universe

During January I was walking daily to receive universal messages and clarity. One particular morning I awoke feeling powerfully drawn outside. Lacing up my sneakers, I ventured out into the fresh, winter air.

Listening to a meditation CD, I allowed the tranquil vibes to filter into my body. Several minutes into the album, I had my awakening. Midway through my favorite song, I looked up to see clouds parting and streams of sunlight illuminating my head. The distinctive words "Get to work, light worker" boomed down upon me. "WHAT!" Frantically looking around my surroundings, I checked to see if anyone was around me. It was in that moment that I realized I had heard exactly what I needed to do!

Instantly I was overcome with emotion and tears started flowing out of me.

♥   ♥   ♥

Later that day I instinctively picked up the phone and called Jude. As I disclosed to her what I had experienced that morning, I could hear her smiling through the electrical currents. "Katie, I have known this all along but being the way you are, you needed to hear it for yourself. Just keep being you, but pay more attention to your surroundings and watch for signs. The universe works in magical ways, and now that you have been awakened, events are going to occur at a very rapid pace."

Hanging up the phone, I felt better after having spoken to Jude.

As I got ready to go waitress that evening, I played the day over and over in my mind. Amid the chatter and noises of a crowded restaurant, I drifted through that night, oblivious to any strife or tension, having been skyrocketed to a new level of consciousness.

My frustration came when I tried explaining this incredible phenomenon to my friends. This led me to feel isolated and alone, unable to relate to them my new belief system.

My meetings with Jude became more frequent as the winter darkened and heavy snowfalls surrounded us. Our lessons became more intense as she began challenging me and questioning my actions. As our bond deepened, I began reassessing my current friendship and realized I had been pouring way too much energy into one-sided relationships. Sound familiar, ladies?

And so began the hardest winter lesson, the art of saying no (and staying **FIRM**).

My first **NO** experience was with a fairly new girl I had met at the college. Though she had a beautiful spirit, she had many fears and created excuses for herself that I felt were a copout. Though I never saw her temper, I felt it.

One particular day I had made plans with her despite having no energy. As I sat in my apartment, dreading our date, Jude's voice echoed through my mind: "Why are you meeting Nomes if you don't feel like it? Are you being true to yourself, Katie? Hmm, are you?"

No, no I'm not, I thought as I phoned Nomes to cancel. Though she said she understood, I knew deep down she was angry and felt let down. As I hung up the phone, I felt a huge relief despite feelings of guilt. This day marked a new beginning as I vowed to assert myself and speak the truth.

The last week of January, I received an e-mail from an old girlfriend of mine. She was working at a heli-ski lodge in Blue River and put out an invitation to go to work there for the winter. The adventuress in me jumped for joy, while the conservative side hesitated.

I headed over to Jude's apartment to discuss my plans. Unsure of how she was going to react, I was nervous. Why? Because her opinion meant a lot to me.

Much to my surprise, Jude encouraged my decision and asked me to feel it out. The support she gave me made my decision easier. The next hurdle was finding someone to rent my place.

The following morning I went to a Kundalini yoga class to meditate. Stretching out on the mat, I closed my eyes and visualized a renter for my apartment. Leaving the class, I felt grounded and knew that I needed to go snowboarding at Cypress Mountain.

Driving up that afternoon, I was excited at the prospect of being outdoors and manifesting a renter. One of my part-time jobs that winter had been serving in that pub. Needing to check my schedule, I walked through the pub and ran into a regular customer.

"Hey, Mark! How's is going?"

Looking up from his beer, he responded, "Not much, just enjoying my day off in the sun."

"Cool. I'm on days off too. We should go for a few runs."

"Sounds good. Let's go!"

♥   ♥   ♥

Faces fresh from the winter air, we headed in after a few hours of blissful riding. Knowing that Mark had a lot of contacts, I asked him, "Do you know of anyone needing an apartment?"

As he lifted his beer glass, he responded, "Actually, I could use a place to study for the next few months."

Sensing he liked me, I took full advantage of the situation.

"Great! My rent is $650 a month and I would be willing to split the payment with you."

Nodding his head, "Sounds good. I will come over later tonight," he replied.

♥   ♥   ♥

That evening Mark came by to check out my apartment. After agreeing to sublet it, he lingered around and watched TV. I knew that I had him due to my manipulative womanly ways. HAHAHAHAHA! Oh wasn't I evil? Little did I know that it would bite me in the bottom.

♥   ♥   ♥

Departure day, I met with Miss Jude at Granville Island for our goodbyes. (Jude always says it is a hello, never goodbye.) As I shyly handed over a card I had for her, I felt sadness. I knew I was only going away for a few months, but she had made such a profound effect on my life. Among the coffee beans and iced mochas, we sat for several hours as she dished out recommendations on how to keep up my spirituality. "Now, don't forget to":
❖ Cleanse your aura every day
   ♦ Visualize yourself lying on your bed. Take a conductors wand. There is a white light on the top of it. You trace the outline of your body with the wand to cleanse your aura.
❖ Detach from people
   ♦ At night visualize one big thread of people that you come in contact with during the day. Image a pair of giant gold scissors and cut the thread.
❖ Visualization
   ♦ Meditate and imagine what you want to transpire in your world
I nodded as we hugged in the crowded parking lot. As I pulled away and watched Jude's blue coat fade into the spectrum of colors, I began to cry.

Leaving Vancouver, I instantly felt relief as the four lanes of city traffic merged into one lonely rural lane. Worries of saving the world, ex-boyfriends, and energy-sucking friends all drifted away as I grooved to soul music on my radio. About halfway to the lodge, I stopped to breath in fresh, clean air and made a wish into the universe. As I stared up into the magical night sky, the full moon gleamed down on my face and illuminated my spirit. I wished to be a children's author and get kids back into their imaginations, I silently explained to the infinite power above. I felt an overwhelming calmness settle into my core as I drove into the starry night. Later that night, I made a quick call to Jude to tell her that I had hit a snowstorm. She calmed me down immediately with her words of confidence that I would arrive safe and secure, in one piece.

Cool, clean air hit my nasal passages as I stepped out into the winter wonderland called Blue River. Though I wanted to stay and explore the small village, I knew my boss was anxiously awaiting my arrival. She had expected me the night before, and by the tone of her voice I could tell she wanted me at the Albreda Lodge on the ASAP. I mentally prepared myself for my new experience as I drove out of Blue River toward Albreda. The lodge was located in the heart of the back-country mountains and was a bit off the beaten track. Reaching the front parking lot, I looked up to fully appreciate the lodge in all its grandeur.

It was magnificent, towering over me with huge beams of cedar and stonewalls. Despite its incredible presence, I felt shivers up my spine as I walked forward to the front door.

♥　　　　　　　　♥　　　　　　　　♥

After a brief introduction and hug from my friend Peggy, a daily routine was quickly established. The job itself wasn't hard, but the living situation soon grew unbearable. In order to save money, I had agreed to share accommodations with Peggy. Unknown to me at the time, our schedules and personalities were opposites, and after three days, I began again questioning the setup. My tension grew as I silently stewed in my new living situation.

Picture this if you will:
One small room, two double beds and one small bathroom. Draw an invisible line down the room. On one side you have bright vibrate clothes thrown every where, jewelry, makeup, and snow board gear in every imaginable corner. On the other side, three rocks, four books on spirituality and some candles. Very different worlds colliding. The straw that broke the camel's back was the nude women's calendar that had managed to find itself on my side of the room. On the third day

of it starring at me, I finally ripped it down, and moved it on Peggy's side. Mature eh!

For the next few days, the energy in the room grew very tense has we both tried to adjust to each other. The second week at the lodge, I noticed that the schedule was very disorganized and illogical. Having a back ground in management, I took it upon myself to rewrite a different schedule and present it to Peggy. Wrong move! Feeling undermined by my offerings, Peggy grew insulted and confronted me.

"What is going on with you? Why do you feel as though you are better than I am? I realize that you have been in management before, but I don't need your help. Also, I don't like having my belongings moved without my permission. Do you have a problem with the fact that I am bisexual?"

Unaware of her sexual orientation, I responded, "Peggy, I didn't mean to insult you, nor did I know that you were bisexual. I don't have any problems with your sexual nature. And in terms of the schedule, I honestly just wanted to help."

Not being used to confrontation, I admired Peggy's honest and direct way of asserting herself.

♥   ♥   ♥

I e-mailed Jude to check in with her and see how life in Vancouver was. After feeling lonely and having a confrontation with Peggy, I needed support now. I wrote about the incident and felt better knowing someone that I respected would understand.

After writing my dear friend, I grabbed a pair snowshoes. The only time I was finding comfort seemed to be when I was alone with nature. About a half an hour into my travels, I came across a stream. The water flowed effortlessly underneath the snow bank, and it had the most calming effect. Little footprints informed me I wasn't the only one to appreciate nature. Three little birds perched on a nearby branch, looking down, nodding their approval. This quickly became my favorite spot when lodge life got too frantic.

As the weeks wore on, I began chatting with the clients and requesting their opinions of what I should do with my life.

It's funny to think about how many other people's perspectives I chased after; in reality the answers were all within me. I have since discovered you have to save yourself first, but try explaining that to the stubborn goat in February.

Halfway through February I began missing Jude and wishing she was with me. We had remained in close contact through e-mail, but I really missed her presence. In her last e-mail, she mentioned her living situation, which seemed to be getting a bit tiring. She was living with a smoking nurse who was very over-protective of Jude. It was at this point that we started planning creative ways to get her a job at the lodge. I began pestering my Swiss boss Alex daily, pointing out that the staff were all burned out and really needed extra assistance. In true Alex fashion, she would ignore my feedback, claiming that the staff was just fine and saying that in Switzerland they would operate with half the staff we had. But I refused to give up. I used visualization with the power of intention. Every night before I went to sleep, I began imagining Jude at the lodge and her being my roommate. After breathing in the crisp mountain air, I would find the brightest star and wish on it, "Please let Jude come up to the lodge". I knew she was such an important person in my mission to help save myself. Her teachings of spirituality and positive energy were infectious. I knew the lodge needed some of her magic, and I got my wish.

One week later, Alex pulled me into her office.

"Katie," she said with her questioning voice. "Do you think your friend Judy would still be interested in working here?" she enquired with her icy blue eyes staring through me.

"But of course," I replied and immediately handed over Jude's contact information. By the end of the day Jude was hired and was due to head north within the week. I was floored. "Hip, hip, hooray!" I chanted as my irritations with arrogant customers dissipated. My anticipation grew stronger for the day when we would met up once again.

A few days before Jude arrived, I had my first encounter with Beetle Juice. I had arrived at work at exactly 5:55 a.m. as usual and had begun my early-morning setup. "Bananas, raisins, cereal," I repeated to myself as I drifted into the mindless monotony of the morning breakfast preparation. I was just in the middle of a spectacular vision of Johnny Depp, when a voice interrupted my bliss.

"Hey, you look pretty tired this morning." Startled, I jumped up and glanced around the dark breakfast room. Up at the counter sat a rugged man in his forties slumped over his cup of coffee. He was one of the guides I hadn't been introduced to. As I turned to see the man who had made me jump, the following words tumbled out of my mouth before I could stop them: "Oh yeah, well, you look like Beetlejuice." Grimacing at me, he cocked his head to one side, as animals do when encountering strange creatures in the wild. He had met someone who didn't believe that ski guides were god's gift to women. "Well, I can't say anyone has ever called me that before," he responded.

"I meant it in a good way," I responded, feeling a bit remorseful at the obvious insulting comment I had made. He grunted a response and went back to his cup of coffee. *Ah, great start to the morn,* I thought as I peeked into the kitchen to test out cook's mood for the day. *Calm with mild undertones,* I noted and went about the usual breakfast duties.

♥   ♥   ♥

During my experiences at the lodge, I began training on the treadmill to keep myself in shape. Also, not having Jude around, I needed to challenge myself somehow. It was on Mister Treadie that I would receive many answers to my questions. Quite often the spirit of my grandfather would visit and encourage me to keep pushing myself. Throughout my life, I have always felt his presence, and since I had embarked upon my spiritual journey, he was coming to me more often: yet another affirmation that I was on the right track.

As the days wore on, I saw many wealthy folk come in and out of the lodge. Due to my own feelings of judgment, I felt anger toward them. They all floated into the lodge with mounds of money, and I assumed that they didn't give back. My assumption was based on my own stuff. Isn't that silly?

♥   ♥   ♥

The morning that Jude arrived, I was super excited. All the girls looked at me as though I had lost my marbles, but I didn't care. I told Beetlejuice about my excitement and managed to get him to raise his eyebrows, which was quite a feat first thing in the morning. "Is she hot?" was the commonly asked question from the godly ski guides and slimy kitchen staff. "Of course she is," I responded. "Hotter than you will ever know!"

Around 3:00 p.m. the head housekeeper, Marnie and I hopped in Cassidy, my green minivan to go pick Jude up from the closest town. I didn't realize my excitement till I saw the flashing lights and heard Marnie saying, "Dude, you were just going 120 kilometers in a 90km zone." Apparently my excitement had channeled itself into my foot, and I sheepishly prepared myself for the encounter with authority. "Good afternoon, officer," I called out in the sweetest voice I could muster. "Afternoon, do you realize how fast you were going?" he responded in a booming voice.

"I sure do. I'm just really excited to get to Blue River, okay!"

He raised one eyebrow while trying not to laugh, "Well, unfortunately going over the speed limit is not allowed. I'm going to have to give you a ticket."

Expecting to hear that answer, I nodded and accepted his words. "I understand, I would give me a ticket too if I were you."

As he was filling out the paperwork in his car, a big redneck truck went flying past us, going way faster than 120. Annoyed, he made his way back, and I made a note to remind him of this complete injustice I had witnessed. Once he made his way back to Cassidy, I looked up innocently and stated, "Officer, he was driving much faster than I had been." Smiling, he shook his head and handed me the ticket. I informed the officer that I would be disputing it in court and turned my van back on. He smiled and walked away...

Once Marnie and I had arrived in Blue River, we found the bus depot and settled in for a snack. Jude's bus was due in at 4:00 p.m., but because of big snow drifts that day, the old Greyhound was running late. We ordered some french fries and gossiped about our roommates while we waited for what seemed like years.

Arriving into the station, the bus sounded its horn as it pulled in. Jumping from my chair, I raced outside to greet my dear friend.

Oblivious to the freezing snow outside, I shuffled my weight from side to side in anticipation. The doors slowly opened and I searched to see Jude's familiar blue coat. First off was a man in his thirties, handle bar moustache and missing teeth. I silently hoped he had not bothered Jude on the bus. Next was a lady with her child, and based on the expression on her face, it had been a long ride since Vancouver. Next down the stairs was a teenage boy who wore a trench coat and looked angrily at the snow. My heart began to sink. Maybe Judy Pants (which was what I also called Jude) missed the bus. My head began to race with negative thoughts. Maybe she decided not to come after all. Maybe she got off in Kamloops and joined the circus. Maybes filled my mind as I silently allowed my imagination to run wild.

Just before I had decided that Jude was a goner, I saw a flash of blue from the corner of my eye. Slowly looking up, I saw my favorite little lady make her way down the staircase, looking very similar to Mary Poppins.

My heart sang as I realized that someone was willing to come all the way to Blue River and support me. Jude had taken a risk by engaging in this act of kindness. Because of her intuition, she knew that our journey together was just beginning and was willing to jump in.

I called out, "Welcome to Blue River, little buddy," once she reached the ground. She gave me one of her famous bear hugs that seemed to last five minutes.

"You've lost weight" were the first words from her lips as I walked into the diner to meet Marnie. All sorts of emotions were jumping in my body. I felt excited that I could share my crazy heli-lodge adventures with somebody who understood me. I was nervous that she would continue to challenge me on a spiritual level and relieved that a woman I cared so deeply had cleared her entire life in order to come support me. As mentioned earlier, I had spent the previous twenty-six years of my life looking after others, so having someone truly care for me was so magical words couldn't describe my gratitude.

Standing up to greet Jude, Marnie looked at her somewhat in disbelief. "I didn't realize you were older," she claimed we all munched on our french fries.

"Yes, I am," Jude responded in her motherly yet firm tone and began explaining her adventures on the bus. She explained about leaving her tense landlady and competitive coworkers and the feelings of relief after pulling out of Vancouver that morning. After we finished our greasy snack, we packed Jude's belongings into Cassidy. As we drove toward the lodge, I felt an instant energy surge as we car-danced to Madonna. Sensing some jealously from Marnie in the backseat, I tried including her in our excitement as she witnessed the unique friendship Jude and I shared. This wouldn't be the last time someone found our relationship odd.

Once we arrived at the lodge, I quickly gave Jude the tour and introduced her to the staff. By the time she had met everyone and got a feel for the place, it was time to go to bed. After our three-hour chat session, I laid in bed counting my blessings that this had happened. I was still unsure why we had been put together. But my growing faith in spirituality informed me there were great things that awaited.

♥   ♥   ♥

Rising at 5:30 a.m., Jude and I shimmied our way to work the following morning. The reason I say "shimmy" is because, due to the maintenance man's laziness, our path to work was covered in ice, making the already unpleasant walk even more unbearable.

Arriving at work unscathed, I introduced Jude to Beetle Juice, who had since accepted his name. He politely shook her hand and returned to his morning bowl of coffee. I noticed two new guys sitting at the counter. They introduced themselves as Brook and Geoff; both dudes were in their thirties. I thought Geoff was cute, but I also sensed he was a player.

Jude informed me that she would be calling Brook "Babbling Brook," and Geoff she called "Sir Geoff." How appropriate. How interesting that she would touch on how he was very into his ego.

Peeking in the kitchen this morning, I saw that Josie the morning cook seemed tolerable, and I sighed with relief, knowing Jude's first day would be good.

After breakfast Alex swooped down to breathe over Jude's neck while she worked in the kitchen. Once Alex determined that Jude was a good worker, she resumed her daily condescending pep talks with me. I found her overall Swiss demeanor very controlling and belittling. Still not having found courage with my words, I suppressed my true feelings, which caused me to feel resentment toward her. Also having a defiant nature, I instantly felt defensive whenever she spoke.

"Katie, good morning! I see your friend, Judy, is settling right in." Annoyed by the interruption to my silver polishing routine, I slowly looked up.

"Yup!" I chirped shortly, hoping she would get the hint and leave me alone.

"Now, about the dining room, Katie, I must remind you we are a five-star resort. Have I told you how much guests spend here in a week?"

Yes, only a million times, I thought to myself as I pretended to nod my agreement to Alex.

Satisfied with our chat, Alex spun around grabbed a Red Bull (at 8:10 a.m., I might add) and retreated back to her office. I silently exhaled and resumed my silver polishing. Besides cookie baking, it had become my favorite part of the day. It was the only time I got to crank my favorite tunes (normally Bryan Adams) and rock out all by myself. It was those times when I would also get my best inspirations on world-saving tactics. Armed with the knowledge I could achieve whatever I put my mind to; thousands of great plans would fly at me as I would rock out. As I was polishing in the empty dining room, these were a few of my many thoughts: *Ambassador for the UN seems to be working out in Angelina's favor. Human rights lawyer?* Since meeting Jude I was learning to stand my ground and assert myself a lot more. *Doctor? Hmm, maybe not. Don't really enjoy the sight of blood too much. Maybe I'll just pass on that.*

♥   ♥   ♥

As we trekked through the freshly fallen snow and inhaled the crisp afternoon air, Jude and I resumed our regular chats on any topic from past lives to men. Walking deeper and deeper into the woods, I felt my insides churning as Jude skillfully pushed my oversensitive buttons.

"Katie, you haven't come very far since you left Vancouver. I know you have been meditating, but you are still caretaking. If you were truly in your own power, what the other staff members are doing wouldn't bother you." Instantly frustrated by her words, my walls went up. I still didn't understand that part of myself.

She continued, "Katie, though I can see you have been working hard on your spiritual awareness, you are still not using your words."

Feeling attacked and defensive, I instantly jumped to defend myself. "I don't know what you are talking about." I replied, "I have been meditating every day, documenting my dreams, and avoiding gossip sessions with the girls." Patiently she waited while I was bumbling and made up several excuses to explain my lack of communication skills.

"You still haven't enlightened me as to why you remain silent while you watch them behave in ways you don't agree with. In order to live in the moment and not carry resentment, you must speak your words. Always remember, speak them with love and compassion."

Though I knew her words were true, my feelings stung as I sulked down the chilly forest trail. It felt so strange to have a close friend challenge me. My friendships in the past had generally involved drinking together, discussing depressing love lives, and planning the next weekend. Now, don't get me wrong! I do adore my girlfriends; it's just that none of them have ever challenged me on my belief system and opinions.

Back in Vancouver, when Jude still challenged me, I would storm off and mull over her words for several days. After several days of analyzing what had transpired, I would phone her and apologize for my behaviors humbly with my tail between my legs.

Every day would bring a new challenge as she pushed me more and more.

"Why don't you like Americans?" she asked one morning as I was raving about our Southern neighbors.

"I just don't," I replied. Ten seconds later I realized how silly I sounded. "Geez, do I always sound like that?"

"Only when you can't back up your opinion up with anything," she responded back through the swinging kitchen doors. Gritting my teeth, I took another bite of humble pie and resolved to rethink several of my opinions. Admittedly a great majority of my opinions stemmed from friends and family, not my own experiences or judgments.

♥   ♥   ♥

Later that afternoon Jude and I decided to bake cookies while Josie wasn't around. It was always a risk due to Josie's mood swings, but my cravings for soft melted delectable goo gave me a new sense of courage as we forged around the kitchen for ingredients. Quickly whipping up the wet ingredients, I was halfway there when from the back door, in walked Josie. *Uh oh, here comes trouble,* I thought to myself as I avoided eye contact and continued my baking.

Not even looking my way, the queen of the grumps turned to the head cook and hissed, "We are already so low on vanilla. Are you going to let her get away with that?" Obviously hearing her spiteful words, I sarcastically answered back, "Don't worry, Josie, I will buy you some new vanilla."

Although I had made light of it, my whole body tensed up as we quickly finished our cookies and fled the scene. Hours after the nasty cookie encounter, it still bothered me. Why did this girl have so much hostility and anger?

Unknown to me, I had the same anger issue but kept it inside.

♥   ♥   ♥

The following morning I was greeted with a stone-cold silence while Josie violently flipped pancakes in a menacing way. "Ah, another great start." Mindlessly I began brewing coffee for the morning skiers and tried to think positively. Noticing my body language, Jude asked, "Why do you give your power up so quickly? What is it about Josie that intimidates you?" Growing huffy, I slipped into a self-pity mood and wondered what I had done to be picked on so much. Remembering Jude's motto of "I ask because I care," I grumpily began serving breakfast.

♥   ♥   ♥

Returning to work at 4:00 p.m., I noticed there were more than the usual amount of people around. The lodge only had accommodations for twenty people, so any extra bodies were instantly noticed. After asking Alex's husband Arman about it, I found out that the general manager, Olf, and several ski guides had come up to dine at our lodge for the evening. Upon meeting Olf, I instantly felt bad vibes. His eyes were sky blue and he towered over me at six foot three. He was also from Switzerland and his voice was one that sounded monotone yet threatening at the same time.

I attempted to make small talk with him in hopes that he would soon leave. Eventually, after he had gathered the necessary information from me, he left my part of the bar. Although he wasn't interrogating me, I could still feel his stone-cold eyes watching my every move. As I poured martinis and margaritas, I looked straight into another pair of blue eyes. These ones weren't cold though no, these eyes belonged to a guide whose picture I had seen but had yet to meet in person. As we said our hellos, I had a feeling there was something different about him. Contrary to all the other guides I had met, he seemed very quiet and comfortable in his skin. There seemed to be a familiarity about him, as though I had known him in a different lifetime. After pouring him a pint of honey lager, I asked him if he believed in magic. Now, before you think of me as the most ridiculous, cheesy cat out there, hear me out. I had recently been reading a lot about magic and was curious to see if he was interested in similar subjects.

"But of course," he answered with a certain quirkiness that made me smile.

"Cool, then we can be friends," I replied as we began chatting about spirituality and life. Just as I was about to dive into my theories on the spiritual movie "The Secret," I remembered that Olf was watching my every move. I quickly cut our conversation short and told my new friend Crosby to have a chat with Jude if he wanted to meet someone cool.

♥   ♥   ♥

As closing time was approaching, I noticed that my new friend Crosby was still lingering around. "Can I help you with something, Mister Crosby?" I called out from behind the bar.

"Nope, I just wanted to check in and hang out with you some more."

Having forgotten that male attention made me nervous, I giggled and stumbled for something, anything cool to say. Nervousness held me frozen in space after his comment. I blurted out, "I'm going to be another twenty minutes; you can hang out till then if you want." So began the saga of Mr. Crosby and myself.

Stepping outside into the cool, chilly night, we began sharing our ideas on helping humanity and the deeper things in life. I told Crosby about my world-saving plans as he told me his frustrations as a ski guide. He had been guiding for almost five years, and he was growing anxious, as the job didn't seem to stimulate him anymore. I understood this completely. Prior to my spiritual awakening, I had always bounced from job to job, never looking for a deeper meaning. I had always worked with people but hadn't been awakened to the true meaningful things in life. Since the fall my outlook had changed; activities and friendships that used to interest me seemed to be quite minor in comparison to the more important issues in my world. As we continued to chat, our quick walk turned into two hours. Our souls seemed to dance and enjoy one another's company.

We made plans to go ski-doing two days later on one condition: Jude had to come. Cocking his head to his side, Crosby agreed, though I'm sure he found it strange.

Being that I am an extremely private person, Jude was the only one I told about my walk with Crosby. Although there had been no monkey business between Crosby and myself, I didn't really want to add to the already raging gossip fest that is a given in any ski lodge or restaurant setting.

Naturally Marnie questioned me in the morning on why Crosby had been sighted on the property the previous night. Playing ignorant, I shrugged my shoulders and drifted into the kitchen to finish my peanut butter and jam toast. I absolutely loved not telling Marnie the fresh gossip as I smugly crunched my breakfast. As I chatted with

Jude about Crosby, I told her about our plans to go ski-doing with him the next day. Silently she raised her eyebrows and consented.

The next morning, Crosby called us with some rather unfortunate news. Due to the heavy snowfall over the last few days, our epic plans to take on the world via ski-do were a no-go. Always having a backup plan, Jude and I suggested taking a day trip to Jasper, the closest town, which was located two hours away. Crosby agreed, and within the hour we set off in Cassidy for a day of adventure.

As we drove northbound, I listened as Crosby and Jude spoke about life. It was a relief to have her attention focused off me and onto someone else. As she asked Crosby why he was a ski guide and gathered information about him, I couldn't help but smile. I had learned so much about myself through Jude's teaching that I liked seeing others receive the same gifts I had. Watching Jude as she enlightened Crosby on particular wisdom, I knew she truly loved what she was doing. As a modern-day fairy godmother, Jude's passion lay in teaching self-empowerment and motivation through responsibility for one's actions.

Crosby was the perfect student; an inquisitive nature and being open-minded made him a fun new friend to have on my spiritual path. "I know!" he shouted as we were getting treats halfway to Jasper. "Let's pretend to view the world through the eyes of a child today!" He looked at Jude and me excitedly as though he had just solved the mystery of why pigs couldn't fly. We looked at him endearingly and agreed. What we didn't tell Crosby was that, as an intuitive person, you should view the world in such a manner all the time. Though was I still learning that lesson, I loved the clarity I gained when peeping at the world in wonderment instead of boredom. We spent a magical day with Mr. Crosby.

Our first stop was at a hat store, where we encouraged Crosby to purchase a new hat. His extra-large baseball hat wasn't working for him and a chic newspaper caddy one was just the ticket. Watching Crosby transform into a confident being with his new hat was superb. It's amazing how the littlest things can change our own self-image.

As we dodged in and out of stores and galleries all day, it was awesome to witness Crosby slip back into being a little boy again. Stresses from work and anxieties about the future seemed to slip away as Crosby opened up. By allowing Jude and me into his comfort zone, Crosby had allowed himself to play again. This was so cool to witness.

Though I am but a lowly island girl, I do have the following opinion on playing. What happened to it? It appears to me that we reach a certain age and suddenly playing stops and big-person pants come on. All notions or concepts previously held about playing are quickly disregarded as we hurriedly grow up and start chasing after external gratifications. For a more colorful description of this allow me to give you the example I often visualize.

PICTURE THIS!

You are a pink-and-green alien from planet Funkdab. As you are orbiting the universe for the eighth time, all of a sudden planet Earth pops up on your radar. Intrigued by the blue-and-green mass below, you begin your descent, landing in the city of all cities, Los Angeles,California. As you place your pink-and-green wheels down on the ground, you begin absorbing your surroundings. As you slowly make your way downtown, a frantic lady runs past you and nearly crushes your foot, without even a hint of remorse or an apology. "Rather rude," you huff, making your way slowly through the crowded, dirty streets. You begin looking for a coffee shop; the boys on the planet Funkdab had told you they were great spots for information swapping. After the initial screams from several customers, you find an average-looking man and ask him a few questions.

"Hello. Research team from planet Funkdab enquiring about your planet's motives, goals, et cetera!"

"Uh, okay, Sir Pink and Green, ask away."

"So I'm here wondering why all these lovely people are running around like crazed zombies."

"Well, sir, everyone is running around trying to make money" replied average looking man.

Intrigued by average man's response, you continue questioning. "Why would they do that?"

"We need money to live."

"Okay, please define *live* for me?"

"Well, there's car payments, cell phone bills, computer bills, insurance, medical bills, designer clothing, perfume, eating out ..." BLAH BLAH BLAH BLAH. The average man continued on for five minutes listing all the "necessary" items one needs to live.

After hearing enough you stop the man. "Now, let me ask you this, little man. Do all these material items led to happiness?"

"Well you know, Mister Pink and Green, I don't know. I have been chasing after material things my entire life; I never sat down to think about it. But now that I am thinking about it, NO! Happiness is when I get to see my daughter and hear her laugh." Average Man gets a dreamy expression on his face as he picks up the phone to call his daughter.

Rather confused by the encounter, you quickly zoom back to your spaceship to input your findings into your database.

Next stop: Vernon British Columbia. Touching down, you are hopeful that your next encounter yields better results. Green trees and a lake surround you. "Certainly smells better," you note, wheeling to the closest public setting.

In the horizon you see a family eating lunch on a cozy blanket. The woman smiles at you as you approach, despite your pink-and-green skin. *Ah, acceptance,* you think as you approach the pleasant family. Again you explain your quest: discovering humans' goals, mission, etc. Smiling, the family nods their understanding as you begin your interrogation.

"So why are you guys so relaxed, at ease?"

"Well, Sir Pink and Green, we are enjoying ourselves with our family," responds the man.

"Now, may I ask your opinions on money?"

Again they smile as their littlest child is busy building a castle out of rocks.

"Ah, my friend, we have had many discussions about this particular subject. Let me tell you our belief. It is this: money is a great tool should it fall into the right hands. However, it can become the thing that destroys man, should he quest solely after wealth. We believe wealth comes from the inside out and spreads itself. Now can we interest you in some homemade strawberry pie?"

Unfortunately for you, pink-and-green aliens are allergic to strawberry pie, but you thank the family all the same and bid them a great day. A feeling of happiness starts building inside you as you depart Vernon, British Columbia and head back to your spaceship.

Later on that night, you are given the task of presenting your fellow aliens with your findings:

"Well, folks, after hitting the pavement on planet Earth, it would appear that the majority of folks are miserably chasing money, and material items. They are in such a mad panic that they have forgotten to smile and care for one another. Very upsetting behavior indeed!

Now, on the other hand, folks living simplistic lives seem to be doing much better, or at least have a brighter outlook. The information I gathered in Vernon was that people cared more about each other and made strong efforts to spend time together playing. The end result was that they had peaceful demeanors and in general much happier dispositions." And so concludes the scientific research of Sir Pink and Green.

What I am trying to demonstrate is that the most beautiful things we experience in life are moments, not money. A moment to tell your favorite friend you love them, moment to really listen to your little one's words, a moment to remember our playful selves, time for yourself. In my opinion, these are all moments that make up a life of bliss and sparkly eyes.

As we drove back to the lodge that star-filled evening, our spirits were high. Crosby had remembered to play; Jude and I got to giggle with him. Looking up at the infinite amount of stars above, I felt the most complete I had in years. It felt incredible to have likeminded people around who shared my depth and belief in spirituality.

We arrived back at the lodge late that night and I said good night to Crosby.

♥　　　　　　♥　　　　　　♥

The last week at the lodge brought with it a bunch of cool lads from down under. After we had weeks of stuffy European visitors, the group of twenty Australians came as a delight. During the first night of pushups competition, I could tell they were going to make lodge life a lot lighter.

Their merry spirits and sense of camaraderie were a welcome change after living in such an alienated environment. In the past I had established that I didn't enjoy Australians, but again my biases were rocked as I was a witness to their big hearts and easy smiles.

Ron, the sheep farmer from the West Coast, soon became a favorite as he enlightened us with his kind, warm essence. The night they arrived, staff went about the usual introduction about who we were and what duties we performed. Despite Marnie's introduction of herself as the "executive housekeeper," the playful Aussies didn't seem to have their socks blown off. I giggled as I watched Marnie's reaction to their unresponsive behavior. Once it got to Jude's introduction, true to form, she spoke clearly and went straight to the point. Instantly respect was gained from the group, and it didn't matter to the Aussies the title you were associated with.

One more piece to the mystery of Jude was discovered that evening as I observed the respect she earned effortlessly by being herself.

Remember that, Katie, I silently told myself as we mingled with the guests.

The more truthful you are, the more people believe in you.

DARE TO BE YOU!
DARE TO BE DIFFERENT!

As Jude and I walked to work the next morning, I made a point to really breathe in the clear mountain air. Though the entire heliskiing scenario had been trying, I was going to miss the healthiness of no electricity in my environment. I was learning the essence of energy and that the less electricity in your surroundings, the easier it is to receive messages from the universe.

Greeting the warm Aussies, I began morning duties for the last week. Backing into the kitchen, I tested the waters to see where Josie's mood clocked in; since the chocolate chip fiasco, interactions had been tense, and this morning was no different.

As the breakfast rush kicked into full gear, Josie's mood intensified while she struggled to make eggs and flip pancakes at the same time.

Snarls began coming out of her mouth and I felt my entire body tense up. After about fifteen minutes of unhealthy tension in my body, I decided to take action. I was not going to allow this dragon lady to ruin my day simply because she was a crankpot and hated women. That was it! I marched into the kitchen and told Josie to calm down.

Actually I believe my words were "Calm down, buddy, it's just breakfast." She hissed back at me, "I am not your buddy!" and returned to her already burnt ham-and-cheese omelets. My famous word, "whatever," popped out as I quickly scooted out of the rage-infested kitchen.

After breakfast I stomped over to Alex's office to explain the situation. As I informed her of Josie's negativity affecting the whole staff, I could sense her attention shifting away. It was only after I informed her of my intention to write a letter to the upper management that she snapped back to life.

"Katie, you don't really mean that, do you?" she said in her silly Swiss tone.

"Yes, I do, Alex. This has gone on far enough and no action has been taken." Leaving her with those thoughts, I turned around and left her office.

The almighty, famous Aretha Franklin's "Respect" began playing in my mind while my stride became more and more pronounced. Yeah. Team me!

♥ ♥ ♥

Over breakfast the following morning, I began more intently observing Jude's mannerisms. As she drifted from table to table with her playful nature, I watched her spread magic and laughter. The Aussies were responsive to her warmth and great attitude.

After doing the rounds, she zeroed in on Kevin, the lovable lawyer. "So, Kev" she asked as a hush fell over the crowd. "I have a question for you." Smiling, Kev nodded, encouraging her to continue.

"How much do you like me so far?"

Cheering and clapping erupted as they adored the early-morning entertainment.

There was that magic I so badly wanted to incorporate in my life; the magnetism. It began dawning on me, it really did stem from have a great self-esteem and saying whatever was on her mind. SO COOL!

While I was restocking the bar with Red Bulls, Alex came running up to me. "Katie, there is room for you to go heli-skiing today. You fly in twenty minutes."

Excited, I finished stocking the cooler and raced to go grab my gear. I had been begging and pleading with Alex all season to get a ride, so I was pumped.

Grabbing my hideous blue fashion coat, I raced toward the helicopter pad.

A tall, handsome man introduced himself as Jesse, the ski guide for the day. Glancing at my ski gear, he questioned me on my lack of warm clothing. Defensive, I responded that I would be fine and sarcastically thanked him very much for his concern. As he stared at me with his intense blue eyes, I felt intimidated. He reminded me of guys from my past whom I thought were too attractive to have time for me. My instant reaction to men like that had been to put up walls and act tough.

As I was watching the lodge grow smaller and smaller, my tummy started churning and I began second-guessing myself. *Hmm, I sure hope I'm not out all day,* I thought as I looked down at my thin blue jacket. Sure enough, as the day charged forward it got progressively worse. Due to our rocky start, Jesse and I weren't exactly on the same page when it came to communication. My stubborn side got in my way as I ignored his instructions and found my own path down the ski run. Ignoring Jesse's instructions to stay left, I swerved right and landed straight in a deep tree well. After fifteen minutes of digging myself out, I sheepishly made my way to the base of the mountain. Red-faced and pissed off, Jesse asked me why I had remained silent while being stuck. I shot back that I didn't realize I was meant to make noise and hadn't heard him yelling. Due to the severe scrutiny of his job, Jesse was just trying to ensure my safety. At the time, I was unable to recognize this concern. I was too preoccupied with my ego-based first impression of him. Reprimanding me in front of the guests, Jesse got his point across and I was mortified. My pride had gotten in my way, and now I was eating really tough crow. I quietly apologized and decided to listen more intently.

I spent the rest of the afternoon frozen and miserable. Not having listened to Jesse's initial concern about my warmth, I was borderline hypothermic by the end of the day. Who was I kidding?

Have you ever allowed your stubbornness to get in your way—or endanger you?

Finally, after what seemed like eons, we prepared for the helicopter ride back to the lodge. Eternal relief washed over me as I sunk into the plush couches of the helicopter. Checking in with my body, I felt my head spinning and feelings of nausea waved over me. *Hmm.* I wondered if this was what hypothermia felt like. Barely hanging on I gingerly stepped out of the helicopter. As I slowly made my way toward the lodge, I saw Jude standing in the doorway, peering out in my direction. Without saying a word, I half-limped/half-ran my way over to her.

"What the hell happened to you?" she exclaimed, warily eyeing the rough shape I was in. Trembling, I clutched onto her arm and told her about the evil tree well and my stubbornness leading to my delusions of escaping Mother Nature. I also added that the evil guide, Jesse, was to blame for my misadventure. Pretty cheeky.

"I was wondering why the hell you decided to go snowboarding," she said, leading me firmly to our home. Drawing a hot bath, she whisked around, grabbing food for me to eat.

My body slowly began unthawing back to human as I sat in the scalding hot water. As I frantically munched on some yogurt and granola, I felt my body coming back from being in a state of shock. Once a few of my wits were about me, I processed what had happened that day. My stubborn nature had gotten me into a potentially dangerous situation and I had been unable to recognize Jesse's concern for me.

Gratitude for Jude shone through me as I again wondered how I had been so lucky to have this real-life fairy godmother in my presence. Her strength was incredible yet foreign to me; I had never truly allowed anyone to take care of me. In the past I had always maintained that I was the strong one and didn't need support.

Such a crock of bullpoop! Even throughout the horrible experience, knowing she was going to be there at the end of the day made the cold seem less chilly.

Now please don't get me wrong. I have great girlfriends and I know they truly care for me, but having said that, I knew the friendship with Jude was very deep. It felt so magical to know someone really cared for me and supported me unconditionally. She knew more about me than I did. Go figure that one out!

Knocking on the bathroom door, she came in to check on me. "Do you even like snowboarding?" she casually asked as I continued munching on my granola.

"You know, little buddy, I don't know! I thought I did, but now that I think about it, I'm not sure." I took a moment to ponder this new thought. Did I really enjoy snowboarding?

As this realization dawned on me, I began wondering how many parts of my personality I had compromised for my friends—probably quite a few.

Jude's voice brought me back to reality. "So, sounds like you and Jesse had some differing opinions today eh?" she spoke with a particular tone that made me reflect on my behavior even though I really didn't want to.

"Yup," I said, hoping to end the conversation right then.

"Sounds like Jesse was coming from a place of concern," Jude persisted in a matter-of-fact tone.

Reality sure bites. I gritted my teeth, as again I knew Jude was right. "Yeah, he probably was, but he also was being really firm and rude."

"It's called being professional!" she shot back. And she kept going: "Can you imagine the expression on his face if you were to apologize for your part in the conflict?"

Taking a big gulp, I considered what Jude had just proposed. Apologizing to Jesse? Was she out of her mind? Then I reflected again. I had put myself in danger and had probably really concerned Jesse. Maybe Jude's idea was so crazy it was genius. Just maybe.

During my bartending shift later that night, I saw Jesse socializing with the guests. Waiting till he had finished, I slowly made my way over to him, feeling very shy and timid. Quietly I cleared my throat in hopes of getting his attention. That tactic didn't seem to be working, so I finally tapped him on the shoulder to get his attention. Turning around, Jesse fixated his blue eyes on me. Stumbling to find the words, I stared blankly at him, momentarily dumbfounded. Jesse prompted me. "Yes, Katie?"

Okay, that was my cue.

"Ah, yes, Jesse, I just wanted to apologize to you for the way in which I acted today. I was being stubborn and my behavior was out of line."

As the words escaped my lips, I felt a huge relief, as I had spoken the truth and there were no hidden motive or agenda. Watching his reaction was magical. Jesse's face softened as he processed the apology I had just expressed.

"You know, Katie, apology accepted. I really appreciate your honesty." With a smile he turned around and resumed conversing with the guests.

What an amazing concept this telling the truth business was. I enjoyed the rest of my shift, knowing I had done the right thing and that the air had been cleared between us.

♥   ♥   ♥

During the last week of the lodge, I manage to grow rather fond of Crosby. Although we only saw each other a few times I truly felt that we has a mutual respect for each other. (I also liked kissing him!) I have been know to fall rather quickly and my experience with Mr. Crosby was no different. Due to my fear of vulnerability, I pretended not to like him and down played our friendship. Having said that, you can imagine my feelings when I came home and heard that he had been caught out all night with a nineteen year old girl. As Marnie sat on the couch, telling me the details of Crosby's adventures I felt betrayed and hurt. As mentioned earlier I have a habit of falling hard and being hurt in the past. Later that evening I told Jude about the latest news about our pal Crosby. Her response had not the being the one I was looking for. Shrugging her shoulders, she answered "So? So, what if he did! It's not as though you and he were married Katie. Also, you gave off the impression that you weren't interested. How was he to know?" Stung by her words, I creased my eyebrows, and prepared for battle. " You don't understand at all. I thought Crosby was different, you know?" More angry at myself than Jude, I starred out into the snow capped mountains and listened to my inner guidance provide with clarity. "Remember, Katie you did only know him for a very short time. Had you allowed yourself more vulnerable perhaps he would have know your true feelings towards him, but what is done is done you must move on."

♥   ♥   ♥

The following night, Jude and I drove out to Blue River for a big city action. The population was about 30, which was huge comparison to Albreda! Knowing that Crosby would be there I put on my best jeans and an attitude the size of Texas. No way was going to show him my vulnerability. Walking into the main lounge, we were greeted to quite the scene. International skiers of all shapes and sizes were gleefully unwinding after along day of powder hunting.

Laughter sprinkled the atmosphere as a cozy fire crackled in the background creating a magical scene. Grabbing a gin and tonic I made my way over to the fireplace. As I slowly sauntered across the room, I silently scanned to find Mr. Crosby. Spotting him across the room, I purposely positioned myself within his range. True to form, Crosby fell for the trap and soon found his way over to the fireplace. Putting on my aloof face, I greeted him with a who cares attitude. (In reality, my nerves were tap-dancing all over the bar, but luckily for me Crosby didn't have the ability to see my molecular makeup!)

After our initial hellos, Crosby looked up at me and denied the tales of the nineteen year old escapades. Shaking my head I told him that I didn't care what he did (a lie!) and proceed to rapidly consume my drink. Pressing the matter further, Crosby continued by stating how much he enjoyed spending time with me and wanting to stay in touch. Pretending to be cool and calm, I nodded. My feelings and ego had being bruised and already written Crosby off to protect myself. As we said our final good-byes, I was sad that things between us hadn't flowed as I wanted. Perhaps, if I had opened myself up more and being more vulnerable…I guess I will never know…

♥   ♥   ♥

The morning before the Aussies left, Jude had found her own form of entertainment. Earlier that day she had been strolling past the gift shop when Guy noticed her.

He called out to her and expressed his need for help. "JUDE! I need your help here. Marnie won't give me a deal."

Turning bright red, Marnie looked over at Jude and said, "I gave him 10 percent off and my rate but that still doesn't seem to be good enough"

Returning Marnie's offer, Jude said "Two-twenty-five and he will take it."

Reluctantly Marnie agreed to the arrangement.

"Oh, thank you, Marnie," Guy exclaimed with his wonderful Australian accent. "You truly are a saint!" He winked his gratitude at Jude and modeled his new orange-and-brown jacket. Happy as a clam, he strolled into the lounge to show off his new purchase.

Jude smiled at Marnie as she left her standing in the gift shop, wondering what had happened.

♥   ♥   ♥

The last night the Aussies were with us was March 16; one day from the jolly Saint Patrick's birthday! There was an end-of-the-ski season party that Jude and I were planning on attending in Blue River. Grabbing green accessories from our closet, we quickly transformed ourselves into green fairies for the night.

After hopping in Cassidy, we began driving west toward Blue River. Small snowflakes started falling heavily as the weather conditions darkened. We soon found ourselves driving straight into a blizzard with absolutely no vision one foot in front of us. Looking at each other, we both decided to pull the plug on the operation and head back to the lodge. It simply wasn't worth the trek.

Pulling into the parking lot, I still felt as though I wanted to dance and be jolly. A quick check-in with Jude confirmed she felt the same way. Just as we were about to head back home with feelings of defeat, we heard faint music and laughing drift out of the lodge.

"The Aussies!" we exclaimed gleefully. Our dream of dancing the night away had not been ruined. We quickly ran up the huge staircase and into the lodge.

The Aussies had taken over the cozy living room area and were having a blast. Kevin and his pals were instructing dance lessons while Rod and Guy were involved in a very serious game of fuseball. As we entered the chaotic scene, they greeted us with cheers and smiles. "Girls, great to see you. Let's get you a drink!" shouted Guy as we ambled our way to the bar. Armed with a green apple martini for Jude and a pink-and-blue martini for myself, we were ready to celebrate with the crew. Immediately Guy challenged us to a game of fuseball and we accepted, seeing as how both Jude and I were rather competitive. We warned the boys that they were in for a heartbreak. As the riveting game began, my competitive streak came out tenfold as I fully immersed in the game.

As Guy yelled in her ear, Jude was a trooper as she maintained focus defended our goal like a pro. As I made the winning shot, I felt a draft come over me. Somewhere between the fifth and ninth goal, my scarf top had unraveled and it now had found a home directly around my stomach. Cheers erupted from team Aussie as I, embarrassed, pulled myself together. After taking a bow, I resigned from fuseball playing for the night and retreated to the bathroom.

Meanwhile, back at the party, Jude and Guy were involved in a nail-biting pushup competition. Completing fifty without taking a breath, Jude became the victorious winner. After five minutes of persuading, the Aussies convinced us to celebrate her win with a shot of some good old-fashioned tequila. Laughing, I felt stoked and happy to see her enjoying herself. Jude was such an important person to me. I knew that she worked very hard. To see her kicking up her heels and playing made me sparkle. She fit in so effortlessly with this group due to her fun-loving ways. Around midnight I began getting sleepy and searched the room to find Jude. I found her ballroom dancing with Kevin and having a blast. Feeling like an ancient corpse, I told her I was heading home. "Ah, come on, Katie! Let's just stick around a bit more." Smiling, I agreed to suck it up and play a bit more.

Jude and the Aussies humbled me as I watched their childlike mannerisms and playfulness in awe. Very cool!

♥   ♥   ♥

Early the next morning, Jude had to work while I stayed in bed. Two hours later I awoke to the sound of Arman, the manager, banging on my door. "Katie, you can go for a helicopter ride. It's leaving in twenty minutes, so you better hurry up." Fifteen minutes later I found myself with Jude, waiting for the helicopter pilot to pick us up. As the copter touched down, a huge gust of wind hit us.

"Now, remember, girls," Arman shouted, "don't tell any of the guests that you got a ride in the helicopter, and do not go in the main lodge." We lifted ourselves in the copter and buckled up, and the pilot informed us that we could talk by flicking a switch and listen to the reply.

At 1,500 feet above the earth, we reached the flight height and relaxed. Beautiful fresh snow and misty fog surrounded the helicopter; it seemed as though we were traveling through time.

Again feelings of complete gratitude rushed over me as I watched Jude. As I mentioned earlier, it was so foreign for me to have such a close relationship with an older woman. My mom and I had never been tight, so until I had met Jude, I found myself disliking older women. But this was different. I knew Jude truly cared for me and I cared for her unconditionally. The concept seemed so alien to me—but a good kind of alien, like the pink-and-green one I spoke of earlier.

For twenty minutes we soared above the clouds and saw the world through the eyes of an eagle. The CN railway train looked little tiny connected pebbles moving slower than any tortoise. Looking back, Jude caught my eyes and we shared a magical moment while floating high above ground. With a whirl of his fingers, our pilot indicated that he was beginning the descent back to planet Earth. Our fantastic adventure was coming to a close. I felt sadness that we couldn't live in the sky forever. It was so free—so light, so far from reality. Once we got the thumbs up to unload, we disembarked the copter and made our way into the helicopter shelter. From there we waited for the company van to come to take us to the main lodge. After we chitchatted with the pilots, our chariot arrived.

Pulling up to the lodge, I decided that I wanted a hot chocolate. Despite Arman's particular request that we not enter the lodge, I felt defiant.

Initially Jude resisted my attempts to convince her we should get hot chocolate. But once I described it as warm, decadent, and tantalizing, I soon gained an accomplice in my hot chocolate mission.

Shuffling our way through the mayhem, we found a table near the back of the lounge. I got us a couple of hot chocolates and sat back down. Just as we were getting into the topic of past lives, the familiar sound of friendly Australians hit my ears.

"Hey, girls, mind if we join you?" Looking up, we saw Guy and Ron in front of us, hands full of food.

"Of course, boys!" we happily exclaimed, moving over to make room.

Staying true to Arman, we didn't tell them how we got to the main lodge faster than they had. When Guy inquired, Jude smiled sweetly and remained silent. While we shot the breeze with the boys, I felt the presence of a dark cloud forming nearby. Just before I stood up to get more hot chocolate, I came face to face with Olf. Remember him? He was the character I introduced earlier as the general manager with no soul. You didn't think he was out of the picture, did you? Oh, no, no, no. Here he was again! Glaring down at us with his big dark persona, he inhaled like he was making an effort to suck away our souls. Exhaling, he started in on his reprimanding. "My staff has informed me you girls have been in here for a while, socializing with the clients."

Being the one responsible for the rule-breaking, I piped up. "Yes, we have."

In his terminator voice, he boomed, "Saturdays are the busiest days of the week. You shouldn't be here. Staff is not allowed to be anywhere near the lounge and are definitely not allowed food. You need to leave immediately." Face flushed, he turned and left our table.

Silence followed as our Aussie friend Rod sat in disbelief. "Did that really just happen?" he inquired once Olf was out of earshot.

"It sure did," I answered. We barely believed it ourselves. Feeling extremely embarrassed and teensy tiny, we stood up to leave. "I guess we better get going," we exclaimed as we hugged our friends goodbye.

♥   ♥   ♥

Later that afternoon we prepared to leave the lodge and head out to Grande Prairie, Alberta to visit Jude's son. Around suppertime we approached the lodge to say our final goodbyes to the staff.

The last task before departure was checking in with Arman and Alex, keepers of the almighty paychecks. The office was unusually quiet as we approached the front desk. Alex emerged from behind the computer and we informed her we were leaving.

She began gathering all of our necessary information for departure. Just as we were about to walk out the door, Arman came spinning in out of left center field.

Rapidly approaching Jude, he swooped down and began reprimanding her for the afternoon hot chocolate mishap.

While Jude and Armin exchanged their words, I cowered in the office, not saying one word. I look back on the day and feel regret for remaining silent. Sensing we needed to leave, I quickly gathered our belongings and made my way to the door. Spinning on her heels to leave, Jude headed toward the front doors. Opening her arms, Alex offered her a hug. Refusing her gesture, Jude quickly strolled behind me after exclaiming her complete and utter disgust with the organization. Closing the huge doors behind us, I felt relief as that chapter of my life had been closed, and so began the new one.

♥   ♥   ♥

As we drove into the crisp, starry night toward Jasper, it felt as though the lodge was light years away. We arrived on the luckiest night of the year, St. Patty's Day, and decided to indulge in our favorite snack, nachos! Looking around the pub filled with green leprechauns and jolly souls, we began discussing future plans. Jude and I both were in the extremely lucky situation of having no responsibilities and open minds from which to allow creative and inventive ideas to flow. Women's retreats, psychic schools for children, and a Bed & Breakfast were all on the list as we munched on nachos with jalapeños and began brainstorming. This reminds me of my favorite quote:

Mediocre minds speak of other people; average minds speak of things; great minds speak of ideas!

Feelings of hope and excitement rushed over me as I grew even fonder of Jude and our future plans. Finally! I had met someone who understood me and truly cared for me.

Hitting a snowstorm, our spirits weren't dampened as Jude skillfully drove us to safety. When we arrived at the hotel at 2:34 a.m., I can only imagine what the desk clerk was thinking as I trudged in looking like a troll just coming from her bridge.

♥   ♥   ♥

The following morning we headed out toward Grande Prairie and enjoyed the first day of true freedom! We pulled into Grande Prairie just in time for dinner, and I got to meet Jude's son. It was an experience I will never forget. I was a witness to the incredible bond that occurs between mother and son. About five minutes after our arrival, Jude had tears in her eyes as she embraced her son. It was so beautiful to witness—one of those moments you hold on to when it feels as though the world is a cold and unfriendly place.

Their relationship seemed foreign to me as I observed how openly they spoke with one another. I couldn't believe that Aaron was allowed to express his thoughts and feelings toward Jude without being punished. It was as though I had just witnessed Martian life. He expressed his feelings of discontent and anger that Jude was living a life he felt wasn't good enough for her. His perception stemmed from concern and compassion, and I could feel his unconditional love for his mom, which was very overwhelming to witness. Spending three days with Aaron and his fiancée Christina, plus Griz, their lovable dog, was such a memorable experience for me.

On the third day, Aaron commented that I seemed confused. Instantly I felt devastated and angry. I thought to myself, *Confused? I'm not confused. I know exactly what I am doing.* Feelings of hurt emerged as I silently fumed about the comment. At the time, I was still in a denial state and didn't recognize that his words were not meant to hurt; they were simply his perception. I internalized his statement and built up walls to shield myself from him instead of expressing my feelings.

The following day Aaron approached me and apologized. Yet another Mars encounter for me! It was a heartfelt apology that I truly believed. Woozers! What a concept! As we prepared to leave Grande Prairie, I was a witness to the strong bond between Aaron and Jude as he urged his mom to stay longer.

Jude declined and we set out once more on the road, toward Calgary.

We arrived in Calgary; my ego got the best of me.

My ego had issues with me staying in a hostel versus a hotel. I felt that I was above hostels, and it bruised my false sense of pride. This frustration, combined with my frugal nature only served to add to my poor attitude that night. It came to a head when I paid for a room for Jude and myself. Expecting her to thank me, I was instantly angered when she remained silent. When I confronted her about this, Jude stated that in her world friendship was unconditional and that she didn't realize that I needed to hear gratitude out loud. Growing up, I had put conditions on everything, especially money. This led me to feel resentment whenever I didn't receive instant acknowledgement. I have since learned that gratitude comes in many shapes and forms, not necessarily from a verbal thank you.

Have you put conditions on your loved ones?

Unsettled from our fight, I roamed the streets of Calgary feeling angry. I soon called Autumn, my oldest friend, to hear some comforting words. Phoning Autumn was my way of distracting myself; instead of going inward, I sought attention externally.

Although we had grown up together, she and I were very different people and our lifestyles were polar opposites. If she was white, I would be black; her apples, me oranges. I think you got the message! Regardless of this, I had grown up not speaking truthfully with her, and the result was that I had allowed her to take control of our friendship. When I reached her, it felt as though she and I were on completely different wavelengths. All I could hear were excuses for why life was so tough for her, and I quickly found myself losing patience. At one point during the conversation, she began enquiring about acquiring plane tickets. (We had planned a three-week trip to Central America together, but I had been feeling bad vibes about it.) Trusting my gut, I explained to her that I might not be going on the trip. The instant the words left my mouth, she began pleading with me and giving me a rather unwanted guilt trip. In the past I would have caved in and gone against my gut, but having found inner strength, I stood my ground. The pleading soon turned to anger as she claimed that over the years I was always the one on travels while she was stuck at school. I responded by pointing out that she was the one responsible for her decisions, as I was accountable for mine. Hearing the truth angered her and she told me I was being harsh. It felt very strange to hear my oldest friend react this way.

When I hung up the phone, sadness flooded over me as I reflected on all the things I had seen in her but refused to acknowledge or discuss. Walking the streets, I reflected upon our friendship. Had we really known one another? I had spent years in silence, not daring to say what I felt about her. As little kids, we had a beautiful friendship filled with magic and imagination. That all changed once we hit high school. Autumn chose the path of partying and drugs for attention, whereas I chose to overachieve in extracurricular activities. Since that point, I had sat back and watched Autumn experience the consequences of poor choices, never telling her how I felt.

Wandering aimlessly, I felt myself being subconsciously drawn to a particular block. Seconds before reaching the corner, I heard glass shattering and the unmistakable sound of metal on metal. I glanced up just in time to see electric headlights making their way toward me. I ran for cover and managed to escape being crunched by the car. I quickly dialed 9-1-1 and disclosed what I had witnessed. After ensuring that everyone was all right, I resumed my wanderings around Calgary.

After wandering around contemplating this, I soon found myself back at the scene of the accident. I felt my guidance telling me I was there to bless the scene and ensure there were no injuries. Although I had always known there were powers greater than myself surrounding me, it still came as an awakening that there had been a purpose behind my seemingly aimless wonderings in Calgary. Tired from all the action, I headed back to the hostel to get a good night's sleep.

♥ ♥ ♥

The next morning I awoke feeling nervous about talking with Jude. I was standoffish and unsure of how to approach her. After eating breakfast we headed west. We spent the first few hours of the morning in silence.

Around midday Jude cracked the ice by pointing out a beautiful view and from there our argument seemed to dissipate.

Yet another gorgeous day greeted us as we cruised west on the scenic 95 and idly made our way to the next destination. Now, please! Don't be fooled by the radiant name of Golden B.C. As we pulled into Golden, we soon saw it was simply an industrial town that had lots of mills and wires everywhere—not exactly a spiritualist's dream. So it came as no surprise as when Jude suggested we only stay for the night and find the cheapest motel. I pulled Cassidy into the dusty parking lot; strange vibes hit me as I made my way up to the front desk. The vibes got even more intense as I rang the rusty bell for service. Out from the stained curtain emerged a young guy dressed gothic-like.

"Yes, can I help you?" he said with an undeniable lisp. Rather entertained by his demeanor, I enquired about a room for the night.

Jude attempted to break the ice. "So are there many bears out and about this time of year?"

The young man seemed arrogant in his demeanor and rudely stated, "They are still in hibernation." He shook his head with impatience and handed me the room key. Deciding not to further engage in conversation with this young guy, we headed to our room. Upon opening the door, we noticed that it felt chilly, so I went to the thermostat and turned it on. After having our usual midnight chat, Jude and I decided to call it a night. Jude, coming out of the bathroom, asked if I was warm now, and she turned the heat off.

At some point in the middle of my sleep, I awoke from my dream. The last vision I remembered had been a cougar staring straight at me, preparing to pounce. Feeling alarmed by the vision, I surveyed the room as my heart pounded. Next to me, Jude had awakened too and was in the process of opening the front door, "I can't believe how bloody hot it is in here," she stated. With a quick step, she went over to check out the thermostat. "It's cranked all the way up! I knew I had sensed some form of entity about us." I looked at her blankly as she continued, "I awoke with something choking me. I need air, so that is why I jumped out of bed so quickly. Sorry for waking you up."

Still shaken from my dream, I answered her, "Don't worry about waking me; I felt a strange energy in the room as well. What is going on?"

She explained that often spirits who die an unexpected death will reenact the scene of death and stay in the very place where they died. This spirit wasn't particularly friendly and needed to be sent to the white light. We knew this because of nature of the hostile feelings we both picked up from this spirit. I absorbed the knowledge I had just acquired. Whoa Nelly! My first ghost encounter; very cool! Rather unnerving but cool at the same time. Our room slowly began cooling down, and after several attempts, I managed to fall back asleep.

My whole life, I had always believed in ghosts, though I had never seen one. That night was the beginning of many new encounters of the mystic kind. I was nervous to be diving into the realm of the unknown, but my excitement overruled as I imagined all the spooky ghost hunts and new adventures I would experience.

Leaving this experience, we climbed into our favorite green machine and headed for Kamloops.

Once we arrived in Kamloops, I pulled out the address of the hotel. Forces seemed to be among us as I pulled up to the hotel effortlessly. Looking at one another, Jude and I raised our eyebrows. "Serendipity!" she said as we unpacked our bags from Cassidy. As I was learning more about living a six-sensory existence, circumstances such as this did not surprise me.

If only I knew what awaited me in room 418.

Opening the door to room 418, I almost jumped directly out of my skin. As I entered the room, fear crept at me as I took in my surroundings. To anyone else the room would have appeared to be a perfectly normal hotel room. Beautiful rose wallpaper and pink frilly curtains were the theme of the décor, but I felt as though I was walking into a nightmare. Please allow me to explain.

Ever since I can remember, I have had several reoccurring childhood nightmares. An extremely distinctive one involved me being trapped in a purely pink floral room with someone trying to get me at the door. Each time I had this dream, the killer would attempt to get at me with a chainsaw. Though the killer never got to me, the dreams would really shake me up to say the least. So you can imagine my sentiments as I walked straight into the EXACT room from my dreams; quickly I felt myself slipping into panic as Jude tried to calm me down.

"Do you know what this room represents? Oh my god, we can't stay here. Sorry, my friend. We have to leave!" I stated frantically, pacing around the room.

"Katie, Katie, let's calm down here and hear what I have to say."

Slowing my frantic pacing, I lifted my head.

"Did you ever try and interpret your dream before?"

"Of course, Jude. Someone was trying to kill me with a chainsaw. End of story. I'm doomed. It's happening tonight. I can feel it!"

(I may have forgotten to mention that I tend to get rather carried away with what Jude refers to as my "imagination market." In other words, my mighty, powerful mind takes over and creates havoc on me.)

Jude rolled her eyes. "Okay, are we done with the dramatics? Now listen, do you ever think that the chainsaw was perhaps an acquired tool you needed in life? Perhaps the fact that we are here tonight is simply to demonstrate to you that you have attained a particular tool you need."

Silently I thought about it. "So what sort of tool do you mean?"

"Well, I don't know, Katie. Perhaps patience or inner strength? What tool you have attained is up to you to determine."

Although I believed Jude's words, I still felt wary as we stepped out for a quick snack before bed. Up until Kamloops, Jude and I really hadn't spent much time discussing what our plans were for the future. I really wanted to start up a business with her, but I was still unsure of what it would or how we would do it. I also had feelings that for some crazy reason Jude would abandon me.

Have you had abandonment issues in your life?

She had become the closest person to me, and it seemed easier to assume we would soon part. Jude had become my rock, which truly wasn't her job. But due to my mom's inability to provide me with the love I needed, I was left feeling unwanted. (I was an experience to her)

Okay, back to Kamloops! We found ourselves a little lounge and sat in a comfy booth. After rehashing the day, Jude looked straight in my eyes. "Now, I want you to be honest with me, Katie, do you think you are up for spiritual work? I'm not sure if you fully understand the magnitude I am speaking of." Taking a sip of wine, I encouraged Jude to continue speaking. "I figure it's going to take you some time and a lot of discipline to acquire the attributes to use your gifts. Are you ready? Are you sure?"

I answered yes without a doubt in mind. I would later discover the depths that she spoke of.

After several hours of discussion, we decided that Montreal would be the spot to start up a business venture due to it's business European influence and open-minded nature. I took yet another sip of wine and stared across the table. I felt like it was one of those moments when you are watching a scene unfold in front of you and you can't believe it is happening. I believe they are called out-of-body experiences, and that is definitely what I was feeling. I knew that during that moment in time my life had just changed. Planets were realigning as I was offered the chance to get back on my destined path.

I know deep down I had longed for someone like Jude to come along for years, to take me under their wing and challenge me. For years I had always felt as though I didn't quite fit in and had been questing to connect with my soul. Now right here in Kamloops, I was experiencing the universe giving me the greatest opportunity ever.

What an incredible day! First I had walked straight into one of my reoccurring dreams, and second, there was the prospect of beginning a business with Jude. Again spirituality was rocking my socks off. Who knew that discovering a belief system could be so wicked? Since having begun my spiritual adventures, I had been ranting and raving to all who would listen about the magical events.

As we headed back to the evil pink paisley room, my feelings went from jumping excitement to utter dread as I remembered the fate that awaited me. I was going to die that night from a chainsaw in a pink room! I have to laugh as I write this because I truly was fearful of this crazy notion. I know that my dream had been a premonition about the future and the fact that I was living it meant I was finally on track.

That night I truly learned about the power my mind had over me. Through logic I knew I would be just fine, and Jude was sleeping right beside me, but fear still had me in its evil clutches. And can you guess who was behind fear's sharp fingernails? Yup, you got it. It was ego! I try not to feed her but find it extremely difficult to tell her to shut up! Darkness filled the room like an old familiar friend as Jude turned out the lights. My mind ran amuck with fear as I drifted into sleep.

A sharp BEEP—BEEP—BEEP woke me from my slumber. My heart beating faster than Roger Rabbit, I leapt out off bed ready to fight the intruder. As the beeping continued, I looked around the room and realized that no one was attacking me. A further glance and my gaze fell upon the alarm clock on the bedside table. It was exactly midnight and the alarm was sounding. I quickly shut of the obnoxious machine and peeked over at Jude fast asleep in dream state. I found it extremely peculiar that Jude had slept right through the alarm going off while I instantly awoke. After about ten seconds of meditation, I came to the conclusion that the alarm had been specifically for me. It had gone off to inform me that I was indeed safe and no evil chainsaw man was coming to seal my fate. Satisfied that I would live to see the next day, I fell back onto the pink bedspread, exhausted after the emotional turmoil I had put myself through.

Rising bright and early, I hopped out of bed feeling exuberant that I hadn't had any nasty encounters with a chainsaw the previous night. It dawned on me that I was indeed quite psychic and had simply been predicting the future as a little girl. Discovering I had this new gift was exciting yet also rather challenging. Now that I knew I possessed certain knowledge, what was I supposed to do about it? This was a question I asked Jude every day as I began putting more and more pressure on myself. If I was a light worker, what was my job? What had the voices meant when they said I should get to work? Those were questions I consistently asked Jude over and over again. The response was always the same: "Look inside yourself, Katie. Ask the question and the answer will come. Listen, observe. The future will unfold itself. Just live in today and enjoy the moments. That will get you where you should be."

Her response would always make me grit my teeth in frustration. Due to my impatient nature, I had become quite accustomed to having instant responses with little to no challenge. Now quite the opposite existed. Every day I faced challenges and was given only slight clues to unravel the mystery of myself. Now, when I say challenges, allow me to explain that through Jude's guidance I had learned about asserting myself as well as my belief system. In the past I hadn't been shown how to use my words properly in order to stick up for myself. So every day since we had been together, she would test me and to see if I was suiting up. Now the challenges I faced were not like the usual test when you sit down, eyes to the front, and regurgitate what you have learned all semester. Oh no, my tests were live, in-the-flesh people who would be deliberately placed on my path to test my new assertiveness skills.

An example that comes to mind is when Jude and I would grab a coffee; quite often it wouldn't be the right heat, flavor, or type. Whatever. In the past I would let it go and miserably sip cold coffee, but now I had the universe testing me on situations such as this one and allowing me to try out my new courageous self.

♥   ♥   ♥

Taking the Duffy Lake road toward the West Coast, we noticed that Cassidy's brakes had been acting funny and squealing like banshees. Retreating from the highway, we pulled into Pemberton, a small community a half an hour out of Whistler. After finding a mechanic, we were left to roam around the village and find some grub. Jude and I found ourselves in a small ma 'n' pa café. Sitting down with a breakfast of a Nanaimo bar and mocha (it's a woman's prerogative!), Jude and I commenced our daily ritual of reading our tarot cards. It was always fun to read them in public places because of the peculiar glances and stares people would throw our way. This morning was no different. Directly across from us sat a First Nations man drinking a cup of coffee. Throughout our readings I could sense he was paying very close attention. Jude had told me about First Nations and their close ties with spirituality because they had deeply rooted customs and rituals with nature. The First Nation culture had always been very open and believed in greater powers.

As I looked up toward him, he shyly glanced away, hiding his face beneath his extra-large cowboy hat. *Hmm! Interesting,* I thought as we put our cards away.

After chatting with a mom and her little boy about astrology, we hit the big town of Pemberton with nothing but time. Three hours later, with no call from the mechanic, two scratch and wins, and two very decadent treats, we sat down on a slab of cement in front of a general store.

Just as I was pondering how the café made the most epic brownie I had ever eaten, the man from the shop walked up to us. He shyly greeted us by taking off his hat and introducing himself as Billy. His words were straight to the point. "I saw you over in the coffee shop this morning. You were reading cards." Though simple words, I could tell he had much to say as he fixated his gaze on Jude. I silently pulled back as I prepared to be an observer of the following scenario.

Jude smiled at him and answered back, "Yes, I noticed you too, Billy!"

Crouching down, he lowered himself in order to look her in the eyes. "You know I broke my back a few years back while breaking wild horses. My back has healed, but I haven't gotten on a horse ever since." In awe of his pure honesty, I remained silent, knowing my role as observer.

"That was your love, wasn't it, Billy? You must have grown up riding horses," she responded.

Instantly Billy grew animated as he vigorously nodded and explained more. "Oh yes, I love horses. I reared wild stallions all my life. That's all I know." Sadness deepened his voice as he disclosed the fate that had torn him from his love.

His humble nature was so beautiful to witness. I had been so accustomed to North American demeanors ego, pride, wealth; witnessing such humble honesty silenced me.

"Well, Billy, it sounds to me as though getting back to your roots would be a great start. I bet you went in a sweat lodge lots when you were younger. Perhaps going back there would bring some clarity to your situation." Nodding, he accepted her advice and sat silent for a moment.

"Yeah, I haven't been to a sweat lodge in years. I used to go all the time with my father when he was still alive. I loved them."

"It's time to get back on a horse, Billy. It's time," Jude advised.

Sensing he had received the guidance he had been questing after, Billy stood up. After shaking both our hands, he thanked Jude and resumed his stroll down the sidewalk. Taking a sip of her coffee, she looked over at me and smiled.

"When he looks past the fear, he will be back to his passion," Jude stated in a quiet voice.

Pure awe came over me as I fully absorbed the interaction. Being First Nations, this man had truly understood Jude's quiet disposition. He had a life-altering event happen and had been searching for an affirmation that he should begin horseback riding again. To most it may seem like nothing huge, but I knew different. It was at this point that I had received insight into who Jude was. I admired Jude for her calm demeanor up to this point; I hadn't before witnessed a complete stranger coming up to her for advice. A spiritual awaking was what happened, and sometimes people just need to hear it from a complete stranger. But is Jude a stranger to others?

❖ Over the past year, I have had the opportunity to research the spiritual realm, which is just as real as our physical reality. Within the magical spiritual realm, there is a order of officials just like here on earth. Difference is that on the spiritual plain, there is a council of elders who all collaborate together to make decisions regarding man's destiny. Although they are ancient, evolved souls occasionally members of the council decide to reincarnate to human form and live in physical realm. Jude is one of the counselors, which explains why so many strangers feel magnetically drawn to her without knowing the cause.

A sharp ringing brought me back to reality. My cell phone jangled in my purse. The mechanic was coming to drop off Cassidy in the village. Pulling up in the minivan, I had to laugh. Picture this: a six-foot-two large man crammed into a space appropriate for tiny Jude. It was perfect: Dumbo in a mouse hole. Snickering to myself, I enjoyed the comical scene. I love stuff like that. Since I had begun to slow down and truly enjoy the present, small comical scenarios like that became more apparent. They can be so slight that often I don't seem to have time to notice them.

♥   ♥   ♥

Once back on the road again, my thoughts drifted to Stephen. Stephen was an ex-boyfriend of mine that I had been obsessively hanging on to. Although our relationship had ended two years prior, we were still playing a dysfunctional game of Ping-Pong with one another. He had recently left for South America and was due back in a few weeks. I had delusions of still being in love with him and was determined to tell him I was once he arrived home. The following thoughts plagued my mind:
What if you don't still really love him?
What if he doesn't love you?
What if now I have changed so much we wouldn't share our past chemistry?
I began what-if-ing myself to death as we slowly made our way toward Vancouver through the windy sea to Sky Highway. After about a hour of annoying myself with obsessive thoughts, I switched my focus to Mom and Dad.
Though I loved them dearly, visits with them had been getting progressively worse since the experience at Christmas. I slowly understood that my parents weren't the perfect beings I had once thought they were. During years of delusion, I had created an illusion that their marriage was perfect. In reality they were simply human and had their daily struggles as well. Nevertheless, as we got closer to the ferry terminal, I felt apprehensive about seeing them. I felt

nervous about expressing how I truly felt. But at the same time, I knew I needed to speak my truth.

Pulling into Vancouver, I could feel the tension of the city overtake me as I found myself stuck in rush hour. My heart rate increased as I weaved in and out of traffic. Amid the chaos, Jude and I made quick plans to have her take Cassidy while I was over visiting Mom and Dad. We pulled into ferry terminal, just in time to catch the 7:00 p.m. ferry to Vancouver Island. I got out of Cassidy, put my things together, and hugged Jude goodbye. I felt a sadness coming over me, being accustomed to having Jude in my presence. I knew this woman cared for me with no strings attached. As we parted ways, she said, "Katie, don't forget to speak your truth of who you are and don't buy into the silence now that you have become accustomed to communicating your thoughts. Don't care-take them; it will take your energy level down. And of course, love them without judgment." With that she disappeared into a crowd of people in true Mary Poppins fashion.

♥   ♥   ♥

As I boarded the ferry, my thoughts drifted into the future as I wondered what Montreal had in store for us. Making my way home on the public transit, I began wondering why my mom and dad never came to pick me up when I came for visits. That realization saddened me as the bus cruised closer to my parents' home. Reaching Apple Street, I opened the front door and yelled a greeting to my folks. Rushing downstairs, they gave me a big hug. I sat down and prepared to inform them of my latest adventures. I had changed in many ways since my last visit, but neither one of them seemed to notice. Given my family's uncommunicative nature, if they did happen to see any changes, they certainly held them in. After updating them on my life and plans to move out east with the Judemeister, I felt tired and declared that I was heading up to bed.

During my visit with my parents, I noticed that they were the exact same people but I was viewing them through different eyes. Understanding that I needed to take the pedestal away from them, I saw them in the bright lights of reality.

For many years my dad had allowed my mom to control him instead of communicating his truth. He had opted out on himself and had become very hermit-like. His renewed love for music seemed to be his saving grace, as he retreated into the spare bedroom instead of allowing himself to speak the truth. Due to his suppression of feelings, he had made himself sick over the years. I had spent years in silence, watching my mom demean and belittle my dad. Though I was learning to speak truthfully, my parents still really intimidated me.

I was raised as an only child and had always felt that my opinion wasn't listened too. As I grew older, I began expressing my feelings less and less due to fear of upsetting my folks. But all that was changing, as I was beginning to speak my mind, feeling more confident.

The following day I got ready for the nature hike Mom had planned. As we drove in silence out to the rugged west coast of the island, I found it strange. Since spending so much time with Jude, I wasn't accustomed to constant silence; we spent a lot time expressing our feelings. Feelings of oppression grew deeper as I played along in the silent game. After all this time I still wasn't ready to fully speak my mind. We began our walk out in the countryside. It was a beautiful spring day and it felt wonderful to be outside. Halfway through our walk, I turned around and asked my parents if they believed in past lives.

As usual Mom answered first as we made our way through the shady, lush forest trail. "You know, I really want to. I really love the idea, but I do find it hard to believe that we have lived many lives and will continue to do so in the future." Typical mom answer. Unless a belief was scientifically proven, she didn't believe it. Silently nodding, I turned to Dad. He remained silent, a normal role, quiet observer. But this time the quiet observer got picked on as well!

"How about you, Dad? Do you believe in past lives?" Surprised that he was being brought into the conversation and included, he asked me to repeat the question. After I enquired again about past lives, he answered, "Yes, yes, I do. I most definitely do believe it's possible." Nodding, I told him I agreed with his thoughts and felt that past lives were most definitely real.

Insightfulness came with this conversation. I realized that two people whom I love the most are losing the most beautiful thing in a marriage: togetherness!

Am I assuming this or judging?

Ending the discussion on past lives, we reached the summit of the mountain. We saw a spectacular view of the island's coastline and ocean as far as the eye could see. Standing at the summit, I inhaled deeply and released my frustration into the universe. As Mom chattered on about everything except her feelings, I began daydreaming again about the meeting day with Stephen.

Because it was the long Easter weekend, we were due for a family visit with my grandparents up at Cobble Hill. As a little girl, I had been very close with my grandmother, but as the years wore on, my visits with her had become less and less frequent. My mother and she had always had their issues, and that had left me directly in the middle. Years of hearing my mom speak poorly of my grandmother had led me to create false impressions of her. Over the years I had believed my moms word about my grandmother without forming my own opinions. Since I had been discovering the importance of having a voice, I have started seeing my grandmother in a different light. She has always been looked upon as the matriarch of the family due to her assertive nature. In reality she only wanted the best for her family and expressed that through honesty. Being enlightened to the beauty of truth, I was seeing my grandmother differently. As I entered their home, she instantly noticed my quieter nature and silently communicated her praise with a smile of approval.

Surveying the traditional turkey feast, I was alive with excitement. When truly appreciating my life and the new leaf I had turned with my grandmother, tastes seemed sweeter that night. Tangy cranberries perfectly complimented the turkey as the mashed potatoes melted on my tongue. Glorious brussel sprouts were cooked to perfection as I enjoyed the meal with my family. After our delicious feast, my grandmother retreated to the kitchen and brought out her famous pound cake. Loaded with raisins and figs; the pound cake had been a Sutherland tradition since the dawn of time. Piling pounds of brandy butter upon the dessert, I felt the sensation of home: sweet, warm, safe, with unconditional love.

That evening I sat beside my grandmother and watched her with my eyes and heart wide open. I finally saw her as the loving woman she had been all along; I had just been too selfish to notice.

As we left that evening, she hugged me tightly and I knew that she understood the spiritual path I was on. When she whispered that she loved me in my ear, I felt closer to her than I had in years. The bridge-building process had begun.

Arriving home that evening, I sat in the living room and tried to explain my relationship with Jude. As we sat in our cozy living room with peppermint tea, I enlightened my parents on the sorts of topics we spoke about and lessons I had learned. I told them about her teachings of aura cleanses, past lives, and meditation; also the comfortable silent times we shared when neither had anything too particularly pressing to talk about. I knew deep inside me that Dad understood this but played the concerned father anyway.

♥   ♥   ♥

Early the next morning, I called Jude to check in and see how things were going with her because ego had put doubts in my mind; I was rather standoffish and guarded as we spoke. Still a tiny voice deep in my tummy told me to trust Jude and follow my heart, I told her I would be on the three o'clock ferry, and she agreed to come get me at the ferry terminal. Today was the last day to see my parents before heading out east, so I arranged a coffee date with Mom and a lunch date with Dad.

Meeting at a busy downtown joint, Mom and I said our goodbyes. Sitting at the table, I began caretaking her by asking her to pursue her passions and follow her heart. This statement angered her and she stood up to leave. "You aren't the one who is supposed to be telling me what to do. It's the other way around." Upon reflection I realize her words were true. The unfortunate reality was that my mom didn't know how to be my mom.

Over the years my mother had forgotten to understand that she and I were equals. A huge reason I have always resented my mom was due to her belief that as mother she had to be perfect. The reality is that all I wanted was her to remember what it was like to be my age and to treat me with respect. Giving each other rather stiff hugs, we parted ways on the busy downtown street corner.

I drove toward my dad's school and wondered if Mom was ever going to understand me. We had lots of talking to do, but unfortunately neither one of us had ever been shown healthy confrontation. At present I am trying to understand my mother's world in order for our relationship to grow.

Walking into my dad's school, I took a deep breath and absorbed all the familiar smells. Awkward feelings, terrible self-confidence, and hotdog days all came rushing back to me as I strolled toward the library. My dad had been a teacher for many years but recently switched over to full-time librarian, his dream job. I felt proud of him as I walked into the library to meet him. He was a man who truly cared about the education system, and it showed in the amount of effort he put into his job.

Sneaking up to him, I poked him on the shoulder as he was stocking books. He jumped a mile high and then landed back with a cheeky smile on his face. "Turkey," he called me and ruffled my hair. "Let's go grab some lunch!" I had forgotten that Dad would get really stressed out at work and that our family was prone to neurotic behaviors, myself included.

We ate a scrumptious lunch at a nearby pub and I again reminded him that I was going to be just fine on my journey. His gray eyes were filled with worry, but I knew he understood. Our time together seemed to be on fast-forward, and just as I was explaining my thoughts on meditation, Dad informed me he had to head back to work. Not wanting the visit with my dad to be over, I decided to go watch him teach a library session. Pride flowed through me as I watched my pops instruct his class. He was teaching them about the Titanic and had created the most magical lesson plan. He came alive as he enthusiastically generated excitement about the old ship in his students. After fifteen minutes I knew I had to leave to catch the ferry. Gesturing to him, I made my way to the door. Stepping outside in the hall, he gave me a huge hug, and his voice got thicker with emotion. "Please, drive safe and say hi to Jude for me" was what he mustered. Tears began filling his eyes.

"I love you, Dad. Please take care of yourself," I said quickly. I made my way out of the school, fighting back tears. At that moment my dad and I both sensed my journey out east would be much more than simply a new adventure. Deep down he knew that the journey I was about to embark upon was a spiritual quest to reclaim my identity.

♥   ♥   ♥

On the way to the ferries, I stopped downtown for a quick coffee. Standing in the line, I noticed a bizarre-looking man flipping through the paper. Gesturing at me, he told me I could go ahead of him. Touched by his gesture, I said thank you and moved forward. Satisfied with his paper flipping, the old man stood behind me and introduced himself. "Hello there. I'm Olar. Who are you?" Curious by his friendly nature, I introduced myself. Our conversation continued, and before I knew it, I was sitting down for coffee with him. As it turned out, Olar was an intuitive man. For the next two hours, Olar informed me about my future and said that I had many doubts. He insisted that I listen to my intuition and never doubt myself.

Because of the power of suggestion, this statement would haunt me for our entire journey!

Leaving the coffee shop, I hopped on the bus to the ferries. Embarking on a coastal ferry sail, I sank into a comfy seat and I thought about future adventures. I was really looking forward to seeing Jude, but I still knew I was holding back around her for some reason. This mystery of mistrust would unfold itself whether I wanted it to or not on the journey.

Ignoring my ego and her whispers of doubts and fears, I gained more excitement as the ferry neared the terminal, and I quickly disembarked the boat. I zigged and zagged my way down to the passenger area. As I walked down the stairs, I felt excited as I searched the crowd for Jude. *Red hair. Nope, that's not her. Pink umbrella. Probably not, Five two with stylish handbag and cool sunglasses. There she is!* Once we made eye contact, we silently greeted one another with twinkling eyes and big smiles.

We drove back to Vancouver in a freshly washed Cassidy and arrived back at the apartment. The reality of packing and cleaning hit me hard. My friend Mark had been house-sitting, so the place was clean, but I still felt there was a lot of preparation to be done before our trek out east.

As mentioned earlier, karma does come to bite you in the bum! Allow me to explain.

While I had been away, Mark had been watching my apartment under the agreement that he would pay half the rent. By April he had only paid for one month and I was stuck with the predicament of getting the rest of the payment. At the time of the arrangement, I had been planning on staying in Vancouver. Not being honest, I had allowed Mark to think that he and I might stand a chance of dating upon my arrival back from the lodge. My latest e-mail to him had informed him about my plans to move to Montreal with Jude. Due to this, Mark played the karma card with me. Over the phone he disclosed that his old drug-dealing friend needed money and said he had given him everything he owned. He expressed that he was going to send the money express post to Montreal as soon as he could. A sinking feeling inside me grew like a contagious monster as I nodded and pretended to be understanding. Feelings of anger and betrayal came over me as I quickly made up some excuse to get off the phone.

"I hope Montreal treats you well, Katie" were the last words from his mouth.

Hanging up the phone, I silently kicked myself for having gotten into such a silly situation to begin with. Had I shown honesty with Mark, this never would have happened. My feelings of anger and betrayal that had been focused at Mark shifted to myself, stupid self. Why wasn't I honest from the start? Sure, Mark had just played me, but I had been playing him too. What a deceptive game! Nobody wins and both parties leave feeling defeated and cheated. I made a mental note to myself about this situation and resolved to remain honest in the future with scenarios involving people's feelings.

♥   ♥   ♥

Heading back to the apartment, I found myself thinking about Stephen. He was due back from South America in less than a week and I was still nervous about his arrival.

To give you an idea of what Stephen and my relationship looks like, I feel it is important to look at my own parents' situation. Often girls will repeat relationship patterns that they see happening at home, and hence I have taken a serious look at my mom and dad's example.

For years I had watched my mother wear the pants in the relationship, and basically my dad catered to her, never standing up for himself. She belittled him in front of me and he allowed it. My father's silence greatly affected me. From him I learned that it was okay for women who loved you to make you feel like a moron. Over time I slowly began resenting my father for having no backbone. Why did this beautiful man allow this woman to speak to him this way? Where was his courage? Why didn't he give his opinions? I love my father dearly, but he definitely demonstrated a terrible role model in terms of an equal partner in a relationship.

By fifteen I had grown so tired of being punished for speaking my mind. I stopped communicating my true feelings altogether. The anger and sadness I felt toward my parents went inward as I slowly began molding myself into the perfect daughter. Wanting nothing more than just love from my parents, I began behaving exactly how I thought they wanted me to: bubbly, carefree, and basically a doormat. Other people's feelings soon became more important than my own, and I quickly slipped into the role of the ever popular "people pleaser."

Here are the following traits:
1. rather wimpy
2. bends over backwards to help others yet can't help herself
3. compromises her feelings for fear of hurting someone else's
4. smiles all the time

Those are simply a few of the traits that I acquired as I metamorphosed into the ultimate people-pleaser, or perhaps I should say caretaker. Great marks, over-achiever in extra-circular activities, athlete: it all looked great on paper. But you know what? It wasn't for myself that I was doing all the overachieving. It was to gain love and attention from my parents.

"Growing up, I learned that voicing my opinion = punishment and suppressing my opinion = love from mom and dad."

So as you can see, I had several issues I needed to work out within myself before I could even dream of having a functional relationship. Firstly I needed to truly love myself, but at the time I didn't even know who I was.

Copying my mother's illustration, I found myself in a relationship with a boy who allowed me to have all the control. I was imitating the same controlling love my mom had shown, with conditions upon it. Knowing that I had Stephen wrapped around my finger, I basically was able to call all the shots and make important decisions. I had created a fictional relationship by convincing myself that everything between us was perfect. Again, as I grew up in a non-communicative family, speaking the truth was a foreign concept to me. So when Stephen did something that bothered me, instead of letting him know about it, I bottled it up, allowing it to grow bigger inside me. Stephen and I spent a one and a half years together never arguing and never having differing opinions. I have now realized this was the control I wielded over him, and I am ashamed at my behavior.

♥   ♥   ♥

Several days later, Stephen arrived back on the west coast. E-mailing him, I told him that I was planning on moving to Montreal and that I wanted to see him before I left. He responded by text-messaging me back. His message read "Want to see you before you go, I'm coming over today on the 3:30 ferry with my friend, could you pick me up?"

As I was rereading the message, a medley of emotions came over me: excitement, hesitancy, nervousness, and curiously all jumped out at me—and dread as I contemplated my response. Of course I wanted to see him. But I also wondered deep down if it was simply to maintain the control I had over him. At the time I still didn't want to shake my control over the relationship. Ignoring my intuition (and

Jude's silent gaze) I responded by stating that Jude and I would be at the terminal to pick him up. Heart pounding, I told Jude the scoop. Shrugging her shoulders, she said, "Well, perhaps all is correcting itself now. I sure hope so for your sake." Nodding enthusiastically, I felt a surge of fake confidence and continued painting the apartment walls. The reason I say I had fake confidence is because nobody but you can make you feel great about yourself.

The rest of the afternoon, Jude and I polished, cleaned, and swept our big hearts out. Though I pretended not to, I had been eyeing the clock every four minutes, anxiously awaiting Stephen's arrival. Finally, at four, I went and found Jude; she was in the bathtub giving it the best scrub it had ever received. Hair disheveled and eyes sparking, she looked up at me, over the French café music. I shouted, "It's time, buddy. We have to go pick up Stephen from the ferries." Nodding, she finished up the tub and made her way to the freshly painted living room.

Driving out to the ferries, I was a bundle of nervous energy; even deep breathing couldn't relax me as we pulled into the lush Horseshoe Bay. Surrounded by green trees and vibrant wildflowers, I tried to concentrate on the beauty of the area. Momentarily distracted, I looked over at Jude, who remained relaxed in the driver's seat *Man, that's got to be nice to be so calm all the time,* I thought to myself. *One day, when I grow up, I'm going to be like that.* Little did I know I had a lot of self-manifested drama in my life to cleanse myself of before getting to that serenity.

Arriving at the ferry terminal, we found a parking spot and made our way to the arrival gate. Feeling super jittery, I began pacing back and forth in a weak attempt to release nervous energy. Finally, after what seemed like an eternity, I saw Stephen's black curly hair coming down the elevator. My heart began beating even quicker, but wait! Something was off with this picture. Upon closer inspection, I noticed there was a girl right beside him. My heart stopped beating; I couldn't believe what I was seeing. Next to Stephen was a girl. As they approached I did the full girl checkout. She was beautiful; long black silky hair framed delicately, petite bone structure, and clear olive skin. *So this is Stephen's friend,* I concluded while standing outside. As they approached me, the girl looked at me shyly with her beautiful brown eyes. I felt like we were back in primal days when two female baboons both wanted the same male baboon. Stephen gave me a hug and turned around to Jude said, "Hi," then brought his attention back to his newfound "friend."

"Oh," Stephen said. "Yeah, this is my friend Harmony; Harmony this is Katie." As I shook her hand and said hello, I felt about as friendly as a cobra after five days of not eating. Declining my offer of a ride into town, Harmony quickly hugged Stephen and made her way toward the buses. As I watched this bombshell walk away from us, a realization slowly dawned on me. Bringing Harmony along was Stephen's way of getting back at me for all the hurt I caused him over the years.

♥   ♥   ♥

That night we went out for drinks at a nearby pub. Deep down I knew things were over with him, but I wanted to sleep with him one last time. It was my way of keeping the power I had over him. As I write this, I am very ashamed of my behavior, but that is what I had been thinking. True to form, we ended up sleeping together and I was left feeling empty. The magic of our past relationship had disappeared, and I realized that I had made a horrible mistake. Stephen had moved on from my control and I could feel his cold demeanor toward me. Dropping him off at the ferries the following morning, I felt about the size of a pea, perhaps even smaller. This relationship had been over for so long, but I had been clinging onto the fictional memories of the past. Although I knew that my relationship with Stephen was over, I still obsessed about him all the way across our Canadian journey (and to be completely honest, I still thought of him into the U.S. as well. Crazy)

♥   ♥   ♥

Later that afternoon I scanned the apartment and my reality sunk in. Yet again I was leaving another city, another cozy apartment, to run from myself. I didn't know this at the time, but indeed I was who I ran from.

Fresh paint smell, boxes of books, letters, and toiletries all stared blankly back at me. Is this what I had become at twenty-six years old? A great painter of apartment walls and professional box-packer, self-esteem the size of a flea. I began crying (AGAIN)! Despite my quick smiles and bubbly nature, I was rapidly discovering I was a rather unhappy camper.

Taking one last look at my apartment I thanked it for the memories and closed the front door. Placing the extra keys in the landlord's mailbox, I was ready to begin my new journey. What lay ahead still remained a mystery, but I was thrilled at the idea of unraveling it.

♥   ♥   ♥

Walking the walk

Unknown to me at the time, the physical part of my spiritual path was about to begin. As Jude and I prepared to leave Vancouver, I had no idea what lay ahead. Let my journey begin:

Getting started:

In order for us to embark on this magical mystery tour, we needed the following:

- ❖ 1 green van named Cassidy
- ❖ 2 girls
- ❖ 2 great spirits
- ❖ 1 jar of peanut butter
- ❖ multivitamins
- ❖ COFFEE!
- ❖ H20 a plenty (especially in the desert)
- ❖ no boys/men (They are way too distracting!)
- ❖ 2 cell phones

- ❖ 1 can of bear spray
- ❖ 1 pocket knife (never been used)
- ❖ wet ones (a girl's best friend)
- ❖ 1 bench seat, 2 bucket seats
- ❖ 1 futon
- ❖ 1 dream catcher
- ❖ many air fresheners
- ❖ Pillows a plenty
- ❖ 1 special blankie and pillow
- ❖ 1 down quilt (extremely useful in heat waves!)

Eliminate:
- ❖ gym workouts
- ❖ baths/showers (Hot water is our biggest dream at present!)
- ❖ hair dryer
- ❖ CD player
- ❖ SANITY! (Lost that very early!)
- ❖ Ego crushed over and over again

Are you sure you have gathered all the essential belongings? Great, then let's begin.

Prior to hitting the dusty trail, Jude and I made various stops in Vancouver. To lighten up our load, we donated all sorts of great treasures to the local Salvation Army: record player, billions of records, microwave, and countless knick knacks were all given in hopes that their new owners would appreciate their talents. Our last stop was a women's shelter where we dropped off some freshly baked chocolate chip cookies.

Exhaling, Jude and I looked at one another, cranked the satellite radio, and made a beeline for the Highway 1 east. Grooving to soul music, the only place for great funk all day long, we pulled into a gas station to refuel Cass for the journey. While I was inside buying water, Jude was busy filling up the back tire. Daydreaming, Jude was startled by a man who appeared beside Cass. Leaning down, he carefully inspected the back tire. Nodding to himself, he turned to

Jude and stated "Yup, you are needed to fix this tire before you get to the Rockies. Having a flat tire on an isolated road, being a woman isn't fun." Jude thanked him and smiled. He disappeared as quickly as he had arrived.

Intrigued by the encounter, Jude recounted the conversation to me. Shrugging my shoulders, I didn't really see the big deal about it. Sighing, Jude began explaining herself: "The spirit world works in very mysterious ways. Often they will send the most bizarre person on your path to relay a message to you. I get the feeling that the man was one of those instances, but you have to remember to pay attention and look for signs. This is very important if you want to live in six-sensory perception." Bewildered with fascination, I responded with my typical "Oh cool." I was still learning so much about the spirit realm that new knowledge soaked into me like a sponge, and I didn't have much to say except "Oh cool."

Pulling onto the Highway 1 east, I felt my spirits soar as the busy, chaotic city backdrop disappeared. Vibrant green grass and tall peaked mountains greeted us as we sat back and enjoyed the spectacular, lush beauty of British Columbia. Worries about the future vanished as Jude and I happily sung along to pop hits on the radio. Around 7:30 p.m. we reached the entrance of Manning Park, a gorgeous provincial park full of majestic mountains and chatty wildlife.

Somewhere along the winding road, Jude began asking me questions about my behavior and particular habits. Growing impatient with her questions, I asked her to stop challenging me. Laughing, Jude looked over to me and responded, "Katie, I'm not even challenging you right now; you are simply getting defensive, for some reason. Why are you so defensive? What's going on?"

Having Jude as such a close friend was incredible but also very revealing. Due to her extreme intuitiveness, she could sense energy shifts from a mile away, especially with those she spent time with. I was no exception. The minute my energy shifted, she would pounce, investigating the reason behind it. As the Manning Park road twisted and turned, I suddenly felt anger making its way to the surface. I couldn't keep it in any longer. "I can't stand the way my mom has no regard for me or my feelings. Just recently she was at a dinner party and when friends enquired about me she responded by saying, 'Oh we don't know about Katie anymore. We just want her to make her mind up.'" My entire body tensed up as I disclosed to Jude my true sentiments toward my mother. "It's easy for her to be honest to a group of her friends, yet when it comes to communicating with me, it never happens." Feeling increasingly angry, I began to drive faster.

Jude calmly responded, "Have you communicated to your parents about how you feel?"

"I don't know," I shot back, now getting really pissed. Glaring at Jude, I directed my anger toward her. I stumbled to find a suitable response to her question but failed. Everything that started leaving my mouth was ridiculous excuses of blaming others instead of me. Flying around corners at this point, I was frightened to discover I had so much anger internalized. Anger had never, ever been an emotion in my range of emotions. At a young age, I learned that demonstrating anger got me punishment, whereas being polite, obedient, and passive got me hugs and affection. It didn't take long for me to learn how to suppress my anger and mask it. Having masked internal anger for so long, I truly believed I didn't have the emotion in my body. Woowers! What a crock of absolute bullpoop that concept was!

Right here on the number-three highway east, I discovered that, yes indeed, there was the scary emotion, anger, right inside my tummy. Similar to a red, scaly dragon just awakening after centuries of slumber, my anger was being revived. Unsure of what to do with this new discovery, I gritted my teeth and growled like a dog. It seems pretty humorous now, but at the time it truly felt like the right thing to do. Jude smiled at me and suggested yelling. Yelling? Was she nuts?

"I don't yell," I stated. The minute the statement slipped from my lips, I realized how stupid it sounded. "I don't yell." I said as though repeating it would add validity to the statement.

Shaking her head, Jude laughed. "Come on, Katie, I'm sure you used to know how to yell." Rather excited at the prospect of being able to yell, I put my window down and took a deep breath. "Ahhhhhhhhhh" came streaming out of my voice box. "Wow, I thought that felt really cool!"

Jude encouraged me to continue yelling. As we drove into a mystical sunset of yellows and blues, I continued yelling out the window. Honestly I couldn't believe how amazing it felt to release my anger out into the universe. It had been lying dormant for so long that the dragon breathed epic fire from its belly.

Around 10:30 that night, we pulled off the road to locate a nesting spot to rest our bones. Satisfied with a quiet country road, Jude and I climbed aboard the floating futon. As I shut off the interior lights, my mind replayed the events with Stephen. All sorts of fears wandered into my mind as I desperately attempted to sleep. Looking up at the ceiling, I began feeling claustrophobic due to my own repression of inner struggles. Hearing the rhythmic sound of Jude's snoring, I sought tranquility to no avail. My ego had now taken over my mind and would not allow me to rest.

♥   ♥   ♥

Brilliant rays of sunshine woke us the next morning. Having received three hours of sleep, I was grumpy to say the least.

We spent the day driving through the beautiful Canadian Rocky Mountains and discussing my previous patterns. Through a long session of truth-telling, I discovered that I had been living with a multitude of masks on. There were many parts of my personality that were completely incongruent with whom I truly was. This is what I discovered:

DELUSIONAL	REALITY
Hippy chick	totally conservative
Always happy	sad deep down
Scatter brained	had poop in a group
Wise beyond my years	oh so much to learn
Love guru	conditions put on love
Extreme Snowboarding	hated extreme snowboarding
Tomboy	girly girl

Ever since I was a little girl, I would wish for happiness every chance I got. Now, looking back, it makes me sad because I realized while writing this book I had wished my life away and stopped living in the now but always in the future. I remember, as a lanky eleven-year-old, staring in the mirror and wishing I was older. Now, here I was, fifteen years later, still making wishes. Another one of Jude teachings consisted of the power of intention. "If you believe, you will achieve, Katie. Just remember that whatever you put your heart and soul into with one hundred percent you will achieve. First, you need to find your likes and dislikes or simply your passion in this lifetime." Jude has given me a book that educated on the magical properties of projection. She had another saying:

"Good intentions, good results; bad intentions, bad results."

Around 8:30 p.m. that night, the sun began setting. We were leaving the ski hill town of Fernie just two hours before crossing the border into Alberta. As Jude maneuvered Cassidy up the windy, steep hill, I turned back to look behind me. Nestled in the canyon was the little town all lighted up with streetlamps and chimneys. Magical twilight illuminated everything around us as we chugged our way forward. It was in that moment I felt complete. The safety of darkness and soft warmth of Jude's friendship encompassed me like my ultimate blanket.

"Happiness is a momentary experience, Katie. It comes from within," Jude commented.

When I was a little girl, I had convinced myself that the only way to be happy was to make others happy. Years rolled on and I was so consumed by pleasing other people I completely forgot about my own happiness and feelings of self-worth. Part of me knew then this journey Jude and I were embarking on was to reclaim me, Katie Sutherland, and discover what made me happy.

As we hit the Alberta border, bright sparking stars twinkled overhead. Finding another country road, Jude maneuvered Cassidy to a spot where we would nestle down for the evening. Looking outside, I could see the faint outline of the Rocky Mountains, a vibrant blue in the faraway distance. Low humming began as we found ourselves surrounded by friendly, singing crickets and frogs. Ensuring the car doors were locked, I slipped under the covers. We said our good nights, and I knew I was going to have a great sleep.

Ten minutes into my rest, Jude shot up like a bolt of lighting. "Katie, Katie." I could hear the urgency in her voice as she woke me. "It doesn't feel right here. We have to go, we have to go now!"

Surprised by Jude's reaction, I giggled nervously, not knowing what to say. "Really?" I asked, still half asleep.

"Trust me, Katie. When my instincts wake me up this quickly, I pay attention. We can't stay here tonight."

Believing Jude's words, I drowsily hopped in the driver's seat and headed further east. Several kilometers down the road, I pulled off down another deserted lane, where we nestled in for the night. Assuring me this spot felt better, Jude rolled on her side and soon the van was filled with her lovely snoring.

The journey through Alberta seemed to go very quickly due to its landscape of flat, flat, and more flat. Images of dinosaurs and windmills welcomed us as we surveyed the big, open backdrop in front of us. That particular morning I had awoken with a pounding headache and sore throat. Unknown to me, due to my obsessive thoughts regarding the Stephen situation, I had made myself sick. Instead of speaking my mind each and every time his face crossed my mind, I suppressed the thoughts back inside—not a good idea. Halfway through Alberta I had to pull over and have Jude take over the wheel.

Upon reflection I realize I had allowed myself to get sick. The power of my mind had been so convincing that indeed all my suppressed emotions manifested into illness. I now understand that the majority of my illnesses over my lifetime were created from not communicating and silencing my emotions.

Lying in the back of Cassidy, I felt so sick and pathetic. Here was this awesome journey with Jude and I was ruining it. Looking up front, Jude forged ahead, taking on the responsibility of driving.

"The universe is always going to take care of you, Katie. You just have to believe in yourself and the fact that there is a greater plan at work here. Keep your senses open and catch all the signs."

For years I had been taking care of others' dreams, and not once had someone truly done that for me. Naturally, when I was sick, my parents looked after me, but they had shown me how to play on my weakness. Whenever something went wrong with my life, I would always head home to the island to be coddled by my parents. Though momentarily it felt great, I began believing I was very fragile and couldn't handle certain challenges life threw my way. And then along came Jude!

Self-proclaimed teacher of tough love, she demonstrates the qualities of real love which are:

❖ patience
❖ loving without wanting anything in return
❖ integrity
❖ honesty
❖ emanating accountability; one's actions!

During the fall, it was Jude's honest words that always brought me back to reality: "You brought this on yourself, kiddo. Sorry to say, but you did know. What are you going to do to get out of it." Her words were packed with just the right amount of love, truth, and compassion. When she spoke she meant every word.

Though her truth did offend me, I always in turn understood that her intention wasn't to hurt but to enlightenment my essence.

The entire day consisted of driving, driving, and more driving. Kilometers slipped away as Cassidy sped farther and farther east.

Reaching the time of our midday coffee craving, we decided to head into Moose Jaw for a quick caffeine fix. After grabbing our standard orders from Tim Horton's, we wandered the streets of Moose Jaw, stretching our weary legs from the long drive across the prairies. Reaching the central park, Jude and I noticed a fountain where we could conduct our daily tarot readings. Blusters of wind brushed through our hair as we interpreted the messages from the universe. Once our readings had been completed, Jude and I began speaking abut my girl friends.

"I find it strange that you have never truly allowed your girl friends see your emotions or troubles. Why don't you let them in? Do you feel scared to show them your emotions?" Instantly defensive, my boxing gloves came on. I couldn't respond to Jude's questions. Following past patterns, my body began shutting down and I got up from the bench. Hair flying crazily in the wind, I started that I needed to be alone.

"Being alone isn't what you need, Katie. You can figure this out with me present the entire time. You have spent your entire life running.

You need to stop and face your issues. They are never going to go away if you keep ignoring them." Ignorant to her words, I ran away. Blinking back tears, I wondered why I was so affected by her words. While I aimlessly walked around town, miraculously I received my answer: *because you know that what she speaks of is true.* Though these were not exactly the words my stubborn self wanted to hear, I had acknowledged my inner guidance. Twenty minutes after my wanderings, I returned back to Cassidy feeling sheepish from my childish behavior. Still too defiant apologize, I silently unlocked Jude's door, climbed in the front seat, and stared straight ahead. Starting up Cassidy, we drove toward the capital city of Saskatchewan-Regina.

After spending the entire afternoon driving in silence, we decided to make a pit stop in Regina. Locating a lovely Irish pub, we sat down at a picnic table with some local Regina characters. Ordering drinks and tasty food for dinner, we began chitchatting with the guys who allowed us to join them. The pub was rocking—Friday (TGIF crowd).

It felt great to have some form of distraction from my own thoughts. Feeling ashamed that I was still concerning myself with Stephen, I didn't tell Jude about my daily inner struggles. Talking about my feelings was so new to me that I didn't want to bore Jude with my worries. They felt small and unimportant, so I decided to keep them quiet.   Sitting back, I enjoyed listening to the friendly guy beside me declare his pride in his hometown. Though, as I mentioned earlier, Canada was mainly a blur for me, I do remember the beautiful people we came across who were quick to offer kind words and actions. Leaving the pub with our bellies full, Jude and I began roaming around Regina, enjoying the warm spring evening. Curious about light workers and our mission, I started asking Jude for answers to my deep questions: "Jude, is Montreal the right place? What are we going to do there? How are we going to do our work? Why was I chosen to come on the mission? What does it all mean?" and so on and so forth.

Eventually Jude grew tired of my questioning and stopped. "Don't ask me, Katie. Look inside. All your answers are there."

Angry at her response, I exploded. "But I don't know how to do that. All these things are happening and I don't know why. Can't you just tell me." With my face a brilliant shade of red, I glared over at Jude.

"Like I said, Katie, look inside," she responded calmly.

Throwing more misguided anger at her, I responded, "Thanks very much, Jude. You don't understand anything. I'm out of here." And with that I stormed off toward the city streets of Regina. Angry thoughts darkened my mood. I stomped aimlessly into town. I noticed a nearby park framed with large green Garry Oaks. I made my way over to find a cedar bench and sat down. My internal questions popped up as I sat down on the bench. Miraculously, when I began repeating the questions over in my mind, the answers echoed from within. Glancing around the park to see if anyone else had heard the voices, I realized the answers were meant specifically for me.

Shocked at my newfound discovery, I remained in the park till dusk. Feeling embarrassed at the way I had treated Jude, I stood up and made my way toward Cassidy, preparing myself to eat humble pie. Once I approached the green minivan, I saw Jude sitting in the passenger seat, patiently waiting till I returned. Sheepishly I handed her a coffee I had bought and apologized for my behavior.

Jude's reaction was "It's not me you want to apologize to, Katie, it's yourself. You want to look outside when all your answers are within. Trust your inner guidance and your intuition. It will never lead you astray."

As my tension from earlier slowly dissipated, I allowed myself to relax as we continued on our incredible journey.

♥　　　　　♥　　　　　♥

We reached Winnipeg, Manitoba the following afternoon. Having visited Winnipeg several years back; I recalled a touristy gathering place called The Forks.

It boasted great markets, fresh fruit, and outdoor entertainers. Once we arrived at The Forks and found a spot to park, carnival music and popcorn smells greeted us. Both desperately needing to use the washroom facilities, Jude and I scoped out the information booth. Curious to see if Stephen had responded to my letter, I made my way over to the computers.

As I sat down at the computer, I felt my heart begin to pound as I typed in my e-mail password. Three new messages were waiting for me in my inbox: one from mom and dad, the other two from Stephen. Hands shaking, I opened the letter from Stephen.

In his letter Stephen responded to a message I had sent to him several days prior. I had accused him of being romantically linked to Harmony. In his letter he denied those words and stated that he was worried about me. He didn't understand my need to rediscover myself and felt insulted that I had essentially chosen Jude over him. Telling me he was still in love with me, he closed off the letter. Deciding to leave the message unanswered, I sat in the Internet station, a jumble of emotions.

Sensing my silent meltdown, Jude walked over to the Internet station.

"You okay?" she asked.

Shaking my head dramatically, I responded, "No, Stephen just sent me a message and I'm so confused. He still loves me and I can feel it. I don't know what to do. I need some time alone." And with that I escaped into the crowded boulevard full of vendors and colorful tourists. Finding some stairs in front of the magician, I tried to distract myself.

After ten minutes of sitting on the stairs, I looked up to see Jude's blue coat and curly dark hair approaching me.

"Well, Miss McGillacutty, have you calmed down?" she enquired with a hint of a smile, sitting down beside me.

"Oh, Jude, I just don't know what to do. What if Stephen is still in love with me?" I searched her brown eyes for the answer.

"What if he is, Katie? You two have played this game of cat-and-mouse for so long it's only thing you know. My recommendation would be to let the chips fall where they fall and not to force things. You seem to always need to have the last say. Why not leave this for a while?" Acknowledging her wise words, I nodded.

Though I knew Jude was right, my strong insecurities got the best of me and I convinced myself I needed to talk to Stephen to clear up things.

Can you see how I had created such a vicious cycle for myself?

Why had I created such a long, drawn-out process for myself? I had been accustomed to always having Stephen as a fallback, so the prospect of finally terminating those ties scared me.

♥   ♥   ♥

Once we hit the Manitoba/Ontario border, Jude began getting excited. "I don't know what it is about Ontario, but I am really thrilled to get into that province." Giggling, she turned up the radio and we began dancing to '70s rock and roll tunes.

After about twenty minutes of driving, completely surrounded by trees, my opinion softened about the big old province of Ontario. Jude and I got out, stretching our weary bodies. In front of us lay the cutest town we had seen since leaving Vancouver; called Canora. In front of us a huge lake lay sprawling for miles. As we walked down to the marina, the sky changed colors from red to pink, then finally decided on a deep, vivid orange. Clouds scattered across the sky as though they were creating messages specifically for us.

Hearing a rumble from my empty tummy, I suggested we grab some food. Across the street from the marina, I saw a quaint little Irish pub with cheerful vibes bouncing off the brick walls. As we sat down, an extremely attractive man in his mid-twenties came to take our drink order. "Good evening, ladies. What can I get for you this evening?" After ordering ice water, coffee, and red wine, we sat back to enjoy our environment. After our waiter scuttled over with our drinks, Jude leaned forward with a devilish gleam in her eye. Jude opened her mouth. "Well, there, young fella, now what's your name?" she said it in such a tone that it would be impossible not to smile.

Blushing, the blonde guy flashed Jude a big smile. "Well, my name is Kyle."

"Well, Kyle, thank you very much for bringing our drinks over. I was beginning to think you had forgotten about us." Due to the confidence and sincerity in her voice, it was virtually impossible for Kyle to do anything but smile. As Kyle walked away assuring us the waitress would visit soon, I shyly avoided eye contact with him.

Growing up, I definitely had a case of the ugly duckling syndrome. Glasses, braces, and pimples were all great targets for bullying from the popular, cute boys at school. Not having fully gotten over my childhood awkwardness, I never felt I was worthy of attractive men's attention. Naturally Jude noticed my shy reaction and investigated. "Hey, Katie, how come you are so shy around good-looking men?" Ah, busted again! Was there anything I could slip past this woman?!

As I explained to her my ugly duckling complex, Jude listened intently. "You know, kiddo, men love to see confidence. Did you notice the way Kyle reacted to my assertiveness?" I nodded my head. "Well, trust me; men love that direct and honest approach."

Throughout our dining adventure, Jude would slyly say comments to Kyle that would make him blush. I couldn't believe what I was watching. A spunky lady in her fifties was charming a super hottie my age. Twinges of jealousy came over me as I envied the way in which Jude became so comfortable. I have since learned it was due to her great self-esteem and open way of talking. As we stood up to pay, Kyle mentioned to us that we should come back soon. Jude replied "Yeah, you'd like that, wouldn't you, Kyle. Trust me, young fella, you wouldn't even know what to do with me!" The entire staff erupted into fits of laughter as Jude tossed her jacket over her shoulder and walked out. Flabbergasted by the whole scene, I ran after her. "Jude, how do you do that?' I innocently asked. She smiled up at me

"Simple. Talk straight from the heart and don't forget to play. Men love a challenge." Yet again, snaps for Jude as she taught me another life lesson.

♥   ♥   ♥

That night we found a super fabulous spot to park for the night. Turning down an old country road, I stumbled upon a spooky forest with darks trees all around. Crooked and gnarled branches swayed in the wind as Jude and I went through the motions of our nightly routine: brush teeth, wash face, turn out the lights, and lock the doors. We were just like people who lived in houses, except it was Cassidy, the minivan.

The full moon beamed its pure white light down upon us, creating a soft glow across the floral bedspread. Jude's words echoed through my mind as I drifted off. "Some people can stay home and fulfill their journey, but not you, Katie. You must physically walk your spiritual path." Her words rang true as I contemplated the many different places I had called home over the years. Although I hadn't been aware of it at the time, my restlessness had arisen from escapism. I was unable to face my own demons and truth. I began moving from place to place, avoiding ever admitting to my imperfections and blemishes. At the time it always seemed easier for me to keep moving, making false friends, pretending to be happy, though in reality I didn't like who I had become and couldn't face responsibility for my own actions.

Jude awoke early that morning and began rustling around, looking for the toilet paper. "Do you need to go?" she asked as she stepped out into the chilly dewy morning.

"Nope, I'm set, thanks," I mumbled out from under my covers. Keeping the door open, Jude began retelling me her dream as she did her business. Midway through her sentence, she stopped and suddenly fixated on something. "Hey, there's a dog over there!" she exclaimed "Katie, come look! He's a beautiful lab." Completely uninterested in moving that early in the morning, I managed to say. "No, thanks" and snuggled deeper into the blankets. Jude continued, "You know this dog looks just like Rex, a lab I knew many years back." She turned her head to talk to me. "He was such a beautiful dog," she said, turning her head back in the direction of the apparition. Rex was gone. Jude noticed that the dog had disappeared. "Now, that's strange. Katie, he just disappeared—almost as though he vanished into thin air." Pausing, she pondered what she had just witnessed. "Often the spirit world will send you images from the other side as guidance, messages, or simply comfort. I have the feeling that Rex wasn't actually a real dog. He was from the spirit realm." Again I thought about how fascinating the spirit realm was.

Jude and I headed out to sniff out breakfast. As we approached the closest town, a vibrant red-and-yellow sign caught our attention. "Tim Horton's!" we cried out in unison as I swerved into the parking lot. Ordering our usual breakfast items, we sat down and prepared for another day on the road. After breakfast I made my way to the ladies room, while back at the table, Jude had struck up conversation with a male employee named Ben.

Due to Jude's intuitive nature, she had sensed a strong sadness surrounding this particular fellow. As she asked how he was doing, he halfheartedly shrugged his shoulders. His response was "I'm okay."

Jude continued "Well, I feel your sadness, Ben. Could you tell me why a girl of your age is with you all the time, from the spirit world?"

As Ben stopped his sweeping, he looked into Jude's eyes but remained silent. She said to him, "Well, Ben, I can definitely feel a deep sadness around you. We are going to be here for another twenty minutes, so if you want to talk, please come back." Nodding, Ben left.

She must have stirred emotions within the young man, because Ben came back to the table. "See, my sister, my identical twin, died when we were four—a drowning accident." He stopped like he was back in the horrific day so many years ago.

Jude continued, "Well, that would explain why this young female presence is around you. She wants you to know that she is fine although she worries abut you."

Biting his lip, Ben disclosed more information. "Ever since she died, I haven't been the same. I have bad thoughts, I think of her every day." He stepped closer to Jude as she relayed a message from his twin sister.

"She knows about your bad thoughts and doesn't want you to think them anymore. Her name is Bonnie, correct?" Ben's face lit up when Jude received her name. He was really listening now. Jude continued on, "She wants you to begin healing, so you can move forward. You have great things to accomplish in this lifetime. Please, Ben, keep talking about that day. I know your Mom and Dad just want to forget, but it is very hard for you. Don't stop releasing your pain. I feel your pain, but I am with you." Extending her arms out, Jude embraced Ben, and with that she whispered he his ear, "Bonnie loves you very much."

As we exited the coffee palace, Jude called out "Remember, Ben, you need to heal your heart now," leaving him with her Mona Lisa smile.

I considered the scenario I had witnessed; the pure compassion and warmth that Jude expressed toward Ben was such a rare experience.

Her words were gentle yet truthful and the fact that she spoke with him that morning may have saved his life. Getting into Cassidy, I was at a loss for words to express what an incredible scene I had observed. As we drove away, I knew another affirmation had been shown to me, disclosing to the true magic of the woman seated to my right.

Thunder Bay was the afternoon destination, and we arrived early in the afternoon. Because my mind was so preoccupied with Stephen, I had been ignoring my dwindling health and soon realized I had been starving myself.

Six hundred forty-nine kilometers farther down the road, we arrived in Sue Saint Marie. All day I had been feeling weak, lethargic, unsteady. Enquiring within, I asked what my problem was. *HUNGER* boomed a loud voice from deep inside my tummy. Looking over at Jude, who was driving, I asked her to pull off at the nearest restaurant so we could chow down.

Spotting a famous steakhouse restaurant, she turned in. My insides were aching from hunger as I unsteadily wobbled over to a booth. Because I had not fed myself for several days, the power of fear within my mind was enormous. Eyes filled with concern, Jude said, "Katie, I have watched you do this to yourself for days. I haven't intervened because you don't listen to my words. It's only when you reach this point that you hear what I am trying to say." Tears filled her eyes as she continued. "Do you know how hard it is for me to watch you do this to yourself? I care for you, kid, but you have to take care of yourself. Now, come on, let's order something so we can put meat on your bones."

Managing a pathetic smile, I sent her a grateful look. "Thanks, Jude". After eating an entire chicken, huge baked potato, beans, and pie with ice cream, I heaved a contented sigh.

"So much better," I said and began humming.

This day stays in my mind; Jude's reaction was so pure. She had been stuck in a car with a grumpy boots all the way across four provinces and still demonstrated genuine care for me. Touched deeply by her kindness, I went to bed feeling warm and fuzzy inside. Actions truly speak louder than words, especially when it comes to demonstrating human emotion. I felt myself feeling love for this woman who had beamed into my life. Miracles truly do occur when you believe!

We awoke the next morning and headed out to locate a tasty breakfast joint. Breakfast had soon become my favorite time of day due to the rediscovery of the incredible peanut butter and jam combination. Over breakfast we discussed where our next location was, south, to Michigan in the U.S. or east toward Toronto. Instantly I voiced my negative opinions about our American neighbors.

Smelling a judgment, Jude finished her toast and responded "So, what's wrong with Americans, Katie?"

Annoyed that she challenged me, I struggled to locate the appropriate answer. Unfortunately a brilliant response did not follow, so I attempted to ignore Jude's question.

Wrong tactic! "What's your problem with Americans?" she pressed on, determined to get a response out of me. Putting down my tasty peanut butter toast, I answered, "I don't know, I guess I have always been told that from my family and my friends."

Raising her eyebrows, Jude responded, "So what you are saying is that you have allowed your family and friends to tell you how to think. Make up your own opinions with experience, then you can form your own ideas, not judgments, Katie."

Scratching my head, I absorbed her wisdom; I honestly had never been questioned on my personal beliefs or opinions. "Yup, I guess you are probably right. I just believed what everyone around me told me without questioning its validity or value."

"And why didn't you question?"

Shrugging my shoulders, I gestured my unawareness of the subject.

"Because you have gotten lazy with yourself, instead of searching for your personal truth. You have taken on others beliefs and thoughts. How are you going to teach and inspire others if your haven't created you own beliefs. It is our beliefs that are the foundation of our identities." With that she grabbed our overnight bag. "I'm going to brush my teeth."

♥   ♥   ♥

We reached Michigan by nightfall. Still suppressing feelings for Stephen, I remained silent as Jude spoke about her family.

Nodding, I listened to Jude talk about her family. I loved hearing about her tales of family traditions and growing up with such a large family. Being an only child, I had longed to belong to a big family more than anything in the world. I fought back sentiments of jealousy as Jude spoke about her sisters and their closeness. Though I am sure there were times weren't always hunky dory, having so many sisters must have been cool. You knew there would always be someone to talk to.

Driving through a rainstorm till dusk, Jude and I discovered a touristy town on the shores of Lake Huron. Both starving, we headed for the only restaurant open in town. Bright Christmas lights and country music were the main ambience-setters as we sat down. Surveying the scene, I could tell it definitely felt different than Canada. Though we were only a few hours south of the border, the whole vibe was different, more relaxed. Our waitress approached us, snapping her blue bubblegum. "Can I get you all something to drink?" she chirped.

As we were waiting for our drinks, my mind began thinking about Mister Stephen. Eagle Eye caught me right away. "What's up, Katie? Still thinking of Stephen?"

Admitting that I was, I struggled to change the subject.

Jude stopped me in my tracks, "Look, Katie, if you miss him this much, why don't you go home to the island?" Though I was tempted, I shook my head. Deep down I knew that if I headed home after coming this far, I would grow resentful of Stephen and our relationship would never work—not to mention the fact that I was on a spiritual journey, and if I aborted the mission I would live in regret.

Even when times had been tough, I knew I needed this journey more than this man or any man. Despite this knowledge, I was still playing a torturous game of internal struggle: ego versus higher self.

This struggle continued into the night as we parked at a nearby lot. Closing my eyes, I obsessed about what to do with my life: return to the island and go back to my old relationship or continue forward with Jude?

Still up at 2:00 a.m., I threw in the towel. My head pounded painfully and my chest felt like there was a thousand pounds of pressure on it; I finally gave up on sleep. In my bare feet, I proceeded to get out of the van. Half asleep, Jude rolled over. "Katie, what are you doing?"

Embarrassed that I had woken her, I responded, "I can't sleep in here. It's too confining" as I stepped outside into the chilly night air. Needing some footwear on my bare feet, I quickly tiptoed my way around to the trunk of the van. Lifting up the hood, I searched for my runners. Exhausted from sleep deprivation and shattered nerves, I could feel my inner rage coming to the surface.

Where are my shoes? I silently fumed, growing more aggressive by the second.

Due to over-packing, one of my rubber boots fell to the ground. For some reason that was the final straw that broke this old camel's back. In a blind rage, I picked up the boot and chucked it as far as I possibly could. Not wanting to leave the second boot out, I picked him up and threw him as well. Can you imagine? It paints a pretty comical picture, doesn't it?

Feeling better after taking some rage out on my boots, I ran after them and put them on. Still feeling the chaos inside my mind, I began sobbing. All I wanted was peace of mind and serenity. In the midst of my meltdown, I heard Jude's voice echoing the following words:

"Inner peace and tranquility comes when you can make a decision and stand firm in it. It comes from using your intuition and trusting in your belief system that everything happens for a reason."

Comforted by such simple, profound words, I took a deep breath and headed back to Miss Cassidy. As I climbed back into Cassidy, I found the inner cavity was quiet, and I instantly fell asleep after exerting so much energy throwing boots.

♥   ♥   ♥

Exhausted from another sleepless night, I awoke the following morning; as a super cranky pants.

And having to go pee. Grumpy and now having to pee, I managed to morph into a raving banshee. Eventually Jude drove us toward the nearest town for breakfast; there she eyed a Big Bob's restaurant.

As we read our cards that morning, I had reached an all-time low. When I took a quick peek at my eyes in the bathroom, the reflection frightened me. My usual vibrant green eyes looked hollow and utterly empty.

"The eyes are the window to the soul" echoed in my mind as I headed back to our booth.

Slumping into the seat, I avoided looking at Jude for fear that she would see right through me. Barely touching my piping hot oatmeal, I listened as Jude began speaking.

"You know, Katie, we often have more than one soul mate in a lifetime. Trust me, Stephen, is a great person, but you need to find you before worrying about something you can't have."

Angry and extremely overtired, I barked back, "You don't understand. We were so in love. Everybody told us. You just don't understand!"

Giving up on the discussion, Jude passed me the tarot cards to provide some guidance for the day. All three cards I drew were ones warning of strife and ruin, describing actions of my soul. Jude's cards were glorious ones, indicating she was on the right path.

Pausing, she looked up at me. "You know, Katie. It seems to me that you are still in love with Stephen even though you say you aren't. I am looking forward to getting to Montreal and having a fresh start. It feels like our paths have come to a crossroads, but I can't stand watching this much longer."

Not realizing it was possible, my heart sank even lower. My obsessive behavior was on the verge of driving the one woman I had grown to love away. Meekly, I answered back, "No, I just really need to talk to Stephen and get this whole mess sorted out. I still really want to move to Montreal with you. This I know."

Jude nodded, but there was a now sternness in her voice "All right, Katie, but just remember you are tortuous on your soul when you behave this way. In fact, I don't believe your soul is with you right now at all. That would explain the empty expression."

Alarmed that she had noticed and even more alarmed that my soul wasn't connected with my body, my spirits felt totally crushed.

Getting up, Jude looked at me. "Come on, kiddo, it's not so bad. You just have to follow your intuition and trust your guides."

Still wallowing in self-pity, I followed her out to the van, kicking rocks along the way.

Deciding that I couldn't stand America, I suggested to Jude that we head back to Canada. We did. (America wasn't the problem; denial of my whole life was.)

Another lesson I learned from Jude was that if you aren't happy, it really doesn't matter where you go geographically; you are still going to feel unhappy. Up until quite recently, I truly believed that particular locations could make me happy. Big NO-NO! However, as a kinesthetic learner, I had to travel all the way across North America to truly believe this.

We spent the entire day driving throughout the Michigan countryside. Due to my self-induced headache/ulcer/nerves, I was a wreck and Jude took over the driving duties.

By nightfall we had arrived in Niagara Falls. *Still* obsessing about Stephen, I had spent the entire day miserable, and by now I had become unbearable. Unfortunately Jude got the brunt of my bad mood as she drove Cassidy into town. Looking for a fight, I complained that she wasn't going the right way. Fed up with my behavior, Jude pulled over and told me to drive. Even more pissed off, I took the wheel and drove to the nearest motel. Once I got the keys to the room, I grabbed my cell phone and stormed off into the motel playground. Sitting on the bench, I prepared myself to call Stephen. This fiasco had gone on way too long and it was destroying my trip across Canada. I had allowed myself to sabotage our adventures due to my inability to let go of an unhealthy relationship that I had created. Feeling ashamed of myself, I realized I wasn't the only one whose trip I had sabotaged. Jude had sat by me the entire trip, being completely supportive the whole time. She had endured as I had many meltdowns and directed my anger at her. Punching in Stephen's phone number, I resolved to terminate this emotional-hostage game once and for all. On the third ring, my heart began plummeting at the thought of Stephen not answering. This inner turmoil had gone on long enough and I needed some form of resolve. *Please pick up, please pick up!*

Finally I heard Stephen's voice on the other end. Relieved that I had caught him, I greeted him nervously. Sounding very distant, he hesitantly spoke to me. I explained to him my inner struggles regarding our relationships and I couldn't carry on that way much longer. He expressed to me his desires to date other girls and I encouraged him to do so. This was such a lie. At the time it still really bothered me, but I had yet to find my truth. Forty-five minutes later, we hung up. It was over finally over. We had resolved to end things, keep in touch, and inform each other if we started dating other people.

Upon reflection I realize I was still scared of letting go of this old relationship. The truth of the matter was I viewed it as my security blanket, a backup plan, and honestly didn't want to release my control. Little did I know at the time I was keeping a door from the past open. This meant I was creating blockages for new healthy relationships to form. The longer I held onto my old relationship with Stephen, the further away I got from meeting someone new.

♥   ♥   ♥

Waking up to a beautiful sunny day, I felt hopeful that my inner struggles had been solved. Over breakfast I apologized to Jude for my previous behavior. Shaking her head, she retorted, "It's not me you want to apologize to, it's yourself."

Magical Niagara Falls was our destination that spring day. Arriving just after breakfast, we drifted to the downtown core. We parked Cassidy and roamed around to find the falls. Jude said, "Katie, I want you to feel its healing qualities when we near the waterfalls."

Jude and I headed straight for the falls, soft spray misting over our faces. As we approached the incredible viewpoint, we found a spot to watch the ever free-flowing water. It was such a magical view to take in. My cares and concerns seemed trivial in the grand scope of life as I inhaled the fresh oxygen from the universe. I was simply part of this incredible universe, not the center of it. Looking over at Jude, I noticed she had her eyes closed. There was an expression of complete serenity over her. Fondness for my dear friend came over me as we stood in silence together, enjoying the healing qualities of water.

Rejuvenated after our walk, we headed to the nearest Starbucks to treat ourselves to two tasty chai lattes. They make the best ones! After waiting in a horrible line, I approached the barista, ordered two chai lattes, and asked the girl to fill my water bottle. Looking at me, she raised her eyebrows and responded snarkily, "Actually, we don't do that here" and swirled around to help the next person in the line. Offended by her response, I made a face at Jude, who had a very low tolerance for poor customer service. Visibly pissed off, Jude grabbed my water bottle and muttered, "This is ridiculous, I used to be a manager at Starbucks, and they pride themselves on five-star quality service." Reaching over the counter, she assertively asked to have my bottled filled up again. The girl repeated what she had said to me. Jude refused to back down. "Well, this is ridiculous. I used to manage a Starbucks and I am going to report this to your manager." With that she swirled around and I followed behind her. Jude's reaction was quite normal, but due to my unassertive manner, her outbursts would embarrass me. "Look, Katie, you have to assert yourself if you want to get your way. I know you think I am acting like a witch, but trust me, it's the only way to get people to pay attention." At the time I had agreed but still thought she was being harsh.

Having traveled across Canada and being a witness to the atrocious customer service, I was learning where her attitude was coming from. "As women we are expected to remain quiet and not have a voice. Well, you don't get anywhere that way, trust me."

Though I was still slightly embarrassed by her outspokenness, I knew that there was backbone behind it.

Despite the bad service we received at Starbucks, Jude and I kept up our spirits as we strolled through the town with our lattes. Two hours of fresh air and healing waterfalls later, we were ready to hit the road again.

Recalling a magical little touristy town called Niagara-on-the-Lake, I suggested to Jude we make a beeline in that direction.

Pulling off the freeway toward Niagara-on-the-Lake, I felt calmer then I had in days. Perhaps it was the chat with Jude that morning, potentially the tasty brownie I had just munched on; I wasn't sure, but I did feel better. Rows of endless vineyards and willow trees stretched for miles ahead of us. The temperature was a perfect twenty degrees Celsius, and even the music on the radio was my favorite, Al Green. As I drove closer to Niagara-on-the-Lake, the strangest notion occurred to me. While driving peacefully toward the town, I distinctly heard the following: "Okay, I am going come back into your body now." Call me crazy; call me nuts, but that afternoon, I knew my soul had finally returned to me. As Jude had warned, due to my self-sabotaging and self-destructive thinking, I had caused my soul to leave my body. In fact, it hadn't been in my body since Vancouver. Feeling very grateful that it had decided to return, I turned to Jude and told her the good news.

Throwing her arms up in the air, she answered, "Well, it's about bloody time! I was wondering when it was going come back." And she gave me a huge smile.

Rolling down the windows, I could hear the rushing of the willow trees and the hum of lawnmowers in the distance. The faint smell of freshly cut grass wafted through Cassidy as we pulled into town. "Since my soul had returned, my senses are much stronger!" I sang out to Jude. "I'm glad you noticed that!" she articulated.

Walking around at the pace of snails, we made the loop of the town. All the houses were perfectly kept, from their tidy gardens to the color of their mailboxes. Old Victorian houses sprawled to three stories high, and one in particular caught Jude's eye. Moving her eyebrows up and down, she exclaimed, "I bet there's tons of ghosts in there, Katie! By the looks of things, it's been abandoned for quite some time." Magnetically drawn to the home, Jude wandered across the street and stood at the rickety old fence, peering into the windows.

Looking around Niagara-on-the-Lake, I knew I could definitely live in a place like that: the cozy familiarity of close neighbors, spectacular lake to provide endless inspiration. Drifting away into the daydream realm, I pictured myself with the perfect family, chasing after a white dog. I will admit it; I had the classic case of the Cinderella syndrome!

Not really wanting to leave, Jude and I slowly hiked back to the Cassmeister.

The rest of our voyage to Montreal was basically a blur as we cruised at 120 kilometers on the number-one highway east.

One hour west of Montreal, we began noticing the sprawl of suburbia as mile after mile of concrete developments surrounded us.

Upon reflection I realize I instantly knew Montreal wasn't for me. At the time, I had so badly wanted to live in a big city and experience the lifestyle. Having also applied to McGill, a prestigious university, I liked the idea of attending not particularly to study but to gain the respect that went along with attending. It was a foolish idea, but at the time I was terribly confused.

About five kilometers away from the downtown core, I recalled the reason I hadn't been an avid fan of driving in Montreal. Total gridlock greeted us as the sun beat down, making traffic unbearable. We passed sign after sign as we tried to determine which exit to take, desperately trying to get a sense of direction, we opted for the exit entitled "Rue Ontario, centre ville."

Heading down the road, we came across a little community with colorful markets and outdoor cafes. We decided to get out and stretch our legs after the crazy morning of driving. We noticed that we had landed ourselves in a rather shady part of town. Sketchy characters and cracked sidewalks were all around us as we pondered our next move. Having finally arrived in Montreal felt very anti-climatic.

Finding a small courtyard to perch in, Jude and I basked in the sunshine, contemplating our next move. Reaching for her purse, Jude rummaged through it to locate her cell phone. "I have an old friend from the fishing lodge days who lives here. Rick has been such a great friend to me over years and he lives here." With that she dialed his number and waited.

Hearing Rick's booming voice on the other end, Jude smiled and told him that we were in town. Hanging up the phone, she stated, "He will be here in twenty minutes" and had a particular glow about her. The infamous Rick showed up twenty minutes later in a huge SUV. Tall and very friendly, Rick introduced himself to me as he walked over, playfully flirting with Jude. Amused by this other side of Jude, I silently giggled as I watched them. Being Taurian (very security- and stability-oriented) Rick immediately asked about our accommodations. When we stated we had just arrived in town, Rick suggested an area of Montreal where we could find a motel. After checking in I began unpacking the van and hauling suitcases up the staircase. Jude and Rick stayed down in the parking lot. Entering the motel room, I felt a shift in my energy as I began unpacking.

A quick check-in with myself established that I was feeling jealous of Rick. After Rick left, Jude entered the room looking dreamy and began unpacking her belongings. Still feeling jealous, I remained quiet instead of communicating my emotions. Instantly my ego started playing with my frame of mind, putting all sorts of delusional thoughts in my head.

Jude only came here to be with Rick. She was using you to get here. She didn't really intend on starting a business with you; she lied. The more I listened to my ego, the more I believed it.

Putting on my best fake voice, I called out to Jude from the bathroom, "He seems nice. I can see why you like him." Jude appeared in the doorway looking rather guilty. "He just kissed me, Katie. That's all." Knowing that Rick was married, my judgments got the best of me as I silently judged Jude for her actions.

She let a married man kiss her?

Who is this woman?

Obviously she can't be trusted!

My ego ran with all sorts of judgments as I remained in the bathroom sulking.

All previous knowledge about Jude's kindness and compassion went swiftly out the door as I struggled to contain my judgments.

"But I thought he was married," I responded, trying to sound calm. Jude's eyes narrowed as she pieced together my words.

"Katie, don't you dare judge me. I have you told you this many times. You do not put me on a pedestal. I am just me, no more, no less. We are equals."

Not hearing her words, I stormed into the bathroom and drew a bath. Heart pounding, I sank in the tub and pondered my reaction.

After my bath I was still feeling rather tense. Stepping out into the room, I warily eyed Jude. As I sat on the bed, she said, "You know, Katie, I don't judge you when you do things I don't agree with. Why can't you do the same?"

Irrationally I said, "No, I can't do that. I can't believe you would kiss a married man. Is he the reason you wanted to come here anyways? Maybe you didn't even want to start a business with me at all." Anger surmounting, I shouted, "I can't handle this, Jude; I'm leaving." With that I stormed out of the room.

Aimlessly walking around the strange neighborhood, I again wondered about my intense reaction. I turned the question inward, and my vibes piped up, *Katie, you view Jude as a role model. You look up to her and everything that she does. You have to remember that she is your equal.*

Acknowledging the truth, I started heading back to our temporary home for the night. The room still felt tense as I entered. Glancing around the room, I quickly noticed that Jude was nowhere to be found.

Stepping outside, I peered down into the courtyard and saw her kneeling on the pavement talking with three women. While I had stormed off on my immature ravings around Montreal, Jude had ventured downstairs to unload her suitcases. As she was lugging the baggage up the staircase, one of the housekeepers came over and asked about Cassidy's Yukon license plates. She warned Jude about the seedy area where we had chosen to stay. In broken English she had stated, "It is not the safest neighborhood, madam. There is much late-night activity around here. I am not sure if you knew prior to moving here; there are many underground, illegal activities occurring all around the city. You are very brave women to move here alone, much courage." Jude had contemplated this newfound knowledge and shifted her attention over to the daughters. As she spoke with the two younger girls, she silently hoped that they did not follow the path many young women desiring money did.

She spent the next half an hour with these girls, reminded them of having choices and telling them to be proud to be women. As she stood up to leave, the mother held on to Jude's arm and stated, "Don't worry about late-night sounds you hear, madam. Just stay in your room and ignore them. I will be sure to inform the front desk not to direct any of the traffic in your direction." As Jude walked toward the staircase, she absorbed the new knowledge that she had received. Although her intuition had already alerted her of the shadiness of the city, the conversation with the chambermaid only served as an affirmation.

Apologizing to Jude for my insane-o reaction regarding Rick, I asked if she wanted to go grab a coffee. Nodding in agreement, Jude grabbed her coat and we headed out.

Locating the Timmy's, we walked in silence over to the entrance. Jude looked remorseful as we sat down with our coffees. After she ate her chili with brown bun, she said, "I promise that will never happen again. My soul had left my body and I'm feeling very sad."

With that she looked back down into her coffee cup with tears falling. Still unaccustomed to public displays of emotion, I wasn't sure how to react. Sitting in silence, I wondered what I could say to ease her sorrow. Guilt washed over me as I considered how harshly I had judged her. Looking at Jude's sadness, I wanted to kick myself for being so ridiculous.

Upon reflection I realize I was very narrow-minded when it came to relationships. Basically it was my way or the highway, and then I met Jude. She taught me that long-term relationships are complex and there are many angles and perspectives involved. "Be careful not to judge. You could end up cheating on your lover." I had shaken my head vigorously. Jude continued "You never know what life will throw at you, Katie. Remember to keep an open mind."

♥   ♥   ♥

Deciding today was apartment-finding day, Jude and I awoke feeling keen and ready to take on the world.

Seven hours later we sat in an Internet café rather defeated and ready to throw in the towel. Having called seven apartments, we were only able to check out one and it was hideous. A family of fleas would have felt cramped, let alone two women. Almost giving up for the day, I decided to search for some part-time jobs. Looking on the local classifieds page, I noticed an advertisement for window-washers. Intrigued, I clicked on it.

"I am looking for hard working individuals to work this summer. No experience is necessary Call Paul today; 514 772-3407"

Hmm, interesting, I thought. Poking Jude on the shoulder, I told her to check out the ad. Scanning it, she looked back at me and said, "Why not?"

Retrieving her phone from the counter, she dialed Paul's number; he picked up on the first ring. Within two minutes we had a job interview for the following day to be window-washers!

♥   ♥   ♥

The following day we headed over to Paul's office. A half an hour before our interview, Jude and I both shifted into a really goofy mood. The combination of van living, city driving, and excitement all played a role in our playful spirits sitting in the waiting room. We began giggling about the fact that we were applying to be window washers. Neither one of us had honestly considered exactly what it entailed. We just did it on a whim.

From the moment we shook Paul's hand, he truly didn't know what hit him. Jude launched into her personal background of owning a cleaning service. Paul didn't know where to cut in between the charged energy level in that room and Jude's rapid-fire questions and job description.

Near the end of the interview, Paul finally spoke his piece: "You know, ladies, I have to be honest with you here. I can't see you two climbing ladders and hauling heavy buckets around all day. I just can't see it, do you?"

Grinning at each other sheepishly, we both shook our heads no. Now Paul continued, "Now, having said that, I can see you, Jude, as the manager for the housekeepers. I have been actively searching for an individual, and you fit the bill. What do you think?"

Leaning forward slightly, Jude responded, "Well, Paul, now Katie and I are living in a van and we need to find accommodations, before we do anything. How about I take your card, think about your offer, and get back to you once we have a home?"

Paul nodded, still unsure of what he had just witnessed. "Sure, Jude, that sounds just fine."

Leaving the office building, Jude and I wandered into the fresh air. "What was that?" she asked me after we grounded ourselves.

"I don't know," I responded, still feeling giddy after our giggle fest.

All of a sudden, I instinctively felt another energy shift. For some reason I began feeling annoyed that Jude had received a job offer and I hadn't. My competitive streak shot out and I started shutting down, not speaking.

Looking back, I know I still viewed Jude as competition, despite there being no logical reasoning for such an emotion. Watching her getting offered a job had made me feel inferior because of my low self-esteem. Still stuck in my childhood, I instantly reacted immaturely.

Naturally Jude coaxed the issue out of me after several minutes of pondering. She explained to me that she hadn't even taken the job yet, but if she did it would be to help both of us.

Snapping back into reality, I realized she was right. It still frightened me how quickly my immature, childish side could snarl its way to the surface. Again I made a mental note to beware my internal demons!

During the interview with Paul, I noticed that my phone had been buzzing, indicating a message. Checking it, I heard a man's voice speaking about an apartment for rent. It had been the apartment that I had called about the previous day. The description had sounded so appealing that I had fallen in love with the advertisement:

"1 bedroom on the 23 floor of down town apartment building, spectacular city views, and bright lighting, pool, sauna and laundry facilities all included. Call Derek."

Quickly calling Derek back, I tried to contain my excitement. Derek picked up on the third ring. Informing him I was calling about the apartment, I asked if it was still available. Telling me yes, Derek launched into the description and details of the place. Growing impatient out of my desire to see the place immediately, I start biting my nails to calm myself.

Writing down the directions, I arranged to be at the place at 5:00 p.m. For some reason I didn't mention Jude, most likely out of fear of not being able to move in with two people.

Pulling out our trusty map, Jude and I astonishingly managed to make our way into downtown and located the apartment effortlessly. Checking the time, we realized we were early, with ten minutes to watch people in the streets of Montreal.

Surrounding us was the most eclectic medley of diversity I had ever seen. All different walks of life seemed to be congregating around the apartment we sat in front of. A pigeon was on top of a statue diagonally from us at the famous Concordia University, which attracted mainly international students.

A rather small Asian man holding a motorcycle helmet walked over. He looked over at us and then proceeded into the lobby. Jude whispered, "I bet that's Derek" as he walked around the corner. Jude made eye contacted with him and he sensed we were waiting for him.

"Are you Katie?"

Nodding I said, "Yup, you must be Derek."

Conservatively he responded, "Yes, I am. Please follow me." On the elevator ride up he apologized for being late. "I was just at a meeting and just got out." Making small talk, we discovered that he was subletting the apartment for his girlfriend who had left for Ireland.

Using her intuitiveness, Jude laid her hand on Derek's arm and said, "I am figuring that this relationship is coming to a close?"

Rather taken aback by Jude's honesty and accurate statement, Derek laughed nervously and answered "Well, I'm not sure, but I have been told I work too much."

With that the elevator reached the twenty-third floor and we got out. We opened the first door on the right. Derek unlocked the door to the apartment. It was everything I had imagined. It had a spectacular view of downtown Montreal, and huge ceilings, windows; the place was bright and had great air circulation. Jumping from one foot to the other, I excitedly decided we had to live there. Expressing my love for the place, I told Derek that I wanted the place. Laughing, Derek told us that the place wouldn't be ready for a few days. Having my heart set on the apartment, I told him that we would wait until it was ready.

Derek ushered us out of the magical apartment, claiming that he would call when the apartment was ready. "Should be within the next three to four days," he said, and with that took off into the crowded streets of Montreal. Although I was excited to have the apartment, I was miserable at the prospect of having to stay in the van. Instead of accepting our current situation and being grateful, I sulked for the rest of the afternoon.

Later that evening Jude had mentioned how she wanted to find the cemetery at Mount Royal and view the city from above. I selfishly sat sulking in the passenger seat while she maneuvered Cassidy around Montreal.

"You know, Katie, I don't know why you are still holding on to the past behaviors and thought processes. It's really not healthy. You have to learn to be flexible."

Angry at myself, I projected it outward at Jude. "Whatever, you don't understand me. I'm just sick of living in this f&$#ing van."

Shaking her head, Jude replied, "You can be so ungrateful at times, Katie. I don't think you realize how much you truly do have and you are completely unaware of it. Let me say this—that universe always pays attention!"

Reaching the top of the mountain, she pulled Cassidy over and parked. I violently grabbed the door handle. I stomped off down a nearby nature trail.

Jude pocketed the car keys and followed behind "So this is really mature Katie. Throwing a tantrum. Is this what you used to do with your parents? Well, guess what, it doesn't work with me. You need to grow up and deal with your issues like an adult. You have been running from yourself way too long."

Infuriated by her truthful comments, I charged quicker down the path. Thoughts swirled around my mind as I allowed my ego to control my thoughts.

You can't do this anymore. You can't live in a van and hear the truth about yourself. You can't handle truth, and on and on.

After I had walked in a complete circle for twenty minutes, I found myself back at the van. Sheer hatred radiated out of me as Jude allowed me back in the passenger side.

Upon reflection I realize my hatred was directed toward me, I had been running and lying for so many years that hearing the truth about me was awful—necessary yet awful. So, instead of accepting Jude's words and reacting like a twenty-six-year-old adult, I acted like a six-year-old child throwing tantrums whenever things weren't going my way. Not a moment went by when I considered Jude's feelings or personal needs. I was so selfish that I didn't ever once thank her for staying with me through my self-induced tantrums and meltdowns.

♥   ♥   ♥

Coming down from Mount Royal, Jude pulled Cassidy over on a busy street. Turning off the engine, she stated, "Well, that's it. This is where we are sleeping for the night." Still in a horrible mood, I climbed into the back of Cassidy and tried to sleep. Due to my earlier rage, my head pounded and I felt lower than low. *WOW,* I thought. *I really do have a lot of anger!*

The next morning we awoke to bright sunshine. Rubbing my eyes, I felt exhausted after only having had two hours' sleep. Negative thoughts had raced through my mind all night, leaving me one super crabby bitch that morning. Miserable about still living in the van, I slowly pulled on some clothing and tied my hair back. After a quick brainstorm, Jude and I decided to head out toward Quebec City in order to make time pass. Due to my terrible mood, the entire van felt heavy as I took over the driving duties.

Heading east on the freeway, I tried to push my feelings of anger down into my subconscious. Healthy idea, eh! After driving through three hours of total gridlock, we finally were cruising along the picturesque Quebec countryside. Tension still loomed over as I obsessed about how much I couldn't stand living in a van.

Completely oblivious to Jude's words, "Stay in the moment," I allowed my mind to wander far off into the future, while I missed many beautiful moments that day.

Reaching a small community that evening, I pulled Cassidy over. We needed gas and had located a service station. Noticing an attractive boy at the cash register, I asked him how his day was going. Without batting an eye, he took my cash and responded, "Long, tired. I am studying to be a doctor at University of Quebec and I have extremely long days." With that he smiled at Jude and continued his job. Offended that he didn't pay attention to me, I sulked back to Cassidy.

Upon reflection I see I had grown so accustomed to tossing my hair, operating through my ego, that I couldn't believe he didn't pay attention to me. It was completely beyond my comprehension that a man my age could be so focused and disciplined he didn't even glance in my direction. Quite an EGO-based reality I lived in, for sure.

As night fell across the countryside, we journeyed up into the Laurentians, a spectacular mountain range in central Quebec. Spotting an unpaved pull-off, we decided this was our nesting spot for this beautiful sunset evening that the universe displayed for us. As soon as we brushed our teeth and climbed into bed, my inner turmoil kicked in again. Like a never-ending Ping-Pong ball, my obsessive thoughts went back and forth as the creatures of the night began voicing their sounds. Frightened by the unfamiliar tones I was hearing, my heart began racing faster and faster. Jude rolled over. *Katie, what did I say about trusting your vibe. Why do you want to feed this unhealthy fear? There is nothing outside that will harm you. Just relax!"*

Comforted by Jude's voice, I sunk deeper into the futon mattress and allowed my heart beat to return to normal.

♥   ♥   ♥

Although we spent a couple of days in the most magnificent, romantic city, I was truly not present, ignoring Jude's guidance. I wandered around the streets, going through the motions but never truly feeling the places we went to. The only spots I can recall that snapped me into the moment were two local churches we visited. The first one was located in the heart of old Quebec City and it was the oldest church in Canada. As we entered the sacred space, the smell of ancient wisdom, passion, and truth resonated throughout the foundation. Taking a seat, I inhaled deeply and embraced the momentary tranquility I found within my own mind. Gone were obsessions and worriment from the past

Clear, crystal truth streamed down upon me as I momentarily stopped my self-induced obsessions. Glancing over, I saw Jude light a candle in the name of hope. The scene stays with me to this day. Though such simple gestures, I could see her compassion as she stood silently by the alter. If asked now what truth looked like, I would answer that this is it: pure simple, truth. As I write this, I find it difficult to express the power and inspiration I felt when witnessing such a simple gesture.

The second church we went to was just on the outskirts of Quebec City. While I pulled into the parking lot, Jude pointed to a nearby sign. It had the name of the church on it along with a local telephone company's advertisement.

"See, Katie, due to many years of sexual lawsuits the Catholic churches have had to resort to gaining capital from exterior sources. It's sad to see that even religion has a price too and can be bought. Completely contradiction to what the true basis of religion is."

Nodding, I listened to her wisdom and acknowledged there was much I needed to learn about religion.

Entering the religious sanctuary, I again felt calm and grounded. The black void that had been suppressing my essence seemed temporarily filled as I sat down on an ancient wooden bench.

Upon reflection I realize I was still living in such a state of denial and self-sabotage. I was not only destroying my potential discoveries in Quebec, I was also firing my fireballs at Jude. The only space at this point where I could find acceptance and love was within a church. Due to my complete disregard for my soul and spirit, I was left to seek peace in a building. I still didn't understand or accept that I was the one responsible for my black void.

On our way back to Montreal, we came across a muddy farmer's field. Sleepy and tired of driving, I pulled off into the field for the night. The undeniable stench of farmer's manure filtered into Cassidy, and I yet again complained about the situation.

Later that evening Derek called me and enquired about several things. Did I want cable or Internet? Answering no, I felt a twinge of guilt for not disclosing that Jude would be living there as well.

Already in a lie, I cowardly didn't get the set record straight. To make matters worse, when Derek asked if Jude was my mother, I had answered, "She is my stepmother!" Yet another lie. The minute it escaped my lips, I regretted it. Here was this wonderfully helpful guy and I had just lied to him, twice! Kicking myself, I wondered why I lied about Jude.

Upon reflection I realize I had wanted the apartment so badly I had lied to get it. Had I shown honesty and integrity from the start, this whole mess wouldn't have been created. I seemed to really enjoy creating messes for myself, and this time was not different.

After I complained to Jude about living in the van, she gave me her typical response: "Gratitude, Katie, remember gratitude." Jude's voice came from underneath the covers.

♥   ♥   ♥

That morning I awoke with the intense sensation that we needed to move Cassidy immediately. Just as I was turning on her engine, a big red truck stopped. An old farmer stepped out and approached the passenger window. Before he had a chance to speak, I began speaking in French, pretending to be lost. Believing the story, the kind old farmer gave us directions to the nearest highway. After thanking him in French, I quickly accelerated off his property.

Later that afternoon Derek called to inform me that the place would be ready the following afternoon. Grateful to soon have a home, I thanked him and hung up. Though I loved being resourceful by living in a van, Cassidy was getting a wee bit tiresome. The prospect of a real bed was sensational.

Halfway between Quebec City and Montreal, the heat was growing unbearable. We agreed to jump into the nearest lake possible. Serendipitously, three minutes after we made the solemn promise, we came across a sparkling lake right on the side of the road. Raising our eyebrows, we quickly swerved off the road and headed out for a refreshing dip.

Noticing a slimer parked nearby (slimers are creepy old men), Jude and I decided to head a little farther away to a more secluded area. Jude spotted a deck close by, so we hiked our way toward it. After gingerly stepping over slippery rocks, we then firming planted ourselves on the dock. Looking rather devilish, Jude glanced over at me and stated, "I dare you to go skinny dipping." Unable to be called a chicken, I accepted the challenge.

Slithering out of my clothing, I quickly took the plunge and it felt magnificent. My body temperature dropped instantly as the water cooled me down. Feeling free and weightless, I floated around nuddlywinks, watching the fluffy clouds up above.

Nuddlywinks was a term my parents used on me when I was naked as a jay bird.

Satisfied that I had cooled down, I swam back over to the dock. After clambering up I quickly covered myself with a towel and basked in the sunshine. Eyeing Jude, I challenged her.

"All right, you, now it's your turn to go winkers!"

"Come on, you chicken!" I called out. "On the count of three. One … two … three!" I jumped in again feeling coolness envelope me. Coming up for air, I noticed Jude still sitting on the dock.

"You are such a scaredy cat!" I taunted while swimming around the dock. Being winkers felt like I was three years old again, playing freely. There is definitely something to be said for the simple pleasures in life. I have often found myself completely humbled by the simplest gestures. They truly are the ones that are the most meaningful. Speaking of simplicity reminds me of a particular situation when I was serving several years back… Allow me to elaborate.

It was a busy, all-you-can-eat ribs night and customers were lined up outside the door and around the corner. My section was full, and I was frantically trying to stay on top of my game. In walked a family of five. As I approached their table, I noticed that one of their sons had Downs' syndrome. Ignorantly I felt a surge of impatience as I began compiling their orders. As the heat rose and plates crashed, I stood at their table, trying hard to keep my patience. As I tried to focus, my mind began racing, as I was mentally in six places at once. When it came to the son with Downs' syndrome, the table went quiet. He was having difficulty choosing between chicken and beef. Biting his lip, he truly was in quite the pickle. As I started silently yelling "Hurry up" in my mind, all of a sudden it dawned on me: *What's the big deal?* So I took an extra few minutes at this table. *I'm not going to fade away and die, am I?* Taking a few deep breaths, I relaxed my super tense body and waited till the son was ready. Chicken was the triumphant dinner choice, the son finally decided. I walked away smiling, feeling calm and more grounded than I had all day.

The funny thing is I know he was my angel that particular day. He taught me to stay in the moment and slow it down—now what a concept!

That afternoon on the dock, swimming winkers with Jude, was another moment. She eventually did conjure up enough guts and bravely took the plunge; she always tells me she is older than dirt!

As we drove further toward Montreal, I felt truly blessed to have someone to share magical moments with.

"You know what you did back there?" Jude asked me as we sped west. I shrugged my shoulders. She answered "You just cleansed yourself, similar to a rebirth. You entered the water as one woman and exited as another, shedding your old skin in the lake."

As Montreal loomed closer, I felt my energy shift. Upon further investigation, I realized that driving toward Montreal was making me feel tense and uptight. Desperately trying to ignore my true feelings, I pretended to be excited as we approached.

Upon reflection I realize I so badly wanted to fit myself into the normal mold that I had idolized for so long: move to a city, go to a great school, find a man, create a family, and live happily ever after. I saw McGill as the golden ticket to my happiness, falsely believing that if I attended school all my problems would miraculously disappear. This was not at all the case. At the point where I was in my life, I was still desperately searching to find out who I was. Going to school is great when you have a particular end goal, but in my case I was assuming it would give me all the answers.

Have you ever tried to fit yourself in a mold that you don't fit into?

Being a fairly spirited young woman, constraining myself to a stuffy school was probably the worst thing for me at the time. But still I persisted in denying my intuition.

As the traffic grew thicker, I soon discovered we were lost. Instead of announcing my frustrations, I held them inside. Unknown to me at the time, we were driving south instead of east, which is a huge mistake in Montreal. Due to its extremely confusing roads, once you got off track, it could take hours to get back. As the sun beat down into Cassidy, I slowly began melting down. Having had no food, emotions suppressed, and tired of living in a van, I grew increasingly aggressive as we sped aimlessly in the wrong direction. Desperate,

I called Derek to gain a local perspective on where I was. As Derek explained to us where we were, I got even more confused. While I looked outside for landmarks, Jude noticed the exit we were meant to take. After several minutes of listening to Derek's instructions, I got fed up and passed the phone over to Jude. She took over as commander in chief and barked out the instructions. Eighteen turns later, we arrived in one piece at the apartment.

Grabbing the keys from Derek, I was ecstatic to have a place to call home. We hauled all our belongings up from Cassidy into the apartment. It felt surreal to see all our possessions in an apartment in Montreal. The past few weeks across Canada had been such a medley of personal discoveries and an uncovering of lies that now that we had arrived, it felt very surreal to be unpacking the basics. Jude and I resolved to rest and unpack the following day.

♥   ♥   ♥

Friday was entirely dedicated to transforming the apartment into a cozy home. Jude and I washed, scrubbed, and cleaned all day long. Around noon I decided to go enquire about a parking permit for Cassidy.

Waiting a century and a half to the elevator, I finally made it to the building manager's office. Mr. Ratte was a short little man who reminded me of a distinctive rodent from the swamps in South America. From the moment I walked into his office, I knew I was in for a treat. Fixating his beady little eyes on me, he hurriedly introduced himself: "HellogoodmorningmynameisTerryRatteandIamthebuildi ngmanagerwhatcanIhelpyouwith?" Since I was accustomed to Jude's methodical way of speaking, my head twirled twice around as I tried to comprehend him.

"I'm sorry, Mister Ratte, but you are going to have to speak slowly. I can't understand you." Looking at me as though I was a complete numbskull, Mr. Ratte repeated himself a fraction slower. After five painful minutes of trying to communicate, I asked about a parking pass. Standing up, Mister Ratte nodded and made some random comment about Keifer Sutherland.

Suddenly I was hit with the most debilitating body odor consuming my aura. After a quick pit check, I established it wasn't coming from me. Stepping out of the office door, Mr. Ratte left a trail of revolting smell that I unfortunately had to follow behind. He led me down four flights of stairs to the very bowels of the building….

Reaching the parking lot, he gestured to the smallest spot on the lot. Quickly he mumbled, "ThisisthisisspotIhavepickedoutforyouItis onlyavailableforaweekPleasepaydepositbeforeyouleavetoday." Again I told Mr. Ratte to slow his speech down, which he did slightly. Climbing back up to the light of day, we headed to his office to fill out paperwork. Glancing at my breasts, he shook my hand and said, "I hope that is all for today, Miss Sutherland. Please let me know if there is anything else I can do for you," and then he mumbled something about car racing, but by this point I had already reached the elevator. Delighted to be away from Mr. Ratte (who soon became known as Mr. Ratty), I sunk into the elevator and went upstairs to grab my keys. Informing Jude I was parking the van, I headed out into the big city.

♥   ♥   ♥

Later that evening we sat in our squeaky-clean apartment and took in our new dwelling. It truly appeared as though a fairy godmother had come in and waved her magic wand: yellow walls, bright flowers, and cozy candles all created a very comfortable feeling. Satisfied with our work, Jude and I changed into our PJs and watched our favorite movie, *I am Sam*.

I am going to explain the plot.

The movie is about a mentally challenged man who raises a daughter by himself. The movie depicts all the challenges he faces along the way. The main theme is that through his unconditional love for her, he proves that love is truly all you need.

Though I have seen the movie countless times, it always brings tears to my eyes. The sheer beauty of unconditional love and determination consistently invokes emotion. After a great big sob fest, I fell asleep, anxious what the new day in Montreal would bring.

Awakening to an overcast day, Jude and I decided to take a stroll in Westmont, the ritzy area of town. We both needed employment and set out to scope out the opportunities. Walking along the Westmount strip, we noticed a dog-grooming store called Bark and Fitz. Entering, we were greeted by three people in their early thirties, one lady and two dudes conversing with them. Jude discovered that there were ample opportunities for dog walking in the neighborhood. Looking at one another, we raised our eyebrows. We both loved dogs; we both love walking. I could hear the wheels turning as we left Bark and Fitz.

On our walk home, we decided to try putting up posters advertising dog-walking services. Jude said excitedly, "I know a lady in Vancouver who was making five hundred dollars a week just dog-walking. Can you imagine five hundred a week?"

Excited about our latest plan, we made a beeline for Staples to purchase poster-making supplies. Later that night we discussed the possibility of doing numerology and tarot readings in addition to dog walking. Agreeing that it never hurt to try, we added psychic readings to our list of professional services.

Finding a copy center across from the apartment, Jude and I headed over to draft up our master plans. As we walked in I noticed a super-hot guy working behind the counter. He was tall and had brown hair and hazel eyes. He was definitely attractive. In true form Jude headed straight for him. "Well, good morning, there. We were wondering if we might be able to use some of your computer services?"

Struck by her direct manner, he nodded and gestured toward three computers in the corner. "Please be my guest." Again I felt jealousy as this man my age was paying more attention to Jude than me.

Several attempts later we had compiled the perfect dog-walking and psychic-readings posters ever. Before leaving the copy center, Jude approached the front counter. The young man appeared to offer his assistance, and Jude looked up at him. "What's your name?" Blushing slightly from the attention, he responded, "Dave."

Jude continued, "Well, Dave, thank you very much for your hospitality; it was greatly appreciated." After making her way to the door, she turned around. "Oh and, Dave? You have a great smile."

Completely flustered by the compliment, our new friend Dave didn't know quite what to do with himself. One of my favorite things about hanging with Jude is watching individual reactions after she gives compliments that come straight from the heart. People always feel them and are touched.

After a quick visit to Staples copying center, we were ready to post our services in the city of Montreal. Making stops at Concordia University and local shops, Jude and I placed our posters wherever we deemed it appropriate. "Now all we have to do is sit back and wait," I said, excited. Checking the time, I decided to find a local Internet station to kill some time. Noticing one across the block, I informed Jude of my plans. Wanting to check hers too, she came along.

Closing down my e-mail, I decided to search the Internet on light workers. Back in Vancouver I had done a little reading but still wanted to learn more.

A website opened immediately to a page dedicated to light workers and their purpose. Noticing an upcoming events icon, I clicked it out of curiosity.

A purple box jumped out advertising the universal light workers conference.

Intrigued, I clicked on it and on a detailed outline of the conference came up:

Where? Boca Raton, Florida

When? June 8-10, 2007

What? A celebration of light forces joining together to create harmonious energy transmissions into the universe.

Hmm, I thought as I tapped Jude on the shoulder. "I do believe we need to check this out further."

When I showed her the website, Jude read the information "Well, kiddo, it's like this. I have told you that I am basically like your shadow. You call the shots and I will go along. So what do you say? Do you want to go?"

Nodding my head vigorously, I responded with a resounding "Yes!" During my awakening in January, when I had discussed my desire to meet other light workers, Jude had nodded yet also issued a warning: "Now, don't get me wrong, Katie, being a light worker means you all have a beautiful qualities and characteristics. Having said that, it has been my experience that most light workers tend to stick to themselves and can be very private. Just remember, not everyone is like you and I."

Remembering Jude's words, I hesitated before registering us for the conference. Florida was a far way to go, and we did need to get summer jobs. But on the other hand, the thought of meeting other light workers and like-minded people truly did pique my interest.

Making an executive decision, I registered us for the conference, putting Jude and myself down as volunteers. My heart beating quickly out of excitement, I looked over at Jude.

"Well, there's no turning back now. We are going to Florida!"

♥   ♥   ♥

By the next morning, Jude and I started to get the feeling that dog-walking and intuitive readings were not popular in Montreal.

We spent most of that day reposting our services on Craig's List but were getting no response. I found this extremely frustrating; in the past things would serendipitously happen.

Feeling sorry for myself, I decided that we should go dancing. Putting on our sexy attire, Jude and I left the apartment to experience the night life. Approaching a bustling pub/nightclub called Thursdays, we decided to venture in for a couple of drinks.

As a tough-looking waitress shoved her way through the crowd, I raised my eyebrows. Sitting down, I surveyed the scene; directly beside us was a group of middle-aged professionals out with their secretaries. Silently I wondered how many professionals cheated on their wives with their secretaries.

After twenty minutes our waitress finally appeared, possessing a striking resemblance to Wednesday from the Adams Family. She looked at us, completely unimpressed. Ordering gin-and-tonics, we didn't let her mood effect us. Another twenty minutes rolled by until Wednesday returned and placed our drinks on the table. She stood around expectantly for a tip. We had only been in Montreal a few days, but already I was getting the impression that the women didn't particularly care for one another. Jude and I were quickly becoming acclimatized to the up-and-down glares we would receive when walking around downtown in our regular clothes.

Finishing our drinks, we searched around for the dance floor, looking to the left, looking to the right. There was no dance floor to speak of. Refusing to give up, Jude and I created our own spot right in the middle of the lounge. As we swayed and cut a rug, pretty soon others started joining in. Smiling, I surveyed the new dance floor we had started. It felt so great to get others involved and motivated. Simply by being ourselves, we managed to attract a fairly large crowd. About five songs in, Jude spotted a handsome man in a baby blue shirt. Signaling to me, she abandoned ship to go talk to him. I simply nodded and shook my head; poor guy didn't know what was about to hit him!

Jude found out his name was Tim and he was an old baseball pro from Arizona. As I grooved with my new dance partners, Jude flirted with her American friend.

One hour passed and I was getting ready to crash. Searching for Jude, I found her still chatting with Tim. When I motioned that I was going to leave, she told me to meet her outside in five minutes. Agreeing, I leaped out to gulp some fresh air. Ten minutes later Jude skipped down the stairs like a young teenager.

Eyes aglow, she exclaimed, "He kissed me. Wow, did he ever kiss me." Amused to see Jude giddy, I asked for more details. She told me about their chats and how Tim had referred to her as Sharon Stone from *Fatal Attraction*.

Walking home, it felt great to be sharing these moments with Jude. After grabbing a coffee on our way home, we waited for our ancient elevator and unwound from the day. Though I was living in the master bedroom, 92 percent of my time was spent out in the living room with Jude. Having been so accustomed to sleeping beside her in the van, I found it difficult to sleep by myself.

Reflecting on our adventures, I think my most cherished memories are of the late-night chats Jude and I would have. When I was growing up, my mother never viewed me as an equal and hence spoke down to me as opposed to with me. Jude was different; our chats could go on for hours as we giggled about sex or goofy men. It didn't really matter to me what the topic was; it was the time spent together I truly cherished!

♥   ♥   ♥

Upon his arrival into our apartment, I offered him some peppermint tea. Wordlessly, he took the hot beverage with no recognition or gratitude. Completely unaccustomed to this behavior, I instantly put up walls towards him.

During the visit with Raj, there were many lessons I didn't catch at the time due to my own head being up my ass.

My ignorance for his Indian culture made me instantly angry and I shutdown. Instead of viewing the whole interaction as a learning experience about different cultures, I opted to retreat to my bedroom like a spoiled child.

Halfway through his visit, Jude beckoned me and asked if I wanted to join them.

Trying to put my arrogance aside, I joined them in the living room. As I sat down, I noticed Raj had his body turned toward Jude. Once again, I instantly felt rejected and resorted to sulking instead of asking questions and learning more about his culture. I allowed my arrogance get in the way. Raj was a perfect example of how the universe was trying to help me learn about other cultures and how I got in my own way.

Upon reflection I realize the universe showed me many, many lessons that demonstrated aspects of my personality, but I choose to ignore them, pretending they didn't apply to me. Essentially this experience was showing me a large dose of the medicine called reality.

I soon leaned that indeed the Indian culture was very different from my own, and I choose to be mindful of this in future interactions.

♥   ♥   ♥

DAVE

Ah, Dave. He was another fabulous lesson the universe showed me, uncovering another aspect of the false personality I was displaying.

From the first moment I walked into the copy center, Dave didn't like me. His normally warm demeanor seemed to turn icy cold whenever I would enter the store. Looking back, I now realize the persona I was displaying was that of a superficial woman, which led Dave to put up all his walls. I have since learned that Dave had been hurt one too many times by superficial women, and he had placed me in that category based on his first impression of me. Instead of showing him my realism and honesty, I had bounced and trounced into the shop, acting like an airhead.

The light bulb lesson with Dave came when I actually allowed myself to be real. I had baked a batch of chocolate chip cookies and brought some down to the shop. As Jude presented the cookies to Dave, he assumed that Jude had made them. When she informed him that I had created the treats, Dave actually saw my real side, not the fluffy exterior persona I had been hiding behind. From that day forward, interactions with Dave changed because I was not being a fake woman.

I learned to be real and have respect for others with honestly draw people closer to me, not away. Dave learned also that his past anger due to pretty girls and the games they played with his heart was a judgment toward me.

This universal lesson was such a great two-way street that both Dave and I learned you can't judge a book by its cover.

♥   ♥   ♥

Derek

Derek was an example of the many qualities I possessed that I denied from the first moment I had meet him. There was something I couldn't seem to put my finger on. As time wore on and we began seeing Derek on a weekly basis, I discovered more about his personality.

Due to his business background, Derek never allowed Jude or I to see his true self, making it difficult for us to truly know him. As I reflect back upon times spent with Derek, the most enlightened experience was when he allowed himself to play.

Two days before we were due to drive south to Florida, Derek and I were out buying paint for the apartment. As we ambled our way through the fresh streets of Montreal we were suddenly struck with the faint scent of smoke. Looking at one another, we glanced around to detect where the aroma was drifting over from. Fifty feet down the road, smoke was subtlety wafting up in the air. Alarmed at the view, Derek and I began running towards the fire. Due to the dry weather, a nearby apartment buildings peat moss had caught on fire and was quickly gaining momentum. Like two superheroes we quickly took action. I raced off to located a fire extinguisher while Derek had other plans.

That particular day Derek had decided to wear his favorite cowboy boots. Little did he know, they would be the heroes of the day! Using his instincts, Derek leapt upon the burning peat moss and commenced stomping about to put the fire out. As the flames slowly admitted defeat, Derek called out triumphantly " Katie!! It's okay! The flames are almost gone."

Stopping in my tracks, I turned back to see one of the coolest things ever. There on top of the peat moss was my friend Derek, Mister Conservative tap-dancing and flailing around in his favorite cowboy boots! It was the best sight ever!

The reason this experience stays with me is due to its authenticity. Running purely on instincts, Derek had put his guarded nature down and allowed me to see his true inner child sparkle and play.

It was beautifully refreshing to watch, and I now know what Jude was talking about when she spoke of realism. Later that day, in yet another random act of kindness, Derek offered Jude and myself one of his computers. He knew how much I wanted to start writing about my adventures on the
road and wanted to help out. Excitedly I accepted his offer and Jude and I fondly named our new laptop "Blue".

Due to my own self-doubt, it took me weeks before I exposed my true self to Derek, and I did it over the telephone, due to my lack of courage. As Jude and I were preparing to leave Montreal, I had called Derek to say my goodbyes. Overprotection and control came over his voice as he questioned our travels down south.

Once again, he gave me advice that I didn't need to hear: "I just don't want you to lose you, Katie." Though his words were meant with warmth and compassion, they frustrated me due to his lack of understanding of who I was. To be fair, I had never truly shown him the real me so; how was he to know. Needless to say that moment something switched inside me and I couldn't hold my truth back anymore. Opening my mouth, I began disclosing truly who I was and said that trying to force me into a mold wasn't congruent with whom I was and that doing so was making me ill.

Once I had finished speaking my truth, Derek had nothing to say. After all, I had spoken my truth, and when it came from my heart, Derek didn't respond. No debating! My foundation was firm, and again Jude was right about having a belief system.

Derek had a great heart, but he also possessed controlling and ego-based qualities. I contained similar qualities, but I didn't want to look at them. Whenever he demonstrated such attributes, instead of calling him on his behaviors, I had chosen to look the other way, pretending not to see our obvious similarities.

Reflecting upon Derek today, I wonder what his true intentions were. Though he had treated Jude and me to many lunches and chats, I wondered how much of it was real. What wasn't he showing us? Was he scared just as I to show his true colors? His demeanor had always been so collected and professional, but when it came to disclosing his private side, he had placed a padlock over the metal door.

He had only allowed us to see one side of himself, which is exactly what I used to do. I had always been fearful that people wouldn't like me if I showed them I was a serious, deep woman, so I had opted to play the role of a scatterbrained free spirit. Unfortunately the end result was that I was belittling my spirit by pretending to be dumb when in reality I was pretty quick (if I do say so myself!).

So the moral of the story is that people are not always what they seem, despite exterior appearances. I am disappointed in myself as I reflect on Mr. Derek, because had I been real from the start, perhaps he would have mirrored my behavior.

♥   ♥   ♥

Sam I Am

Lesson #432: Sam. He came blasting out of nowhere one night while Jude and I were at a nightclub. This man with a huge heart had many lessons to show me—insights into my character. From the moment he caught me flirting with a coffee shop attendant, I knew our first date would be an experience different from anything I had ever known. Sam was forty-two and had been hurt many times in love. Due to his numerous heartbreaks, his demeanor toward women had shifted from loving to predator. I had played the same role with men over the years. I would often date someone, grow bored, and drop him like a hot potato with little to no explanation. Sam had the same qualities, but because he had been playing the game longer, he was definitely the predator while I was the unaware prey. Over the course of our extremely short-lived romance, I was shown what I would look like if I had continued on my path of lies and deception. Sam had many obsessive qualities especially when it came to his appearance, often exercising seven hours a day to maintain his athletic exterior appearance. This self-absorbed behavior was very unhealthy, and I could see he was driving himself crazy with his rigid routines.

Upon reflection I realize I had the very same qualities in my personality. My obsession with Steven, my exterior appearance, unhealthy patterns: I was on the exact same path as Sam. The universe was simply showing me how my self-destructive behaviors could continue well into my life. Sam and I essentially mirrored one

110

another's personalities. There are two major fears I had surrounding this relationship. For as long as I can remember, I have always been attracted to many, many different men, and the idea of committing to one really challenged who I was. I saw the exact same qualities in Sam and therefore felt I couldn't trust him with my heart. The second fear regarding Sam was related to his ego. Like me, Sam operated in a predominantly ego-based reality, based on money and exterior possessions. During our first date, he had given me many compliments regarding my appearance, which only seemed to inflate my ego. As I reflect I realize, had Sam and I stayed in a relationship together, it would have been based entirely on ego, not truth, which would have led to my demise.

♥   ♥   ♥

Army Men of Montreal

During one of our first weeks in Montreal, Jude and I went out dancing at a nearby club. Within thirty minutes of our arrival, we had been approached by a group of men in the army. The first two guys to approach us were very friendly and introduced themselves as Daniel and James. After several drinks, Daniel started flirting with me and telling me his thoughts. Instead of being straightforward and honest with him, I enjoyed the attention and again slipped into my role as the dumb blonde. I could tell he really dug me, and I played on it by acting.

I continued flirting and acting interested when in reality his attention was only inflating my ever-present ego to epic portions. As the evening progressed, Daniel eventually grew bored with my mixed signals and wandered over to another group of women.

A new guy, Kevin, had taken his place and was sitting beside me. Because I wasn't attracted to him, I let my guard down and conversed with him as my true self. At some point in the past, I had convinced myself that attractive men wouldn't like the real me; hence my bimbo persona. As I showed more of my real self to Kevin, he responded with genuine interest. It felt so great to actually disclose my true colors and have a male respect my words.

Although I showed my true self, I was still playing a Ping-Pong game with my behavior. Even though I wasn't interested in Kevin, I began leading him on, unaware that I could simply have a conversation with a male without it being flirting. Again my need for attention was the driving force behind my flirting with Kevin. Needless to say, I wasn't behaving like a mature, honest, twenty-six-year-old. Nope, I was sending out crazy mixed signals, confusing all who came around me, especially myself. Even as I write this section, I have to laugh. I completely assumed that Kevin was into me when in reality I'm sure he was simply enjoying the conversation. See how my ego could get me in trouble?

By assuming Kevin liked me, I allowed myself to again inflate my ego, instead of stay in my shoes, and as Jude always says, "When you assume things, you make an ass out of you and me."

♥   ♥   ♥

Simon

Lesson #716: Simon played a small role in my path, but he did teach me about myself. The same night I met Sam, Simon and his friend had approached Jude and me; Simon was in his forties and exuded great wealth. I could tell this instantly and decided to have a drink with him. As I write this I have to laugh. For years I had loudly announced to all who would listen that I didn't give two toots about a man's wealth. Was that ever a bunch of bullshit. Pardon the French, but seriously, the minute Jude told me he had money, my interest in him instantly increased.

As I sat across from him, playing the role of a pea-brained blonde, I was becoming the very person I had announced I was not. As the evening progressed, I felt smaller and smaller due to my performance. I started feeling guilty. Simon was married, but his wife had left him because he cheated on her, so please tell me why I would make an attempt to be used for my body. Because I was running with my ego and he was paying attention to me. Simon was a great lesson to show me how confused I truly was. As I gave him my phone number, I gave off the impression that I truly wanted him to call. In truth, I never wanted to see him again, but instead of being honest, especially with myself, I acted like a bimbo, and this behavior has a name, folks: attention-seeking! In the future I am going to recommend to myself that I invest in a dog instead of seeking men's approval. Dogs are a lot less harmful, and cuddlier!

♥   ♥   ♥

charlottes web!

Observation 1,234: One particular Montreal evening, Jude and I decided to rent a couple of DVDs to pass the time. *Charlotte's Web* had always been a childhood favorite of mine, and I excitedly brought it home. As the film rolled forward, I began noticing many similarities between Charlotte the spider and Jude. I know it sounds silly, but I honestly did. Allow me to explain. Naive throughout the film, the pig is introduced to the big bad world of farming. Although it was upsetting, he had the loving guidance of the barnyard spider, Charlotte. During the course of the film, Charlotte teaches Babe about patience and loving himself for who he is. She would patiently create masterful spider webs depicting the inner beauty she said was within Babe, a simple, everyday pig.

After the movie, I told Jude that I saw many similarities between her and Charlotte. Smiling, she began explaining her views on life. "It's a tangled web we weave, but it's also as tangled as we want to make it. Spider webs are made up of two parts; sticky and non-sticky. Everyone has a choice of how they want to live their lives; either getting stuck in the sticky web or choosing to live unstuck. It's always a choice."

As our journeys continued, those words stayed with me. Every single situation I had gotten myself into was of my own doing. For years I had created quite the tangle for myself, and Jude was in the patient process of unwinding the damage.

♥　　　　　♥　　　　　♥

Janna

Lesson #985: Janna. She was such a monumental lesson for me during my Montreal experience. Since the moment I had seen her in the gym, I felt jealousy and judgment toward her. Though I had barely said ten words to her due to my low self-confidence, I felt threatened by her. She was a young vibrant woman who had recently moved from Vancouver with her husband. She was starting to work on her second degree and was a very motivated, positive woman. She was an example of exactly the kind of women I needed to surround myself with, but instead of opening myself up and connecting with her, I began avoiding her eye contact and acting stand offish. As my wacky behavior continued, Jude asked what was up with the weird vibes I was giving off. All this time I was honestly oblivious of the shield of "leave me alone" I had created toward her. It took me until our last week in Montreal to finally turn the switch with the Janna situation.

I had entered the gym and proceeded to start my usual cardio routine. About fifteen minutes into my workout, I noticed Janna glancing over in my direction. Instead of avoiding her eye contact, which was my usual reaction, I decided to smile. Well, can you believe it? And she smiled back, then started to approach me. For the next thirty minutes, we had a glorious conversation and I could honestly feel the connection. Why did I feel such a magnificent connection? you may ask. Because I dropped down my walls and spoke honestly with her.

Placing to the side my judgments and jealousy, I soon learned that she was a beautiful spirit with similar concerns and opinions.

So lesson learned: put aside your bullshit at the door and be real. End of story.

♥　　　　　♥　　　　　♥

Katie versus the City of Montreal

Folks, please prepare yourself for the wonderful tale of how I, Katie Sutherland, learned to wear big-girl underpants.

For years I had thought I was above the law and conducted my life with a false sense of pride. Avoiding parking tickets, ignoring rules, I was always dodging societal responsibilities. All of that dodging came to a close as I got caught in my game in Montreal.

Unlike most cities and townships I had lived in, Montreal was extraordinarily diligent with their parking enforcement.

City of Montreal 1 versus Katie

The very first day I arrived in Montreal, Cass received two tickets in one day. Falling into old habits, I automatically threw the tickets in the garbage, completely unfazed.

City of Montreal 2 versus Katie

The very next day, I received another ticket. First thing in the morning, cocking my head, I looked at the ticket and didn't want to deal with it.

Again I threw it in the garbage. This little game of escapism continued all week until finally I had received quite the collection of tickets. Earth to Katie, Earth to Katie. This tactic simply isn't working, girl. Go figure out another one! This seemed to be the message the universe was yelling at me louder every day.

City of Montreal 3 versus Katie

After I received my tenth ticket, Jude suggested that we go down to the City Hall and purchase a parking permit. Following the rules? I had thought at the time, What a concept!

That same afternoon, to attain my pass, after waiting thirty minutes (which in my world felt like to ten thousand hours), my number was finally called out. Approaching the front desk, I explained my situation to the clerk on duty. Nodding, she requested two pieces of mail proving that I was a Montreal resident. I can promise you at this point I had smoke coming out of my ear, pretty impatient bugger I was. Shaking my head, I told her I had hadn't acquired any essential documents. Apparently my bargaining tactics were lost on this woman, and she told me to come back when I had proper information.

City of Montreal 4 versus Katie

Seething, I walked back to Cass. Glaring at my beautiful van, I directed my anger at her.

Upon reflection I realize poor Cass must have been suffering from feelings of neglect and abandonment. At this time I was truly angry at myself but again too up my own ass to admit it.

One week later, I once again found myself waiting impatiently at City Hall. One hour and two bitten thumbnails later, my number was announced. Finally I received my parking permit and proudly placed it on Cass. It had taken me fourteen parking tickets to finally understand it was easier to play by the rules than defy them. Having said that, I have quite a bit to explain to the credit agency!

♥   ♥   ♥

Montreal Departure Day!

Jude and I bounced out of bed this morning, excited about the upcoming Florida adventure. Earlier that week we had gone in to see Dave about making business cards. Rewarding Dave for doing such a great job, I gave him cookies, and Jude made him blush with a compliment that only she could give, right from the heart. One thing I should share with you all is that Jude gives respect to all without strings attached; sometimes I believe she is too humble at times.

Cassidy looked raring to go after having been parked in the streets for several weeks. My attempts to sell Cass had gone sideways, and after posting her ads for two weeks, I had finally given up, not without a struggle though. About ten days early, I had thrown a fit after receiving my eighth parking ticket. Silently yelling at the universe, I questioned why I couldn't get rid of the van. Storming home in a terrible mood, I told Jude about my frustrations. "Why can't we get rid of it? I don't understand."

Calmly Jude looked up from her tarot reading and said, "Katie, the universe works in many different angles. Perhaps you aren't meant to sell her. Did you think about it that way? Remember the dream you had about, Cassidy not being fully unpacked. That could mean that you aren't finished with her quite yet."

All the time I was still struggling with my back-to-school-dilemma and didn't want to admit I might be leaving again. I was still fighting a battle against my intuition, but if I had been truly listening, I would have known deep down that Montreal wasn't resonating with me. I have compiled a list of the "subtle" universal messages I received:

1. didn't get accepted into McGill
2. couldn't sell Cassidy
3. couldn't find work as a waitress, which is pretty unheard of
4. complete energy drainage
5. waking up not feeling right
6. creativity not flowing

And the list could go on and on. Needless to say, the universe was obviously trying to articulate its opinions regarding Montreal.

As we hopped in Cassaroni, I thanked the universe that I hadn't sold Cassaroni; she had been such a great companion to me, and I vowed not to speak so harshly about her again. I asked myself why I would sell such a great companion because I couldn't stand driving down into the bowels of the Amityville horror, a.k.a. the underground parking lot. With a spiraling ramp that twisted and was the width only an import car could maneuver around, the parking lot, with dark shadows, created feelings of claustrophobia and suppression.

We left Montreal at the worst possible time: 5:00 p.m. rush hour. To quote Frank Sinatra, "I did it my way." This was our way. As Jude and I had never preplanned any of our departures diligently since leaving Vancouver, another lesson was that when it is time, then we go.

Cranking the satellite radio, we sung our way through rush hour and straight down to the New York state border.

♥   ♥   ♥

Border Crossings #2 down to Florida

We arrived at the New York state border after supper, and my adrenal glands kicked in, creating anxious vibes all over my body. Since I can remember, authority figures—any shape or size, pink or green—have always intimidated me, and I know authority scares most people. But trust me; I am really scared of authority. Allow me to explain. Due to my terrible habit of lying, I have always had the feeling I am going to get caught by someone. Don't ask me who, but someone. Needless to say, when I get interrogated by border guards, they definitely freak me out. So as Jude and I approached the guards' booth, I was not a happy lying camper.

A man with a fabulous handlebar moustache stuck his head out and started asking questions. Jude and I must have had a lucky penny hidden in Cassaroni that evening, because the guard was a real softie. When I explained to him we were traveling to a universal light workers conference, he enquired if we were electricians, Ah, thank the heavens for lighthearted government workers!

Needless to say, I had put my entire body through an anaerobic workout for absolutely nothing, and what do we call this, folks? FEAR! And what is it good for? NOTHING!

I think you get my point.

Having spent countless hours driving on endless freeways, I felt overjoyed at the vision of rural Florida roads. Coastal beach on one side and palm trees on the other created mellow vibes as Jude and I sped south toward warmth. After several hours along the country road, I noticed red rocks jumping in front of Cassidy.

Confused at the odd visions, I squinted my eyes and focused my attention on the unusual bouncing rocks. Upon further investigation, I realized these weren't rocks, no man! These were crabs frantically scuttling across to the safety of the sea. Swerving Cass left and right, I desperately tried to save the little crustaceans from impending doom. Laughing at my antics, Jude suggested we pull over and observe the critters. Finding a safe spot, we stopped Cass and explored to find the curious crabs. Peeking out from their underground holes, the crabs looked primal and snapped me back into survival mode. These crabs' sole mission was to cross the street so they could jump into the salty ocean and recreate.

Pretty simple existence, eh?

As we pulled away, I tried to envision my life as simple as the crabs'. Nature truly does have many insights into our souls if we are paying attention.

♥ ♥ ♥

Beach Bums

Once arriving in Florida we were met with several drizzly days. One particular day, we decided to relax with an afternoon matinee. Two hours before the movie started, Jude and I headed out to pick up a few groceries. After grabbing some tasty deli treats and plenty of grapefruits, we had a picnic lunch in the parking lot. While nibbling on chicken wings, Jude and I brainstormed more ideas for a business. Creating our own life-coaching organization came up as an option. We continued on eating. Jude had been unofficially coaching people for years. I began asking her how she would approach new clients.

She responded, "Well, first you have to establish why they are coming to see you. Introductory questions are always important in order to establish a relationship." Nodding, I asked her to continue.

As Jude spoke more about being a life coach/strategist I happily sat listening to her every word. When I was growing up, my mother and I didn't talk much; hence our current relationship suffers from it. Like most kids, I simply longed for time spent with my mother, but she never seemed to want to spend time talking with me.

Since having met Jude, I realized she hadn't replaced my mom, but I did feel as though our daily chats were making up for lost time from my childhood. Jude would tell me about her father and mother; all the wisdom truly passed down to her. Because she is a very descriptive storyteller, I would listen intently as Jude recalled old memories.

The coolest thing about my chats with Jude was that she listened to me as an equal, not someone greater than her. Many adults I have encountered have spoken down to me, insisting they possess more knowledge simply because they are older. Although adults may be older, this does not automatically mean that they are correct. In fact, truth be told, the wisest words I have heard came from the lips of a ten-year-old boy at summer camp last year!

Needless to say, to me, being treated as an equal was very important, and I respected Jude for her ability to truly listen to my viewpoints.

Prior to entering the old movie theatre, we decided to sit at a nearby patio and enjoy a cup of joe. While sipping on our coffee, I noticed an odd shape fidgeting underneath the table. Intrigued, I glanced downward. To my astonishment, I was met with a pair of beady red eyes that belonged to a pigeon. Rather startled, I shot back from under the table and informed Jude of my discovery. Since I can remember, birds have always frightened me and this time was no different. While I was explaining my childhood fear to Jude, the pigeon decided to hop up onto our table and truly make his presence known. Heart beating rapidly,

I leaned as far back as humanly possible in a desperate attempt to hide from the winged creature.

Jude noticed my reaction and told me to breath and calm down. "Remember Katie, we are all connected so there is really nothing to fear. "This statement did serve to relax my mind a fraction. Sensing my heartbeat returning to normal, I took a breath and investigated our new friend. The sight that met me brought tears to my eyes. The pigeon was covered from beak to claw with dirt and grim. It's piercing red eyes told me that his time on Earth was coming to a close. My sadness soon turned to anger when I realized that it's horrific condition was a product of man and his wasteful, self consuming ways. Beautiful creatures of the earth were slowly being destroyed by man and this pigeon in Fort Lauderdale was no different.

Suddenly, the coffee shop door swung open and a man in his twenties walked out. Dressed in ratty old clothes, he was not exactly the picture of cleanliness. Glancing in our, he noticed the pigeon and jumped about 50 feet in the air.

"Whoa! Dude! Be careful. You don't want to get close to that thing. It's disease ridden." And with that, he hopped on his skateboard and rode off down the busy street.

Rolling her eyes, Jude responded, "Rather ironic that he speaks of the bird being disease ridden when it's his garbage that is polluting the animals environment to begin with. That's the problem with the planet today. Everyone is so quick to judge and point fingers but few actually want to be active participants in making our world a cleaner place."

Several minutes later, the pigeon hopped down from our table and continued on his path down the polluted road. As I watched him waddle away, I noticed some similarities between the two of us:

Katie	Pigeon
Living in unhealthy environment	Living in unhealthy environment
People judging by exterior appearance	People judging by exterior appearance
Developing illness due to my inability	Developing illness due to my inability
to handle toxic energy	

At precisely 2:53 p.m. Jude and I walked into the movie theater and caught the last five minutes of the movie. We looked at each other and made faces.

"Well, this is rather silly," I said as we remained seated, trying to sort out what to do.

Taking action, I sprang up and wandered into the front lobby to enquire about movie schedules. The lovely girl at the popcorn counter assured me that, yes, we had caught the last five minutes, but not to worry; the three o'clock show was beginning in two minutes. Relieved we hadn't missed the show, I returned back to our seats.

The following two hours consisted of an adorable movie about a waitress; the storyline went a little something like this.

A waitress who made extraordinary pies discovered that she was pregnant with her husband's baby. Because she loathes her husband, the news about the pregnancy was devastating, and then came along the doctor. New to town, Dr. Smith and the waitress soon developed strong feelings for one another. An affair developed and the waitress felt happy for the first time in her life.

Throughout the movie the owner of the restaurant served as a guardian angel. In the end he passed away, leaving the waitress enough money to raise her child without her horrible husband and doctor. She could open up her own restaurant and raise her baby.

By the closing credits, I had tears of happiness and understanding in my eyes. As Jude and I left the movie theater, she looked over to me and asked, "So, Katie, what was it about that movie that seems so familiar?" her eyes twinkling the whole time.

Recognizing the cool universal lesson I had received, I responded, "A few weeks back when you kissed Rick, I judged both of you very harshly. Even though you told me Rick helped you with advice to leave your ex-husband, he was also unhappy in his marriage. I still frowned upon it. Now, watching this movie, I got to see more angles to the puzzle. This woman was married to a man who was verbally and emotionally abusive. She was completely miserable in her life."

Love and relationships are very complicated; who was I to judge when I have exhibited the same behavior even with the last boyfriend I had, flirting with another boy when I knew my date was coming to meet me.

♥   ♥   ♥

PEDRO

During the next few days, Jude and I basically became professional beach bums. Our days consisted of rolling out of bed, sweating from a stifling-hot nights, and swiftly jumping in the ocean to cool down. One particular afternoon we came across an interesting fellow who was originally from Peru: Pedro.

While I was walking along the sand, Pedro approached Jude and I and began disclosing strategies for proper crystal cleansing. "You must take it out on the full moon and place it in a cup of saltwater in order to fully cleanse the toxic energies," he said with his brown eyes gleaming. Excited to meet fellow spiritualists, Pedro followed us to Cassidy. During the walk we got on the topic of Reiki masters and their teachings. Pedro disclosed that his mother possessed her black belt in Reiki, and she had been born into natural gifts, not commercialism. He went on to discuss his dislike for commercialized spiritual practices that seemed to be appearing around the globe. Astrology, the healing touch, and wisdom all seemed to be for sale as marketing corporations were tapping into the energy phenomenon. Spirituality was losing its ancient authenticity through courses that taught anyone the art of healing and intuitiveness.

Jude has often told me the physical damage that is spawned from unskilled healers who are spreading toxicity because of their own negative blockages. "The healing touch is not something that you can learn in a book. It is an inherent gift passed down from the universe. I wish people would understand this. You can't read about having healing hands. Either you have or you don't."

Pedro agreed completely with Jude's words and proceeded to walk us down the beach. He began articulating his frustrations about being an immigrant from South America. As his words gained increasing anger, I started feeling uncomfortable and impatient.

Upon reflection I realize I saw a lot of myself in Pedro. I had many anger issues that lay dormant within, but I would never admit it.

Pedro, on the other hand, was articulating his feelings by discussing them out in the open.

Now who's the healthier one with anger issues? Definitely not the Canadian iceberg! Nope, indeed it was our newfound South American friend. I now know my frustrations with Pedro's anger stemmed from my own inability to express my emotions.

At the time, I was unfamiliar with such direct expression of anger, so instead of accepting it, I repeated old patterns by removing myself from the situation. I regret this, for I am sure that Pedro had many other enlightening topics to discuss with me.

♥   ♥   ♥

ELLIE

Oh, dear, sweet Ellie. Jude and I met Ellie at the local Penny's in Fort Lauderdale. During our morning ritual of card readings, Ellie quietly interjected her intuitive spin on my personal reading. Shocked at such accurate honesty, I looked up at her with a very inquisitive expression on my face. Shyly she had pushed her glasses up on her face and apologized for such direct feedback.

Ellie went on to explain pointers about intuition and how to trust your vibes. I sat in awe as this older woman stood at our table and explained all about her gifts and psychic visions that she had received over the years. Noticing dark spots on her arms, Jude inquired what had happened. Self-consciously Ellie covered her arms and disclosed that the spots were form a skin condition called eczema. Also adding to her unhealthy state, Ellie revealed that she had been a smoker since the tender age of fourteen. Shaking her head, Jude lightly reprimanded Ellie, reminding her that she of all people should know better. Agreeing sheepishly, Ellie stated that smoking was her release. As Jude has mentioned, "As people who handle energy, psychics have to remember to release it properly. Many intuitives release energy through smoking, which only serves to trap even more toxic vibes within your body. The best way to release is by placing your palms toward the sky and allowing energy to flow upwards."

Seeing Ellie, I fully understood Jude's explanation of unreleased energy creating sickness within. I was doing the same thing through remaining silent and obsessing in my mind instead of expressing my thoughts.

Watching Ellie that morning, I was reminded of all the "behind the scenes" intuitives who were out spreading warmth and wisdom simply because it was who they were. Inspired by such humble kindness, I imprinted the memory of her into my conscious mind.

♥   ♥   ♥

Florida Good Times

On the last day before the conference, Jude looked up at the sky and stated, "See those dark clouds; looks like we going to be treated to a rainstorm pretty quickly."

As if on cue, the low rumble of thunder resounded as we walked. Both being avid lovers of nature's elements, Jude and I exchanged excited glances as we felt soft raindrops start to that float down from the heavens.

"Mother Nature is so cool to cool us down," I shouted as we hurriedly put our belongings into Cassidy. Within two minutes the soft raindrops turned into heavy big drops as the dark clouds opened up directly.

Throwing our hands in the air, Jude and I gleefully jumped with delight at the sudden rainstorm. Splashes upon splashes came down while most people ran for cover, but not us. No, we stood out in the storm until it passed by us, ensuring we were completely soaked. With my eyes closed, tilting my head up toward the sky, I felt a part of the universe as the rain poured down. Being out in the rain took me straight back into "prehistoric times," when the main focus was survival. No cell phones, televisions, personal computers running the show—no sirree, BOB! Simple survival was the name of the game as animals either ate or were eaten. As the downpour continued, I wondered how I had allowed my life to get so complicated with other factors. As I looked inward, my vibes told me, "You believed everybody else but yourself. You bought into the concept that you need all of these items and machines. But at any given point, you can return back to days of simplicity. The choice is always yours." And with that, the huge raindrops slowly transformed into little ones and then eventually ceased altogether. Feeling refreshed and chilly, Jude and I grabbed some warm towels to dry off.

Later that evening, we decided to take Fort Lauderdale by storm. Within twenty minutes, Jude and I magically transformed ourselves from scruffy van ladies to breathtaking divas. Armed with scarves and angel perfume, we approached the nightclub.

As I watched men and women filter out of the bar, I began feeling nervous. In the past, I had always been fairly tomboyish and hippy-like. Never would I care much about my appearance or the way in which I carried myself. All that had changed since Jude had been teaching me about belief in oneself and caring about your appearance. Though I was dressed in beautiful clothing, I still felt uptight and nervous as if I was an imposter sneaking into an exclusive party.

Jude noticed my jitters and said, "Come on Twinkle Toes, don't pay attention. Let's just go in there and have some fun!" Nodding, I followed her past the fancily clad doorman and into the club.

Looking around, I felt as though I had crashed a Hollywood celebrity party. Every single woman in the club was tan, size two and talking on cellphones. There were many slimers lurking around hiding behind white suits and sunglasses. As a group of girls walked by dressed entirely in Gucci, I looked over at Jude. She motioned toward the bar and I gladly followed. Perhaps a drink would relax my nerves and stop my body from moving like a robot. Sipping on a rum-and-coke, I did feel a bit better. As the band started up, Jude and I found a patch of floor to claim as our spot to listen to the great rock music pouring out from the stage, and soon I felt the urge to shimmy down in my fancy sandals.

Using our scarves as props, Jude and I began dancing in our own little world. Our dancing moves soon caught the attention of many slimers. Within a few moments, Jude and I had several offers to dance; declining each one, we both determined that dancing with each other was the way to go. After about five minutes of dancing, I eventually stopped caring what others thought about me. The less I cared, the more I moved and the better I felt.

Glancing up, I noticed a very tall guy directly in front of us. He was wearing very chic clothing and chatting with blonde women who'd definitely had some work done, if you know what I mean. As he scanned the room, his eye caught Jude, who was dancing directly behind him. Excusing himself from the ladies, he swirled around and started smoothly chatting with Jude. It was a pretty funny sight to witness. This six-foot-five man was bending down, talking to a five-foot-two lady. Strategically placing himself in between the two of us, he introduced himself as Jeremy. As the evening progressed, Jeremy soon became a fixture attached to the Katie and Jude combination. At one point Jeremy peered down and enquired what we did; I responded that we were writers as well as psychics.

The usual "can you read my mind" comment followed as Jeremy tried to test my abilities. Laughing, I told him I was in training and still learning the tricks of the trade.

As we made our way to the washroom, I felt very self-conscious as we waited in the line. Beautiful girls in beautiful clothes surrounded us as we slowly made progressed in the line. True to form, Jude complimented many of the girls, telling them they looked radiant or commenting on their accessories. In awe, I secretly hoped that one day I would have enough confidence to do the same thing.

Back on the dance floor, Jeremy soon found us and shimmied his way over. "I missed you! Why don't you come home with me tonight?" he exclaimed as we danced to loud rap music. Rolling my eyes, I responded, "I don't do that sort of thing." I pretended to shake my fist at Jeremy and shook my head no.

Upon reflection I realize I was trying so hard to up keep the good-girl persona I had created for myself. Deep down part of me craved the excitement of a one-night stand, but I had been so right that I should never allow it. I judged others so harshly for engaging in one-night stands I knew I would be even harsher on myself. Also, due to the fact I was traveling with Jude, I didn't go home with Jeremy. This was delusional thinking. I still saw her as my mother and was fearful that she would judge me were I to behave frivolously.

♥   ♥   ♥

Light workers conference

Two days later, Jude and I headed north to Boca Raton for the conference. To off set the admission fees, we had both signed up for volunteer duties.

As volunteers for the conference, Jude and I were due at the hotel room orientation and introductions. Pulling into the hotel parking lot, I felt butterflies in my stomach; Jude smiled and said, "This should be interesting, Katie. Pay very close attention to what you see and don't be nervous, just be you."

The hotel doors swirled open as we walked into the front lobby; black and white tiles below us created the feeling of entering a medieval ballroom. Straight ahead of us was a water fountain that sprayed a spectrum of colors from yellow to deep violet.

While Jude and I advanced through the lobby, the concierge seemed to appear from thin air. A rather tall man, he had gray hair and a nice smile. "Good afternoon, ladies. Can I give you a hand finding anything?" When we informed him we were volunteers for the conference, he nodded, gesturing toward a long hallway to the right. "I believe Robin is over there. Let's go see if we can find her, shall we?" And with that he ushered us into the main vendors' room, which was in the process of being set up.

As we poked our heads into the main vendors' room, we saw beautiful brightly colored scarves, jewelry, and massage tables. Other vendor tables consisted of psychic readings, clothing made from batik, and hobbyists. Outside the vendors were the speakers with tables of DVDs and books.

Just as I was about to locate Ted Andrews's (an incredible spiritualist author) booth, a blonde woman approached Jude and me. In a singsong voice, she called out "Hi, there, I'm Robin Rose, the coordinator for the weekend. You must be Katie and Judy. Very nice to meet you two." Shaking her hand, Jude asked if there was anything we could do. "Not right at this moment, but we are having a volunteers meeting in the front lobby in about fifteen minutes. So in the meantime, you can just explore around and check out the booths." And with that she checked two things off on her clipboard and was off.

Noticing an outdoor garden, I mentioned to Jude I was going to step outside for some air. We had only been inside for twenty minutes and already I wanted fresh air. Taking a seat in the sunshine, I took a deep breath and enjoyed the clean summer air. Checking in, I said to myself, *this is what you have been wanting. Now you will be able to see for yourself what other light workers are about.* Continuing to ground myself, I heard nearby birds chirping their support.

As we prepared to hear Robin's instructions I sat and pretended to pay attention. My mind wandered as I contemplated different people's belief systems. It appeared to me that the lighter workers' predominant belief was in the almighty one being, God. As mentioned earlier, I was raised as an atheist, so praying and religion were brand new concepts to me. I began wondering about the universe and how I had been so blessed to experience all the serendipitous events that had eventually led me to this conference. I wondered if the universe and God were the same. After pondering this for about three seconds, I drew my own conclusion. Whatever belief one person has is their own, whether they believe in the universe, God, or nature. It really doesn't matter, but what did matter was having a strong belief system. As Jude had taught me many, many times, "If you have a strong belief system, no one can rock your boat."

Reflecting on the statement, I agreed, yet I was still learning to fully trust in a power greater than myself. During the past year of discovering the universe and the power of intent, I noticed that most loved ones in my life didn't have any beliefs at all. They simply went about their lives and potentially ignored the many signs the universe would be showing them.

It is my humble belief that it is due to this lack of belief system, which can get people off their course. I am the perfect example. For years I had been searching high and low, near and far, to discover who I was. Having no belief system in place, I often felt very alone and felt that I was questing in this world alone.

Then one magical day in September, Jude and her belief in spirituality came along, revealing a whole new world of possibilities and wonders. The key to being a spiritual being was simple:

Believe and it will happen;
disbelieve and it won't.

So there I was at the universal light workers conference, June 8,2007, exploring spirituality ever further. The guest speakers I am about to describe are amazing. They came from all walks of life; Jude always told me that science, religion, and medicine form the triangle that the world should realize is the foundation of spirituality.

Our first presenter for the night was a doctor of psychology by the name Dr. Raymond Moody (very cool name). His entire presentation involved his theories on "nonsense." As Dr. Raymond Moody put it, the combination of nonsense and logic actually creates a genius combination and should be used as methods for teaching children. He used the example of Dr. Seuss and his magical ways of teaching children valuable lessons through rhymes. Absolutely captivated by his theories, I remember how I adored Dr. Seuss for the exact same reason that Dr. Raymond Moody was speaking of. Dr. Seuss had an incredible way of articulating an essential teaching in such a manner that intrigued both adult and child alike.

Just as I was grabbing my pen to write notes, a man beside me poked my shoulder and whispered under his breath, "Oh, I get it, so what he is saying is that I should be actually listening to what three-year-olds have to say, actually playing with them! According to this scientist, three-year-olds possess a certain wisdom we don't!" Gleeful at his discovery, he resumed his position, facing forward, frantically scrabbling down notes.

Flabbergasted by his comments, I tried desperately not to giggle and embarrass myself. *Of course, three-year-olds are wise, silly,* I thought to myself. *They haven't been exposed to all the fears, doubts, and insecurities that the big bad world places on us.* Hearing that doctor make that claim about children served as an affirmation to me that no matter how much studying one does there are many universal wisdoms that you can't learn in a classroom.

Fast-forwarding several weeks into the future, I indeed met a little intuitive boy who held the secrets of the cosmos simply in his eyes. Little Jack would have been a great character for this silly doctor to meet.

♥   ♥   ♥

Little Jack, the Wise One

During our Canadian road trip tour, Jude and I came across the spectacular area called Digby. It was nested in glacial mountains and sparkling clean lakes. One particular scorching afternoon, Jude and I took advantage of a chilly refreshing lake. Along the lake front, Jude befriended a very intuitive two-year-old named Jack. With crystal-clear blue eyes, little Jack radiated ancient wisdom as he constructed a sand village by the shoreline. His parents, Ken and Jenny, stood by this little man, exuding gorgeous parental pride. They were both spiritual beings who believed in past lives and sixth-sensory perception. Since discovering Jack's intuitiveness, they had found a healing doctor who taught them methods of protecting and enhancing his energy. Deep down I know this little soul had chosen these parents due to their spiritual openness and understanding.

After Jude and I left the lake, I was embarrassed by my feelings of envy toward little Jack. I couldn't help but wonder what my life would have been like had my parents nurtured my sixth sense. As I went into sadness, Jude instantly noticed and asked, "Why the long face?" Feeling very childish and embarrassed, I explained that I felt jealousy toward the little boy we had just met due his deeply spiritual parents.

Nodding, Jude responded, "Katie, don't feel embarrassed by this admittance. Just don't let jealousy pull you into regret. It was in your life plan to be born into your family, just as it was little Jack's plan to be born into his. You obviously have lessons to teach your family, just like I teach you lessons. Remember, we all choose what families we are born into in order to learn lessons we didn't capture in past lives."

Hearing Jude's words comforted my feelings of jealousy as I earned a deeper understanding of why we choose certain families to be born into.

♥   ♥   ♥

Looking over at the man beside me (whom I later found out was a doctor of child psychology), I silently pondered why he didn't have such basic knowledge. I honestly thought everyone knew that children were smarter than we were in some areas.

The doctor's reaction also triggered something else in me. For several months I had been struggling internally in regard to going back to post-secondary school. Because I was raised in an intellectual family, there had always been the silent expectation that I would follow in their footsteps and get my degree. Up until recently I had bought into the mindset that without a degree I would never amount to anything. It sounds all fine and dandy, but in reality, most of my friends who had quested long and hard for degrees were working in fields completely unrelated to their studies.

♥   ♥   ♥

Kay

Kay was a beautiful intuitive, Jamaican woman whom we met at the conference. She was a fellow volunteer comrade, and what a spirit did she have. Kay taught me several lessons throughout the June weekend.

The first lesson was again another affirmation about Jude's character. During a coffee break, the three of us had sat at Buck's, and all of a sudden Kay looked straight at Jude and stated, "Your eyes. There is something so familiar about your eyes."

Smiling her Mona Lisa smile, Jude answered softly, "I know we've met." Nodding in acknowledgment, Kay understood completely in yet another affirmation of Jude's old soul.

The second lesson was in reflection of my constant search for answers from external sources. As I questioned Kay about being a light worker and how she knew she was one, she looked at me and answered, "You just know, child. To thine self be true. That's all you need to remember." Her kind, patient words stay with me as I reflect upon my search to find myself.

The third lesson I learned from Kay was that I was still projecting a false impression of myself. The first time we had coffee; she turned toward me and said, "You know, Katie, you are so sweet. I can't imagine you ever being in a bad mood." Ho, ho. Did I have her fooled! Although this statement was said as a compliment, I realized I wasn't showing the true colors, which were still masked behind many masks of falseness—KINDA LIKE A DANCER AT A MASQUERADE BALL.

♥ ♥ ♥

The morning presenter was Ted Andrews, a clairvoyant who has written numerous books. His talk was about nature. He said that if we pay attention we get signs every day from trees, flowers, animals, and insects, they are symbols to be acknowledged.

Jude had introduced me to his writings, which were full of knowledge and sprinkled with magic. His books are both informative and fun to read, so I couldn't wait to listen to what he had to say.

As Ted commenced his presentation, he instantly held the crowd's attention. Being a children's storyteller, he had been reciting and sharing stories and fables for years. In the perfect stage voice, he told the legend of the eagle and two little village children to a captivated audience. Not missing a beat, he added pauses and sound effects to create a dramatic feeling to his presentation. After Ted finished his legend of the eagle, he launched into the second part of his performance. Having a strong background in working with animals of all shapes and sizes, Ted held an infinite amount of knowledge regarding animals and our connection to them. Using excerpts from his book *Animal Speak*, Ted skillfully spoke about nature and its subtle ways of communicating with us.

One of the examples he used was paying attention to types of animals that cross your path. Often they are a representation or lesson for you at that particular point in your life. A couple of examples he used were:

	Representation
Vultures'	Purification-death and rebirth-view vision
Cats'	Mystery, magic and independence
Raccoons'	Dexterity and disguise
Elephants'	Ancient power, strength and royalty

He shared that creating a harmonious relationship with nature was a guarantee to feeling more connected to the power greater than us. My favorite quote from Ted Andrews is:

"Nature is talking to you all the time, are you paying attention?"

Ted repeated this motto several times during his presentation, and it soon became a slogan Jude and I would use.

Finishing his presentation, Ted took a bow and humbly hopped off stage. Feeling extremely inspired, I nodded my appreciation and checked in with Jude. "I just loved his presentation and he is so right. Mother Nature is communicating to us all the time. But most of us are so busy we don't make time to explore deeper." Jude expressed her appreciation for his presentation as well.

After Ted's presentation, I again reflected on the state of nature and its rapid demise due to our depleting ozone layer. Driving down the coast of Florida was simply a taste of other disasters I would see.

Lunchtime came and went. By 2:00 p.m. it was time for me to report to my volunteer duties. A physicist by the name of Marcus Masson was presenting his information on astrology, and I was his timekeeper.

Marcus spoke of the universe, its infinite solar systems, and their relation on our genetic bodies. He spoke about the importance of paying attention to particular planetary shifts, as they often play a role in our lives. Though a bit on the dry side, I did find his information very informative and thought-provoking. After gesturing to him that only fifteen minutes remained in his presentation, he announced that he was going to guide us on a meditation to travel to the center of the universe.

Leaning toward me, Marcus whispered, "Your duties as timekeeper are done. You can join us in the meditation if you like." Thrilled at the thought of traveling one million miles to the center of the universe, I gladly put down my time cards and positioned myself. Using a drum as a guiding tool, Marcus led us through many different realms of the Earth. Checking into my body, I realized I could actually feel different parts of my brain being activated. Blood was pumping in the back of my mind as we continued deeper into the visualization. With a resounding BANG, Marcus stopped his meditation and allowed us to explore what we saw. After several minutes of taking a roller coaster through my mind, I faintly heard Marcus starting to bring us back into a conscious state. The very last thing I remember before opening my eyes to the light of day was seeing one single eye in the middle of my forehead. Due to my background in Kundalini yoga, I knew this was my third eye finally being awakened. I opened my eyes. I felt groggy from a deep sleep. As we filtered out of the room, Marcus gently reminded us to drink some fresh water and eat some food.

♥ ♥ ♥

After a long day filled with spiritual universal truths and understandings, we enjoyed a fabulous evening of laughter and play.

During our dinner buffet, it was announced that each table would be responsible for creating a charade that depicted a presenter of the conference. Looking around our table, we saw there were many jovial women who started sharing opinions of particular presenters they wanted to imitate. Ideas of animals and nonsense floated around the dinner table as women announced their favorite speakers. Out of the blue, Jude burst out in laughter that resounded throughout the entire dining hall. One thing about Jude's energy level is that she has the ability to spread positive energy to all she is in contact with. One by one the ladies at the table joined in, mirroring Jude's giggles.

Before long, magical vibes radiated from our table while a creative brainstorming process took place. Although our table didn't take the cake for best skit, I know we had the best energy levels and the most fun, which was better than any prize any day!

♥   ♥   ♥

We arrived the following morning at 8:53 a.m. after having a glorious breakfast session at Denny's. Diane and Nancy greeted us as we checked in for our volunteer duties. With a quick glance at the schedule, I saw they had me down as a timekeeper for the "Real Love" presentation.

Grabbing the electric pink laminated sheets, I made my way over to the main hall.

Gregg Bauer was the speaker's name; he had created an entire series of books and tapes that taught his secrets of real love. He was previously a brain surgeon whose life had changed seven years ago with a divorce and cocaine addiction. He went to rehab and discovered with clear eyes how he had let materialism and ego take over his life. His teenage children didn't listen to him and had no respect for him. This is when he discovered real love through clear eyes and began his research.

Though a fairly simple concept, Greg stated that 90 percent of relationships lack real love. He spoke about people's perception of idealistic images of love and said that this has little or nothing to do with real love, which, as Greg put it, involve tough love. This meant lots of:

1. Listening
2. Patience
3. Communication
4. Firmness

"I have seen so many people blame everyone else for the problems when in reality they need to be checking their own actions. Countless women I have consulted have complained about their men neglecting them yet when I asked them what they have done lately for their man, they are silent. Look guys, this isn't rocket science, it really isn't. We just got to start listening, truly listening to what our loved ones are saying."

Real love defined is the desire for another person's happiness without wanting or needing anything in return.

Watching Greg Bauer, I had yet another one of those incredible light bulb moments illuminated my world. As he passionately spoke about real love and its qualities, I completely understood what Jude's methods were based on. For years I had bought into the artificial concept of what true love looked like: butterflies and rainbows.

Since having met Jude, I was learning that real love was spending hours upon hours with a person and speaking the truth; not only that but showing patience and placing absolutely no conditions upon the person. While Greg continued I thought more and more about how Jude's wordless way was teaching me real love through her actions. "It's not what you say, Katie; it's what you do. Always remember that love is an action that is instinctual. There should be no thought process involved."

Aha! I thought, *yet again another affirmation from the universe about the fairy godmother they had sent me.* Very cool beans.

♥   ♥   ♥

At eleven o'clock we had our final closing ceremony in the main hall. Scanning the room, I found my new friend Michelle and Jude at the front. Slipping between rows of chairs, I made my way over to the girls and waved. Robin Rose stood on stage and again thanked everyone for coming; she expressed a big thank you to the volunteers and then welcomed Arman and Angelina for the last performance. As the duo played the Beatles' "All You Need Is Love," everyone joined hands and sung along. Holding on to Michelle and Jude's hands, I could feel the warmth and love channeling through our bodies. Near the end of the song, my friend Michelle started crying. Wanting to take her sadness away, I held on to her and gave her a huge hug. Though I knew I couldn't take her sadness away, I wanted to comfort her. After a five-minute hug, Jude and I both decided it was time to go.

We had made plans to head down to the Florida Keys and were ready to head out. Saying our last goodbye to Michelle, Jude and I walked out to find Cassidy.

♥   ♥   ♥

Michelle

Michelle was my fondest memory of the light workers conference. I had spotted Michelle early on Friday and was immediately drawn to her sparkle that radiated through her from within. We had bonded on our mission to the grocery store and quickly became inseparable during the conference. The lessons I learned from Michelle was her pure, honest genuine nature and her trust and true compassion. One of the exercises during the conference was to look into one another's eyes and disclose our fears, sorrows, and anger without saying one word. As I telepathically told Michelle my most intimate, deepest issues, tears sprang to her eyes; at the time, I was still in such a state of denial I didn't understand what she saw that would lead to tears. As we reversed roles, I could see many childhood fears and sorrows in her eyes. What I saw saddened me greatly. No tears came from within after the exercise. I hadn't cried as she had.

As I write this, I see many lessons and beautiful gifts Michelle gave to me during that exercise. She showed me how to let my guard down and allow other females into my guarded world. Her genuine tears were generated by the sadness she saw in me, which also created an awareness of how deeply I had hidden childhood sorrows. At the time of the conference, Michelle had cried many times in front of me, teaching me the beauty of allowing yourself to cry and be vulnerable.

Although I had spent the majority of my time with Michelle during the conference, I began slowly detaching early out of fear of getting to close. Sound familiar? This was a habitual pattern of mine that was coming back to rear its ugly head. On the very last day of the conference, I remember saying goodbye to Michelle by the pool. As she was preparing to leave, I could feel my distance between the two of us. My biggest fear was being revealed to me right in my face: **abandonment.**

Instead of admitting it to myself and diving in anyway, I emotionally shut down and became a cold stranger. Sensing my emotional shutdown, Michelle quickly said her goodbyes and left. It was my inability to be real that created such a distance between us. To this day I wish to send her love and tranquility, wherever she may be.

Right before we left the parking lot, we saw Diane and Nancy preparing to leave. *How appropriate,* I thought. *They were the first people we met now they will be the last ones we see.* When we honked at Diane, she turned around to investigate. "You! It's you girls. Have a safe trip back to CANADA!" We told her that before leaving home we wanted to go swimming nuddlywinks in the Atlantic Ocean. Raising her eyebrows, Diane responded, "Well, you two be careful. Last time I went nuddlywinks the coast guard found me! Exploding into fits of laughter, we had imagined the scene. Feeling uplifted Jude and I headed south.

♥   ♥   ♥

Driving down to the Florida Keys, Jude looked up and noticed big dark storm clouds. "Its hurricane season down here, so we are going to have to watch the weather patterns very carefully." As soon as the words left her lips, we heard a resounding BOOM and the sky opened up on us. Fearful of being electrocuted, my whole body tensed up in anxiety. Trying to appear tough for Jude, I casually started humming along with the '70s rock station. Out of the corner of her eye, Jude sensed my tension. (Was there anything she didn't notice?) "Now, Katie, don't worry. We are going to be just fine. Don't you trust your vibes? It would have warned you if you were going into great danger. In order to live a fully spiritual life, you must trust in your guides and in your belief system."

Nodding, I agreed, but after a ginormous lightning bolt struck in front of us, I grabbed Jude's hand tightly. She allowed me to behave like a little girl, and we continued driving through the eye of the storm. As the wind was gusting and trees were swaying, we were truly witnessing who was in charge of the earth. *We are definitely small potatoes,* I thought to myself as the wind blew harder.

After what seemed like forever, the wind died down and the dark clouds rolled away; streams of sunlight broke through the clouds as we continued our trek southward. Getting the growlies mid-afternoon, we decided to stop in a funky-looking beach hut called Boon Docks. I pulled Cassidy into an almost empty unpaved parking lot. Top 40 hit music blasted out as we walked into a grass hut. It was so cool; like stepping in time warp. A waitress turned and smiled to acknowledge us; she wore a black tennis shirt with black skirt and a pair of pink crocs. We sat down at a table in the center of the hut because the weather was not finished with us yet. We were feeling a little chilled due to hunger.

Introducing herself, she said, "Hi, my name is Sonja. What can I get you to drink?" She handed us menus. I ordered a lime margarita and Jude ordered a lime martini; we sat back and reveled in what a great life we were living. I felt complete and had no desire for anything else. When I explained my feelings to Jude, she nodded and responded, "Now hold onto that feeling, little one, and don't let anyone take it away from you." Immediately I felt very protective of my feeling and decided to guard it with my life. That is yet another lesson I learned from the Judemeister: you and only you are in control of your own happiness.

Sonja came back to the table and asked if we wanted something to eat. I acknowledge that we sure did. "May we have twelve hot wings, plus twelve honey-garlic wing. Thank you." With that Sonja left.

Within ten minutes we were eating the crispiest, most flavorful wings. You can imagine how many miles we had to go to get the best! To the very last wing, we smacked our lips and licked our fingers; we were thankful for all we had for now and would have in the future. Having paid the bill and saying our goodbyes to Sonja, we wished her well in her future.

I turned Cassidy right so we could investigate more of the Florida Keys. We drove about a half an hour when we hit a town called Marathon. By this time I looked at the thermometer. It read 36 degrees Celsius.

I turned to Jude. "Let's find a beach to cool off." As soon as I spoke those words, Jude piped up. "Look, a sign. I believe it says … yes, Sunset Beach access, next left at the lights."

"Great work," I said as I gave Jude the knuckles.

"Right back at you, girl friend."

I ambled my way toward the ocean for a dip. Jude soon followed and we checked out the stunning view that surrounded us: aquamarine water, white sandy beach, big palm trees, and motorboats towing water skiers in the background. Suddenly Jude announced, "Katie, this would be a great spot for a healing, come on." Never one to say no to a healing, I paddled over to where Jude was. As she positioned me with my back facing upward, Jude began with my feet. As she applied pressure, I let out a yelp in protest, feeling the intense blockage within. "Ah, Katie, this is where all your tension blocks the flow of energy (chi) throughout your body; both arches need a healing."

She applied her healing hands to all the points where I needed to be healed, head to toe. By the end of the healing, I was very relaxed. She said softly that she was done. "I will release you, so please give yourself time to stay on your back, in your floating position, for how ever long as you wish." Jude released me and I opened my eyes to see her release the blocked energy from her body to the universe above. Rubbing her hands together, Jude looked down at me as I floated in the waves. "Now, how does that feel, Katie?" Katie!"

It was too late; she had lost me to the tranquil motion of the ocean swaying all around my body. With my ears under the ocean, I listened to every little sound that vibrated underwater. The healing had totally rejuvenated me and I was capable of hearing my inner vibes crystal clear.

♥   ♥   ♥

Healings

Jude's healings would often last from two to four days. The reason the healings didn't last longer was my inability to actively release my old energies into the universe. I have since learned that the more frequently old energy is released outward, the longer the affects of the healing last. Everyday habits such as remaining silent, holding tensions, and carrying others' issues were all sneaky contributors to blocked energy. For months Jude and I played the marvelous game of catch and release; I would unblock my energy and then fall back into old patterns of creating blockages. Ah, good times. The trials and tribulations of a spiritual student; constantly reminding myself to not carry others issues.

One very important aspect of energy healings was to place my hands upward toward the universe and allow it to release all toxic energy from my physical body.

After a healing took place, my creativity and inspiration would flow. Each healing would bring incredible clarity I longed to maintain for the rest of my days. The clarity can remain as long as I stay true to myself, not others. As more time passes within my spiritual ventures, I am discovering that the more anger, sorrow, and frustration I release through meditation, writing, and speaking, the less blockages I am carrying.

Pretty sweet, eh?
I dare you
to be different!

Moral of the story: heal yourself through releasing negativity and manifesting positive vibes from within.

♥ ♥ ♥

Upon the conclusion of our Florida Keys tour, Jude and I resolved that the next stop on our marvelous adventure was going to be crocodile alley in the Everglades National Park. Crocodile and alligators had always fascinated me, and I was excited to go check them out in their natural habitat. Cruising back north, five hours later, the view from the car window had changed drastically from palm trees and beefy lifeguards to muddy swamps and lush green forest.

As I drove past the sign that said "Welcome to the Everglades," Jude and I squealed with excitement, wondering how big the crocs got. I peered out the windows in hopes to catch a glimpse. Half an hour later, there was still no crocodile sighting to be had. Announcing that she had to pee, Jude turned off the highway at an Everglades tour company. Scrambling toward the front door in her girdle,(bathing suite) Jude was met by a tall man in jeans. "Place is all locked up for the night, ma'am," he said and left Jude standing in the parking lot. By this point I had jumped out of Cass to stretch my legs and shoulders. Five hours of straight driving wasn't exactly great on the skeletal system. As I bent down to stretch out my body, I noticed that I was standing right beside a small white fence. Beyond this small white fence was a pool of water stretching out into a swamp. Raising my eyebrows, I quickly put two and two together.

Everglade company + white fence + swampy background = potential crocodile sightings!

As Jude walked over to where I was standing, all of a sudden five bubbles bubbled their way to the surface. Thrilled at a possible crocodile viewing, I craned my neck to catch a better view. Just as the bubbles' ripples were vanishing, I saw it: two black eyes surfacing to check out its environment. Soon the two black eyes turned into the head of a crocodile as he fully emerged to survey his territory.

Standing at the edge of the fence, Jude and I peered out at the prehistoric creature. It was six feet away from us and our only protection was the white picket fence that suddenly looked very puny. Finding an adequate spot on some rocks, the croc slowly turned his head in our direction. Black beady eyes stared right at me as he sized me up. Looking at that crocodile was an experience I will never forget for the rest of my life. The cold penetrating glare from Mister Crocodile instantly reminded me of my rather humble placement within the food chain. He certainly didn't care about my registered retirement savings plan, life savings, or satellite radio.

Nope, all Mister Crocodile wanted to do was eat me, and he made it very clear. Suddenly feeling very vulnerable, I turned away from his penetrating stare. As Jude observed the scenario, she commented, "Can you imagine how much simpler life would be if everyone would remember that we are all essentially animals? Though we had supposedly evolved over the years, when it comes right down to it, it's either eat or to be eaten. At least the crocodile is honest. He isn't pretending to be something that he is not; he fully intends on eating you and is communicating this through his direct eye contact." Hearing Jude's comment, I nodded, still feeling very unnerved. After another two-minute staring contest with Mister Crocodile, I decided it was time to leave.

♥   ♥   ♥

Primal Animals and Katie's Theory

We are all part of the animal kingdom, but man has somehow forgotten that. "Katie's theory of survival" stayed with me as Cassidy drifted into the ancient swamplands of the Everglades. Let me share my insightfulness on Katie's Theory: years of running from situations had given me absolutely no backbone. Instead of digging my heels in, I would run and avoid my issues. Determination and dedication were not my reality, and I found it easier to run than face my inner demons straight on. During the Everglades adventures, I still had mistrust of Jude, which only added fuel to my doubt fire. Disbelieving her intuition, I was creating extra turmoil within.

Although the entire experience was rather unnerving, it also served to teach me how truthful nature was in comparison to man. Through intense eye contract, Mr. Ally, the ancient alligator, was being very honest with me: "I want to eat you, little girl. Yes, I do!"

Upon reflection I realize Mr. Ally had much more honesty than I did. For years I had been pretending to be someone I was not, hurting many in the process. Had I projected honesty with myself and others, I could have prevented several awful situations. Taking notes from my new predator, Ally, I learned that honesty is much simpler than deception; it may seem cold, but in reality, expressing your truth creates instant understanding.

SCORE BOARD

Primal Animals   1   Katie's Theory   0

Although I thought the vultures were intimidating, I also had much respect for their incredible instincts. What I learned vultures are the most resourceful creatures within the animal kingdom. After they consume their feast (Mr. Ally), vultures pee over their legs and feet to sanitize themselves. Vultures' cleaning process aids in the delicate balance within the natural everglade environment.

This experience served to show me how wasteful man is. I myself have thrown away countless meals, products, or material items because I didn't necessarily need them. Buying into my consumer-based attitude, I was contributing into the evil cycle that only added to the growing wastelands. So lesson from the vultures: waste not, want not!

SCORE BOARD

Primal Animals	2	Katie's Theory	0

Another creature that made itself quite pesky during our adventures was the ever-annoying mosquito. Although the mosquito definitely favored Jude's blood over mine, I still allowed them to get under my skin (metaphorically speaking)! Doing a bit of research, I discovered that mosquitoes are in fact the most dangerous animals on the planet.

Upon further research into the vampire insect, I discovered that only the females BITE!

Now isn't that interesting?

Again, I could see a comparison being drawn between me and the mosquito; as a female, I had learned to manipulate and "bite" my way out of countless situations, often leaving quite a lasting mark upon men. My ruthless behavior harmed many people, and in the past, I came across as very cold-blooded, just like the mosquitoes, feeling little remorse for my actions.

SCOLE BOARD

Primal Animals	3	Katie's Theory	0

♥   ♥   ♥

Offering to drive, Jude took the wheel as I observed the swamps from the safety of the van. As Cass cruised farther and farther into the prehistoric land, I became increasing aware of my minute existence within the grand scope of nature. Looking out onto the main highway, I saw we were surrounded by complete darkness. Just as my heartbeat had returned to normal, I heard a booming man's voice coming from the outside my window. Though I couldn't make out the words, I knew it was a spirit. Quickly rolling up the windows, I frantically looked over at Jude and hissed, "Did you hear that? It was definitely a man outside my window. Please tell me you heard that."

Slowly nodding, Jude answered, "Yes, Katie I did hear it. It was a spirit. It was a question. And now I feel he came to you because of your white light that beams out like a lighthouse. Remember Katie, you are from the fairy realm and were reincarnated as an earth angel. Katie, I just sent him to the white light. I feel he has been in this area for a while and didn't know he was in the spirit world."

Eyes as big as saucers, I continued driving into the dark, eerie night. After an hour of driving, my eyelids began growing heavy and I decided to park in the next closest town.

After searching high and low for a spot, we finally settled on the back parking lot of an old building. It was rather sketchy, but being exhausted at the time, I didn't care!

Taking off my clothes, (the new code word, nuddlywinks), I prepared for a restful sleep. Just as I was becoming engaged in a vivid dream about sailing, swirling lights outside of the vehicle shone down and woke me. The distinctive sound of police radios crackled in the background as I quickly searched for my clothing. As I frantically searched for something—anything—to put on my body, a sharp knocking on the window stopped me in my tracks. Abandoning my clothing search, I grabbed the comforter and guarded my winkers body. When I opened the sliding door, two policemen greeted me.

As I peeked out into the parking lot. "Evening, ma'am. We were just driving by and I happened to notice your van parked here in the abandoned lot. When we saw your windows down, we thought it looked suspicious, so we wanted to come check things out."

Mortified by the entire experience, I managed to squeak out, "Oh well, we really appreciate the concern. We were just really tired from a long day of driving and thought we would grab a few winks before heading out." Giving them my best "I'm innocent" smile, I silently hoped they would retreat. No such luck. "Yeah, see, in the State of Florida, you aren't allowed to park within the city limits. You are going to have to keep moving. I'm afraid we need to see your driver's licenses, from the both of you."

After rummaging around Jude and I both handed over IDs. As the police were scanning our photos, I hissed at this so embarrassing moment. "I know, kiddo, I know, but they are just doing their jobs." Stifling a yawn, I nodded, wanting the whole fiasco to be over. Ten minutes later the policemen returned and handed us our IDs. "All right you ladies have a safe trip back to Canada. Just remember no parking in city limits."

Embarrassed at the police encounter, I started Cassidy and headed out into the dark night, searching for a rest area. At exactly 5:46 a.m. we arrived at the roadside rest area and crashed out.

♥   ♥   ♥

Disneyworld Ticket Fiasco

Disney World was the priority the following morning, as Jude and I made our way toward Orlando. Visions of pirates and Splash Mountain emerged in my mind as we pulled into Kissimmee, the neighboring city to Disney World. My inner child cheered as we neared the universe playground.

As we traveled to the almighty, famous Disney World, I was determined that we would get to experience the magic for the day. I was so determined to go to Disney World I was willing to pull out manipulation and deceit all in the name of saving money.

Roaming around the streets of Kissimmee, Florida, I began searching for discount tickets. Spotting a man with sunglasses, I approached him with my best innocent persona. He introduced himself and he said he would have some discounted tickets for me the following morning. Not truly using my intuition, I trusted him and returned the next day. Handing the tickets over, he told me that he trusted me and that I could pay him once I returned the tickets that evening.

Over breakfast Jude had warned me, "I don't know, Katie. These could very well be illegal, stolen tickets that could get us in a lot of trouble."

Sloughing off her concern, I said, "Nah, don't worry, its fine." My desire to save a few bucks had completely overruled my common sense and conscience.

Luckily for us the tickets worked; no problems at this point. The problem came later, when I tried to return the tickets to him. After calling him three times, he finally picked up, completely hammered. As I tried explaining to him where we were, he began getting increasingly angry and rude. Hanging up the telephone, I thought to myself, *you get what you paid for.* The universe was laughing at me as I marched back to the van.

Irritated, I told Jude what was happening, to which she responded, "Well, let's think about what happened. You trusted a man on the street, not great idea to begin with. All you could see was saving money. That's okay, that was the lure for you. He trusts you to give them back. The game of deception is one to one at this point. But you forget that the universe is watching, so right now we can't seem to find this man, so I feel he loses the tickets and we both live with the fact that we got free tickets."

"I gave him my promise to return them!" I hissed at Jude.

"Well, Katie, let me say this. Give the money and tickets to charity." Lesson learned by all.

Upon reflection I realize I can also see the similarity had with this fellow. Although I wasn't swindling Mickey Mouse tickets, I was behaving with malicious intentions.

♥   ♥   ♥

The Disney World morning started out with our usual IHOP pancake breakfast. Still feeling guilty about my ticket fiasco, I attempted to make small talk with Jude. Having recently checked my e-mail, I had news to report about a mutual girl friend, Sandy.

Sandy had mentioned that she was starting her own wellness company called "Stay Grounded". Jude shook her head and said, "It sure makes me nervous to hear about Sandy starting her own business. Now don't get me wrong, but any healing of any sort requires a complete cleansing of negative energies within. I don't feel as though Sandy has fully healed her past."

"Well, I thought it sounded cool that Sandy had created her own business. I thought maybe we could join forces with her, seeing as how we know about spirituality."

Glancing across the table, Jude replied, "Katie, you are nowhere near ready to begin spirituality work; you have to get outside of your box or bubble. You speak about making a difference. I know you intentions are all good. Please challenge yourself with making a plan of action. Picking up garbage is great. It helps with the environment issue, but the scale you talk about is going further." I nodded my head.

Jude continued, "I was watching this show last night. It spoke about how five kids were shot in Brooklyn yesterday. Five kids. These are the areas that you should be focusing on. You haven't even tried volunteering yet, so how can you call yourself a spiritual being." Sitting back after being blasted by truthful words, I stopped eating my breakfast. The whole world seemed to stand still as Jude's words sunk in.

"Look, Katie, I can see you volunteering at an inner city location showing by example with real kindness, hope, and as a positive role model. Look inside yourself, not outside, to find the things you think you need. Put action in your words. For once that is my challenge to you!"

As Jude finished speaking, I was speechless. Strong emotion washed over me as I felt teardrops come. Trying to hide them, I quickly raised my hand to my face. Jude stopped me. "Don't stop them, baby girl. Just let them flow. Who cares if anyone can see." Hearing her words, I let down my guard and allowed myself to cry; big alligator tears fell down as I envisioned myself giving love to children who really needed it. Jude had just touched on a very tender subject close to my heart, my love for children.

The restaurant scene with Jude is a perfect example of how she does her teachings once she establishes your depth. She then pushes and challenges to your appropriate breaking point. Jude's intention was never to break anyone; it was simply to push them to be the greatest person they could be. With me, Jude knew exactly when to push and when to ease up and did so throughout our journeys. After I wiped the teardrops from my face, I gave Jude a big hug and whispered "thank you" in her ear. Trying to explain the relationship I have with Jude is like trying to define the color yellow; it's virtually impossible. The depth at which she knew me was deeper than I knew even existed. She exposed and demonstrated characteristics of my soul I had forgotten for many years. Feeling drained yet optimistic, Jude and I paid the bill, then left the restaurant.

♥　　　　♥　　　　♥

Disneyworld Adventure

Finally arriving within the Magic Kingdom, we pulled out our trusty map and decided to check out Adventure Land first. Adventure Land was home to both Pirates of the Caribbean and Jungle Cruise, two of the greatest rides ever. Big green tropical bushes surrounded us as we found ourselves at the entrance to Pirates of the Caribbean. Looking at each other, we shrugged and decided to start the day off with sailing around in a pirate ship.

During our wait we got to know the little girl behind us. She was very nervous about Captain Hook and his surprise attacks. We both were fond of little ones. Jude and I tried to put her mind at ease. We assured her that Captain Hook was on vacation in the Bahamas and that the other pirates were actually really nice people. I shared with her that I was a pirate, and upon hearing this, she wanted to be one too. After giving her the nickname Captain Twinkle, I carried her on my back as the line wound into a dark cellar.

As I walked with Captain Twinkle on my back, I realized how little I knew about children. Though I adored them, I was also unsure of how to act around them.

Upon reflection I realize my mother didn't know how to interact with children. Although she had me, I don't recall being touched by her as a child; hence as I grew older, I didn't learn how to interact with children or touch another female. I remember watching girls my age playing with each other's hair and giving loving touches, sharing feelings. As an adult I still maintained my standoffish persona but didn't like it. I remember the first time Jude touched my hair. I almost jumped out of my skin. Since then she has been trying to touch me to let me grow accustomed to it.

Once the pirate ride was over (and Captain Twinkle survived), Jude and I headed over to Splash Mountain singing along to "Zipadeedodah." We playfully danced in our tugboat. As we crashed down into the Briar Patch, cool, refreshing water splashed us and cooled us down.

The rest of the day was spent frolicking around the many different magical lands and playing with kids. As the sun dipped down, fireworks began exploding from behind the magic kingdom. Jude played with nearby children as I peered up at the fantastic castle. Mickey and Minnie were singing about dreams coming true, and as I reflected upon my latest years, I agreed with them. Dreams really did come true when the dreamers believe. As I gazed at the fireworks in wonderment, I thought about the companion with spirituality.

"If you believe, you will achieve." Jude's famous words rang true as I continued to ponder the statement. Since I discovered spirituality, magical events had been happening all the time. Every day I had been writing a universal wish list, and every day the universe would provide me with what I had asked for. I wondered if Mr. Walt Disney hadn't been a bit of an intuitive spirit HIMSELF.

As the mice continued their song about dreams, I felt warmth come over me. As I checked in with my vibes, I realized that the warmth was coming from my heart.

"Your dreams are coming true, little one; you just have to believe everything is taken care of. Just do your part and believe." Promising that I did, I watched in childlike wonderment at the enchantment of Walt Disney.

At around 8:30 p.m. Jude and I decided to go on one last ride before leaving. Space Mountain was chosen as our final hoorah and we made our way through the thinning crowd to its dome, walking across lime green Astroturf. I smiled at a man behind an information booth.

"Nice crystal," he said as we walked past him. Stopping in the middle of the Astroturf, Jude and I both turned around and looked at him. Like any other religion, spirituality had its symbols and signs, which served to identify believers. My quartz crystal had been with me since November, and I rarely took it off. Crystals were one of the tools intuitives used to guard against evil spirits.

The man towered over us at six foot five and looked to be about in his late fifties, his nametag read "John Allen." He seemed grounded as we approached his booth. Jude and I introduced ourselves. After the formal introductions were over, Jude and John Allen began discussing different concerns and opinions regarding spirituality. It was very interesting to witness Jude interacting with older psychics. Although she enjoyed being a teacher, it was always refreshing for her to meet an intuitive close to her age group. Jude enquired, "Why do most psychics seemed to keep to themselves, segregated from other psychics, not wanting to help each other out? I have found that unless I am paying them, they are usually unwilling to offer assistance or guidance."

Shaking his head, John Allen did not have a response. Partway through their conversation, John Allen enquired if we were going to Cassadega. Unsure of what or where it was, we shook our heads. John Allen explained "Cassadega is a spiritual community that is about two hours from here. It is out in the countryside and has beautiful energy about it. There is an old hotel and a bookstore that offers courses and workshops on different aspects of spirit realms."

Looking at one another, Jude and I instantly agreed that would be our next stop. As Jude touched John Allen goodbye, his eyes welled with tears, having felt the warmth she had. It was such a beautiful sight to see a man shed tears, completely proud of his emotions. Armed with universal understanding of projection and manifestation, John Allen chose to live a humble life spreading warmth and passion to all little ones who came within his vicinity. Again, he was a marvelous example of an intuitive spirit doing his mission on earth: spreading love.

Continuing on our path, we soon reached the magnificent Space Mountain. As we waited in line, I asked Jude about fairies and their characteristics. Smiling Jude, looked at me. "Come now, being from the fairy realm yourself, you know what the characteristics are."

"I know, but it would be cool to meet someone else from the fairy realm too just so I could try to identify them." As soon as the words escaped my lips, I heard a loud giggle coming from my left.

As I turned around to investigate, I saw an eleven-year-old-girl in a pink dress. Grinning from ear to ear, she pushed back her long blonde hair and said confidently, "Hi, my name is Kali, and I love this ride. Have you been on it before?"

As I answered, "Yup." I knew I had just gotten my wish to meet another fairy. The line moved slightly while Kali and I began talking. "I bet you're more scared than I am to go on this ride," she challenged me while swinging around a pole. Biting my tongue, I thought to myself, *Yup, this is definitely a fairy!* Fairies are known for their mischievous, charming demeanors. They're tiny and often have sparkly eyes and a small bone structure.

As I watched this little girl swinging around the pole, my guidance confirmed that indeed I had met a fellow fairy creature. Kali and I continued on playing back and forth, teasing one another about everything and anything. "I bet I'm more popular," I stated, munching on pink bubblegum.

"No way. I am," she shot back, enjoying behaving like an eleven-year-old.

Finally, after a thirty-minute wait, we arrived at the front of the line. "Let's go beside each other, okay?" Kali asked as we stepped into our space shuttle.

"No problem," I answered while mentally preparing myself for the roller coaster.

As the ride zoomed throughout the incredible bends and twists of the universal solar system, I could hear Kali giggling behind me. "I love this ride!" she screamed as we whizzed past one million light years of galaxies. Several light years later, we came to a screeching stop, ending our ride. "I love this ride," Kali exclaimed one last time before we left. Before saying goodbye to her, I told her to believe in her wishes because they would all come true. Feeling satisfied that I had instilled a little knowledge into her realm, I grabbed Jude's arm and headed for the exit. Yet another affirmation from the universe had demonstrated its magical way of creating serendipitous events.

♥   ♥   ♥

Wishes

Oh my favorite topic in the whole wide world! Boy did I ever discover the power of wishing throughout my journeys. As a little girl, I recall finding the brightest stars out in the night sky, closing my eyes, and wishing, wishing, wishing!

At some point along my path, I stopped this magical ritual because of societal norms, expectations, and ego. All that changed this past year when I rediscovered spirituality and the power of thoughts and intentions. In the fall I began writing down my wishes and dreams and watching in complete awe as they manifested themselves before my very eyes. Honestly, they truly do come to life, if you believe. I can't stress this enough: believing is the most important magical ingredient that needs to be added into your wishes. I had countless examples of this as I reconnected with my inner child. Just to give out an example, I will tell you about New York state. Man, did I ever get us in trouble that morning through my wishing practices.

Picture this if you will.

There was boiling heat and we were driving south toward Florida. I casually mentioned to Jude how much I wanted to drive through New York City. Looking at me as though I had grown three heads, Jude quickly responded, "Ah, Katie I'm not driving through. New York is such a great idea. I think it would be best to drive around and visit New York by foot in the future." Hesitantly I agreed. I agreed, but unknown to Jude, I had already secretly wished to drive through NYC. Silly rabbit, careful what you wish for.

Five hours later, guess where were? Not Paris, not Rome; no we were in NYC. Unknown to me, I had managed to maneuver us straight into the heart of downtown traffic during the lunch hour!

As we drove 10 kilometers per hour through the gridlock, Jude looked over at me. "You had to wish about driving through NYC, didn't you?" Shaking her head, she began searching for the appropriate exit signs.

So the moral of the story is be careful what you wish for, because it will come true! Cross my heart. I promise it will.

♥   ♥   ♥

Cassadega

After our epic adventures in Disney World, Jude and I made an executive decision to travel to Cassadega. Trusting John Allen's advice, we allowed our spirits to lead the way.

Cassadega was a tiny little town nestled away from the main highway; it was lush with green trees and beautiful tropical flowers. As we pulled into the bookstore parking lot, we noticed two men sitting outside on a bench. As Jude and I walked toward the entrance, the older man smiled and greeted us.

"Hi there, you folks visiting from somewhere?"

Nodding, Jude answered, "Yes, sir, we are visiting from Canada."

Impressed with this particular piece of knowledge, he raised his eyebrows and smiled. "Well, welcome to Cassadega. It's not a big place, but people here are real friendly."

Reaching for a local paper, he added, "We have a really nice church service on Sundays, complete with healings and messages. I'm Rufus, by the way, and this here is Stan." He pointed to the man sitting beside him. Introducing ourselves, we sat down and chatted with our newfound friends.

As Rufus chattered on about Cassadega and its history, I began tuning into the energy. Jude had told me about positive energy, fueled by individuals and the spirit world. I could feel warm surges of positive energy filter into my body, swirling, and atoms bounced freely through my body. I truly felt a part of this earth, being an entity that was there to witness this amazing positive energy. It was the sort of energy I will never forget, I knew to the deepest part of me that it was something unseen but felt.

"I bet this place has lots of spooks," Jude whispered as we climbed up the front stairs.

The front lobby looked very old, from the antique furniture to the creaky baseboards beneath our feet. To the left was a pink dining room; to the right the hotel reception area. Hearing our tummies grumbling, Jude and I decided to head for a mid-afternoon snack.

An older lady with soft brown eyes and a cowgirl hat approached our table. "Howdy, there, girls. What can I get for you?" I ordered our afternoon coffees, then enquired about a sweet treat that they offered. Eyes gleaming, the lady smiled and said, "I think I might have just the trick for you two. Our chef has made himself quite famous in these parts due to his coconut crème pie. It is out of this world! What do you say, girls, want to try it out?"

"Yes," Jude exclaimed without even a second thought. Laughing, the cowgirl turned and retreated into the kitchen.

A few minutes later, she returned with two fresh cups of coffee and one colossal piece of coconut crème pie. My mouth instantly began salivating as I stared at the work of art towering at about seven inches high. The pie looked absolutely delectable. Clutching my fork, I cut off a morsel and placed it my mouth. Instant joy spread around my taste buds as I savored the flavor of the pie. Armed with the secret ingredient of cream cheese, this pie soon became my favorite food in the whole world. It even beat our chicken wings!

While Jude and I savored this epic dessert, she mentioned a nearby posting she had seen. "Katie, I just noticed that there is a woman here who does past life regressions. I think that may help you with some of the fears you may have. Past life regressions are a great way to uncover a lot of fears we often bring back from previous lifetimes."

Clearing my throat, I responded "So, yeah, I noticed that posting too, but I don't know; I'm kind of scared about what she might uncover. What if there is stuff I don't want to know about?"

Jude took another bite of the pie and replied, "Sounds like you are letting fears rule you. Trust me, this is something I think would release a lot of blockages for you."

My initial thought was the cost. I know, I know, as a student of spirituality I shouldn't concern myself with money, especially not when it comes to enlightening myself with information about myself.

After ten minutes of battling with my cheap, frugal self, my higher self won out. "Okay, Judepants! I'm going to do it. I am going to go make an appointment right now." After taking one last bite of the pie, I trekked over to the front desk.

A plump, friendly-looking lady greeted me with a genuine smile. "Can I help you?" she asked.

"Yeah," Nervous about following through, I answered, "Yes, I wanted to have a past life regression done. Can I make an appointment through you?" Nodding, she reached for her appointment book marked *readings*. "I don't have any spots available for today, but I do have one at eleven a.m. tomorrow morning. Could that work for you?"

Nodding, I told her "No problem" and began filling out the paperwork. Once all the necessary information had been gathered, she handed me an appointment card and bid me good afternoon.

Proud of myself, I headed back to the pink dining room to share the news with Jude. Clapping her hands together, she said, "Oh, Katie, this is going to be awesome for you!" My curiosity started kicking in as I wondered what we would uncover.

Leaving the dining room, we decided to head for the nearest body of cool water. The temperature was 33 degrees Celsius, with absolutely no breeze to chill things down. Walking across the streets, Jude noticed that Stan was still sitting on the bench outside the bookstore.

As she called out a greeting, Stan waved and beckoned us over. As I approached the bench, I noticed that Stan had vibrant yet sad blue eyes and a unique crooked nose.

"Hi, girls, how is Cassadega treating you so far? Staying out of trouble?"

I replied, 'Well, the delicious coconut crème pie did get the best of us! I hope you have checked it out. It's incredible."

Stan shook his head. "Actually, I'm a chef myself and plan on opening a café right here in the bookstore. So, I don't really go over to the dining room very often at all. In fact, I think most of the people over there are weird." Silently I wondered who Stan would be friends with if he was boycotting the only hotel in town. As though he was reading my mind, Stan looked over and said, "Yup, I tend to stick to myself around these parts. I have been classified as the black sheep around here. Due to the fact that I have many lady friends, my nickname has become The Casanova of Cassadega." He smiled shyly after revealing his title. Jude and I continued chatting.

Jude and I leaned forward toward Stan and Jude said, "You know, Stan, there is something, terribly familiar about you. I get the feeling you are meant to be telling me something."

Peeping at her with his bright blue eyes, Stan shrugged his shoulders. "Not that I was aware of. Maybe it will come to me later."

Starting to feel overheated, I recalled our original plan to find some water. "Hey, Stan, can you tell us where the closest ocean is from here?"

Nodding, Stan gave us directions to Daytona Beach, which was located forty miles away on the east coast. Before we left, Jude enquired one more time, "Now are you sure there is nothing you feel you have to tell me."

Stan smiled sweetly and said "Ask the question."

Jude grimaced and responded, "But I don't have a question right now!"

"Well then, I don't know what to say to you. See you later, girls, and have a nice swim."

♥   ♥   ♥

Daytona Beach Walks

By the time we reached Daytona Beach, we were really ready for a dip. "Could it be any hotter?" Jude challenged the universe as we parked Cassidy. Adjusting her girdle, she continued, "Oh I am sticking to the seat, GROSS." Snickering to my friend, I jumped out of Cassidy and started walking toward the ocean. On the beach was the typical Florida scene: cars parked on the sand, stereos blaring, beach bunnies scantily clad on white towels, and Baywatch lifeguards flexing their muscles atop their towers.

Running toward the ocean, I instantly felt my spirit, enlighten and soaring; the undeniable healing qualities of the ocean were magical. Drifting with the current, I looked up and watched pelicans soaring overhead, searching for their supper, serenity and completeness encompassed around me as worries about school, men, and the future seemed to wash off my body with every new wave.

After our dip, Jude and I decided to go for a walk down the shoreline. It stretched out before us spotted with colorful umbrella's and hotdog stands as far as the eye could see.

Jude and I walked for miles as we chatted about spirituality. "Don't ever forget these moments, Katie. All these awakenings and clarity you have been experiencing have been wonderful. I want you to remember from this day forward, you are in control of you. Nobody else can dictate to you what to do with your life. You do what you want to do. The reason I push you so hard is because I know you can handle it. You have great things ahead of you, but you have to remember to strive for excellence. Given the nature of your personality, you are always going to be searching and questing after universal truths. It's who you are."

Looking at Jude with a shocked expression, I said, "Am I ever going to settle down, ever going to stop moving around?"

My expression must have made me look horrified, because Jude started laughing. "Now, Katie, don't look so dismayed. At some point down the road I'm sure you will stop. But given your thirst for life, you will always be looking for the next challenge, and by the way, you don't have to actually physically move in order to gain further spiritual knowledge. Some people remain in one place and still manage to challenge themselves every day." With each step we took, Jude provided more and more wisdom about life and spirituality.

Ah, the magic that occurs within the simplest gestures; I do believe that is what life is about! What do you say?

Upon reflection I realize these moments with Jude had been exactly what I wanted my entire life. Her kind gestures and simple honesty provided me with the grounding I needed in order to flourish. Though my parents loved me, Jude understood me and accepted me exactly the way I was. She gave me her time, which was the most precious gift I had been missing. Our marathon gab sessions were actually providing me with a concrete foundation of who I was and what I stood for.

♥   ♥   ♥

We arrived back in the spiritual community just in time for dusk. Twilight illuminated the sky as frogs croaked their greeting to the silvery stars. The energy felt fantastic and that night I had the most vivid dreams about ghosts and baseball teams.

At promptly 11:00 a.m. the next day, Jude and I sat in the lobby, waiting for my past life instructor to appear. Jitterbugs flew through my tummy as I nervously twitched my legs.

Jude gave me a little pep talk. "Just remember to relax and enjoy yourself. This is going to be such a great experience for you, Katie." Just then a woman with pure white hair came floating down the stairs. Her hair pulled into a old-fashioned bun, she looked very sweet and soft. Peering down at us, she turned her gaze toward me and said, "You must be Katie. Please follow me." Anxiously I got up and began following her up the old staircase. Jude called out one last time, "Katie, I will be waiting right here for you when you are done, okay. Have fun!" And with that I soon found myself in a small room overlooking a courtyard. The white-haired lady introduced herself as Patty and commenced the session by explaining the procedure.

Taking a seat in the large overstuffed pink chair, I assumed the position, placing my palms downward onto my legs. Patty began by having me visualize a garden full of rainbow-colored fruit and described the taste and smell. Once we had made our way through all the colors of the rainbow, Patty began putting me into a trance. As I imagined myself swirling back in time, I suddenly found myself soaring over London. As the trance continued, I identified myself as a male named Sebastian. He was dressed in a tan robe and sandals. Throughout my regression, I uncovered many mysteries that had lain dormant in my subconscious mind.

After one hour of being hypnotized, I was brought back to consciousness by Patty. Slowly opening my eyes, I peered around her office and felt very at peace. Patty smiled and said, "That was great work, Katie. Due to your openness, we were capable of going very deep into your soul." After quietly thanking her, I walked downstairs feeling like I was floating on a cloud. As I reached the main floor, I saw Jude sitting patiently, coffee cup in hand. Once she saw me appear, she nodded. It was such a heartwarming moment for me. Throughout all my self-searching, transformations, meltdowns, and hissy fits, Jude had stayed by my side, patiently riding out the stormy weather.

As we started to eat yet another piece of the glorious coconut crème pie, I explained to Jude everything I remembered. "I actually saw fairies, too, drifting throughout the entire progression, and then I saw a unicorn, dragons …" My excitement went on for hours as I relived my past life experience with my teacher and dear friend Jude.

Backtracking, we walked over to check in with Mr. Stanley. "Hey, girls, how was your swim yesterday?"

Jude answered, "Lovely, thank you. We were actually just heading back in that direction."

Stan looked sad. "Does that mean that you are leaving for good? You're not going to stay for awhile? You're not going to stay for the service tomorrow?" Sensing that Stan and Jude needed to chat, I excused myself and walked over to the washrooms.

When I returned a few minutes later, Jude and Stan were still chatting. As I approached them, Jude looked over and said, "Stan has opened up his home to us, offering full use of his shower. What do you think? Do you want to stay another day here?"

Floored at the prospect of a shower, I jumped at the offer. "Absolutely. Thanks, Stan, that's a really kind offer."

Stan responded, "Hey, I know what it's like to live in a van, trust me, I have been there. Plus, I really enjoy your company."

Before we headed out to Cassidy, Jude asked one more time, "Are you sure there is nothing you wanted to tell me, Stan?" Obviously this issue was still bothering her.

Smiling smugly, he responded, "Ask the question." Frustrated, she spun around and head toward Cassidy.

Around suppertime we pulled Cassidy up to Stan's house and unpacked the bare necessities. As I gleefully showered with hot water, Stan and Jude chatted in the kitchen. Once I emerged, Jude took her turn at the glorious hot shower game and I cleaned up around the kitchen.

Fifteen minutes later Stan returned home after a quick mission to the pizza parlor. Digging into the delicious supper, I slowly began listening to Stan's story. As it turns out, he had been a very unfortunate victim of Hurricane Katrina. It had completely destroyed his home, leaving him with nothing. After moving to Cassadega, Stan slowly began rebuilding his life within the spiritual community. Just as life seemed to be looking up, Stan's house was struck by lightening. As Stan told his tale, I wondered what he had done to the universe to be the recipient of such unfortunate events. While he recounted his life story, I couldn't help but notice there seemed to be an undeniable sadness about him. Never having married, he had spent his entire life being taken advantage of by manipulative women. I felt a pang of guilt as I wondered if I would leave that bitter taste in the mouth of Stephen.

Eventually moving off the topic of women, Stan disclosed that he was a wanderer who was never fully satisfied with where he resided. Europe seemed to be the only place where he had found memories of feeling complete. As I listened to Stan express his viewpoints and attitudes, I began seeing an increasing amount of similarities between the two of us.

Allow me to demonstrate:

Stan.	Katie.
Sadness from years of aimless wandering	Ditto
Big heart that people had taken advantage of	Ditto
Desire to fit in and be a part of something	Ditto
Traveler	Ditto

Regardless of the fact that Stan was a fifty-two-year-old man, we had many resemblances.

About halfway through his tale about playing his guitar for supper in Greece, Stan announced that he wanted to record Jude's and my tales of how we managed to come in contact with the town of Cassadega.

As he positioned the video camera toward us, I felt a surge of excitement; I loved being on camera and the center of attention. After announcing "Ready and action," Stan sat back and watched the display of the indescribable energy between Jude and myself. Springing into action, I started recounting how we met, adding brief character descriptions to provide more flavor to the tale. As our moods got sillier and sillier, Jude and I burst into laughter that we couldn't contain. Throughout tears of laughter, I began explaining about Jude's girdle and our daily morning rituals. After describing what *nuddlywinks* was, I couldn't carry on.

Looking across the room, I saw that Stan had abandoned his duties as cameraman and instead had opted for rolling around on the ground, holding his belly as he roared with laughter. That moment with Stan and Jude is one that still brings a smile to my lips. Watching Stan roll around the floor, I realized how magical it was to uplift spirits. Though Jude and I only stayed with Stan that one night, we allowed him to play and be a kid again: such a beautiful thing to witness. Shortly after our tummy workout, I excused myself to go to bed.

The universe wanted to show you this man to demonstrate the similarities in your lives, no matter what age you are. You both have lots of potential but can't seem to release toxic energies. Better get your poop in a group, KIDDO. The Universe is talking to you!

Upon reflecting on Stan, I realize the lesson learned is you should release old hurts and disappointments before they permanently affix themselves.

♥   ♥   ♥

catherine

Catherine, Catherine, Catherine. She is quite the interesting woman to say the least. Our last morning in Cassadega, I decided to attend an information session about the spiritual church and their ten main principles. As I sat in the empty room, I noticed a woman enter from behind. Knowing that she wasn't a local, I introduced myself. She introduced herself as Catherine and went on to explain that she was a millionaire life coach and writer.

As my eyebrows shot up, I felt as though I had hit the jackpot: a life coach and writer. What were the odds? As I began pumping her for information, something simply wasn't clicking properly with her words.

Ignoring my vibes, I introduced Jude to Catherine later that morning to see what her opinions were. As the day charged forward, Catherine offered to give Jude and me a crash course in writing techniques. Intrigued, we took her up on the offer and met her in the hotel lobby for a brief session.

As Catherine began explaining how to write creatively, I noticed how formatted her system was. This seemed contradictory to the whole creative writing process, but Jude and I pressed forward anyway. Midway through our session, Catherine began speaking about her past and displaying feelings of anger. Creative writing had been placed to the side and her true feelings began flowing out. For the next forty-five minutes of listening to her issues and problems, Jude and I simultaneously resolved to exit the situation.

Looking back, there are many lessons I learned from Catherine. Her rigid creative routine mirrored my rigid routine of pretty much everything. Over the years I had created standardized routines in my life, similar to that an eighty-year-old woman. Cool, eh? Seeing Catherine's intellectual approach to creative writing also showed me my own tendency to use my head instead of heart when in the creative process, which, by the way, never works out! In order to be creative, I have discovered it has to come straight from the heart, never the brain, especially when expressing your love or feelings. For me the brain makes me go into perfectionism!

Okay, back to my similarities with Miss C. During our visit, she spoke of being a life coach, yet she displayed the qualities of a very unhealthy person. I did the same thing. Due to my denial, I was unable to comprehend that I had past issues I needed to resolve in order to coach others on their lives.

Catherine served as a great indicator of what can happen if you decide to live in your head instead of going with your heart: suppressed emotions, manipulation, and unhealthy lifestyles. NO THANKS! I'll take heartfelt!

♥   ♥   ♥

The following few days, as we cruised back north to Montreal, were a blur to me. My enlightened spirit began darkening as the great north loamed. Deep down I knew I wasn't going to attend McGill. But I still struggled with letting go of my control of delusional thinking. Why did I want to go in the first place? "In order to reach your dreams, you have to shut your door on your past, Katie, being truthful to yourself first" repeated in my mind.

Driving through Georgia, we again approached dark rain clouds that threatened thunderstorms ahead. I recalled the last storm experience in Florida, remembering Jude's advice to check in with my vibes. I did just that. Inner voices responded, "Don't be scared. Everything is fine. You are safe." Believing in the advice, I took a deep breath and drove straight into the eye of the storm. Lightning bolts exploded beside the car, but I remained calm, relying on the divine message I had heard. Trees swayed as the wind blew at gale forces, threatening to uproot them from their earthy home. Still I remained collected and drove on. As the rain slowly dissipated, the gray clouds magically rolled away, making the storm less threatening. As we drove through the wet countryside, I felt proud of myself for having conquered my fears of electricity striking the van—at least from this storm.

As mentioned earlier, the closer we got to Montreal the darker my mood turned. The looming reality created inner turmoil as I realized that once again I would be leaving another situation. My feelings of failure pulled on my spirit, manifesting them into a rotten mood. Again, instead of talking about my feelings of failure to Jude, I remained silent and hid behind many masks.

The night before we reached Ontario, we approached an old country road that seemed deserted. Pulling Cassidy into a vacant patch of land, I looked up and saw magical sight: green sparkles of light that surrounded us as Jude and I peered out the window. The green strikes of light floated all around the car. "I think they're fireflies," I exclaimed excitedly, recognized the enchanting insects. After we turned out the lights and locked up Miss Cassidy, I laid awake mesmerized by the spectacular creatures. It's amazing how such a little discovery has the ability to completely uplift spirits. Nature is so beautiful!

♥   ♥   ♥

The following morning we had reached the Canadian border. Driving through with confidence, I silently gave myself a pat on my back for not getting shaky around the border guard. Heading east on the Highway 1, I decided to take an alternate route toward Montreal. Bypassing the chaotic clutter known as Toronto, we steered our way down toward Kingston, the oldest town in Canada.

Just before we drove past Kingston, Jude suggested pulling in to grab some supper and exploring. Agreeing, I turned Cassidy onto an exit ramp into town. As we drove in, I noticed all sorts of old churches and heritage homes. Streets were lined with tall trees, and perfect flowerboxes framed the outside of many character houses. Finding a spot in the downtown quarter, I parked Cassidy by a cobblestone church. Jude looked around. I could definitely feel a chill and some form of presence. I said, "Well, I can feel something, but what I'm not exactly sure."

Jude nodded, "That is usually a sure sign of ghosts. This should be interesting."

Glancing across the street, we noticed a lively looking pub with an outdoor patio. "Shall we?" I said as I heard my tummy growling, advising me that it was famished. "Absolutely," Jude answered, and together we made our way across the street.

At the pub we met a glorious girl by the name of Lindsey; she was our waitress and had a fabulously outspoken personality. After determining that she had beautiful red shoes and nicknaming her Unicorn, we ordered some food and took in our surroundings. As I sat in Kingston, Ontario, I could hardly believe that just three days prior I had been in the sunshine state of Florida; our three-week trip had been such a whirlwind of emotions and diverse sceneries that I had barely time had time to process it.

Watching our new friend Unicorn flutter from table to table, I felt a twinge of jealousy. Since having embarked on my journey, I had gone to the very depths of my soul and unraveled many mysteries I had once pondered. That said, there were truths and discoveries I now knew that I couldn't take back; a certain sadness about myself and regrets about decisions I had made. Being a deep person, I had been profoundly impacted by the scenarios Jude and I had witnessed on our journey.

Awareness is a double-edged sword; on one side it was glorious to be enlightened of my own self-destructive patterns and behavior. Once being made aware, I had the option of resorting back to old unhealthy scenarios or creating new functional ones. On the other hand, the awareness of my reality saddened me for I had been living in such a delusional mindset my entire life, making bad decisions based on my unhealthy self esteem, I felt regret that I had manifested countless situations that could have been avoided had I communicated my true feelings and sentiments. As I said, enlightenment is an outstanding process, but I was still learning to forgive myself for my mistakes. Having said that, I watched Unicorn float from table to table, completely contented in her own world.

Since meeting Jude, my rose-colored glasses had been removed and I was seeing the world as it truly is, a mess. The knowledge of this is devastating, though as I reflect, I realize I knew all along that things weren't right in the world. There were many injustices, inequality, and imbalances. My initial dream of saving the world was rapidly growing smaller as I was learning the true reality of our earth.

Jude often says "Animals are perfect because they are born without words to dictate or bully others. Animals don't have choices, just instincts; man does what he chooses without thinking of the consequences."

So, anyway, back to Unicorn. Halfway through our fish and chips, Unicorn's father came in to say hello. As I observed their interaction, I noticed how openly they communicated. He allowed her to speak honestly and vice versa. As a child I was often silenced for my opinioned voice, and hence, as I grew into an adult, my feelings were accustomed to being suppressed.

Due to my fear of communicating my true feelings, I had allowed other people to walk all over me, and I found myself in situations I wasn't comfortable in. The skill of communication has only recently been introduced to me, and already I have noticed incredible differences in my ability to connect with other women. By speaking my truth about insecurities, mistakes, and fears, I am finding that other women share similar sentiments. What an incredible discovery it was that I wasn't the only female on the planet to have made mistakes I wasn't proud of. Communication truly is a wondrous skill that can be learned at any point, and it has most definitely positively transformed my relationships.

After our delicious meal, we said good night to Miss Unicorn and decided to stroll around town. About two blocks into our walk, we came across the Old Kingston Ghost Tour, which boasted spooky walks into and around the haunted areas of the town. Glancing over at each other, Jude and I both raised our eyebrows and approached the booth. Upon inspecting it we were challenged with the decision of "Haunted Fort St. Henry or downtown graves." Deciding upon the haunted Fort we bought our tickets. The tour was due to leave at 9:00 p.m., leaving us with two hours to continue our exploration of Kingston.

Feeling deprived of e-mail messages, I suggested to Jude that we search out the public library to see if we had any messages from loved ones. Casually we strolled several blocks till we reached the old historical library. Carefully walking up the broken cement stairs, Jude and I entered.

As I signed into Facebook, an online photo album of friends and family, I noticed I had a message from Autumn. Eager to read what it said, I clicked on my inbox. After I read the first two sentences, my heart sank. Her message was full of anger and guilt toward me, throughout her letter, she blamed me for not being available to her during her latest disaster.

Accusatory words stung me while I continued on reading her angry letter. Autumn ended her message by telling me she was very disappointed after all the care and support she had provided me with during my difficult times. Sitting in disbelief, I reread Autumn's message. Was this really my best friend? How dare she blame me for her misfortunes?! Hurt washed over me as I slowly began seeing Autumn as she truly was: a girl friend I had allowed to walk all over me for years.

Flashbacks of our childhood came rushing forward as I sat in the Kingston Library wondering what happened to our magical friendship. When I checked in with my vibes, they informed me of several truths: "Katie, Autumn has been this way for many years. You simply never truly communicated your feelings toward her. For years she has controlled your relationship and made you feel bad about yourself. Now that you are finding your own voice and empowering yourself, she can't stand it. Her words of anger and blame are based on fear; laying a guilt trip is the only tactic she has toward you. Just remember, stay in your power and speak your words. Don't allow her to make you feel bad. This is your journey and you need to stand up for yourself."

Empowered by the truthful words, I shook my head and jumped back into reality. Without a thought process, I allowed my fingers to type out a response to Autumn's angry message. After I finished, I felt great. I had spoken my truth and asserted myself.

"No one can touch you if you maintain openness and honesty all the time. When you express your truthful opinion, how can anyone tell you you're wrong? Your truth is your own and nobody can take that away from you."

Leaving the library, I still felt angry about the message and decided to talk to Jude about it instead of letting it remain in my mind. While Jude and I explored the neighborhoods of Kingston, she encouraged me to talk about my feelings.

"So why are you allowing this to bother you so much, Katie?" Jude enquired as we crossed into the old part of Kingston.

After contemplating this for a moment, I responded, "I guess it just really hurts because I have known Autumn my entire life and have always considered her my best friend. But after receiving such an accusatory response from her, I am wondering what our friendship's based on. It just seems so strange. I have embarked on this journey with you to truly discover who I am, and all the folks I considered my loved ones seem to be the least understanding. I guess I'm finding it disheartening to discover that Autumn is so self-consumed."

Nodding, Jude gestured to a coffee shop, claiming, "You know, Katie, it's one of those hard life lessons about detachment and letting go of relationships that are unhealthy. You have spent your entire life caring about other people and what they thought. How about taking care of you for a change? The people who truly love you are always going to be around and support you no matter what your endeavors. That's unconditional love."

Stepping into the cozy coffee shop, I felt my anger slowly dissipate. My talks with Jude really did help me to process and eliminate toxic energy and thoughts to keep them from staying inside. After a quick glance at the time, we realized that our spooky tour was due to start in thirty minutes. Quickly adding sugar to her dark roast, Jude grabbed her coffee and we set out to find Cassidy.

♥   ♥   ♥

Fort St. Henry was located atop a hill, overlooking the entire town of Kingston. As Jude and I neared the front gates, I was amazed by the spectacular vista; we looked down upon green soccer fields, the twinkling city lights, and the view of Lake Ontario's massive circumference.

Looking out toward the lake, I actually felt as though I was home on Vancouver Island, a great place to experience a beautiful summer sunset. In the middle of the lake across from the Fort St. Henry was an island, which had an amazing love story about a man's death and his true love and how she died trying to find him.

A couple hundred years have passed, and now it's a national park.

We reached the massive doors of the fort. They opened with such a grinding sound that my hair stood on end. I pondered supernatural entities. A black cape behind the wooden door caught my attention. Under the cape was a young lady who, I assumed was our guide. She introduced herself as Kirsten and proceeded to lead us to the office to check in. As we entered the inside of the fort, I peered around its stone walls. This was such a dramatic setting, I thought as I felt twinges of apprehension.

Earlier that morning I had wished to see a ghost and it appeared as though my wish was coming true. Yet another of my wishes was manifesting itself into reality. Goosebumps quickly took over my arms as the wind picked up and blew through the barracks.

Jude roamed the courtyard while I stepped into a ledge to look out across the lake. As the wind blew, my hair swirled around my face and

I felt as though I was being watched. Instantly, I remembered Jude's advice about communicating with the spirit world. "Now remember, Katie, if you ever feel the presence of a ghost, ask for their name. Also, ask if they have a particular message they want to communicate."

Recalling Jude's words, I felt prickles up my spine. I decided to investigate what was around me. Feeling rather goofy, I silently asked the ghost what its name was. To my complete and utter astonishment, I received an answer: "Sylvester." Unsure if I had manifested this name from my imagination, I asked again. Again the voice repeated "Sylvester." This was followed by silence. Amazed that I had made contact with a ghost, I rushed over to find Jude.

I found her on the other side of the courtyard, looking in a window where old artifacts were displayed. She was lost in time. I tapped her on the shoulder. Jude turned. "Hey, Katie, you look funny. What's the matter?"

"Well, I met a ghost, Sylvester." I was so excited that I could barely stay in my shoes.

"Did you ask him what he wanted?"

"No, I didn't."

"Well, that's okay. Next time try asking what they want." Jude turned back to the window and peered back in.

At precisely 9:30 p.m. our tour guide, Kirsten, emerged from her dark little office. Black cloak fluttering in the wind, she dramatically began her tour. Armed with a lantern, she briefly explained the general history of the fort. As the wind picked up, I shivered, anticipating the eerie vibes that we would feel. Upon the completion of her introduction, Kirsten led us into the main courtyard, which the soldiers used when off duty.

The first room she took us into was the old bake shop that had a huge oven. Across from this was a preparation table for making baked goods. There was another long table with two long benches. Above the preparation table were shelves where the baker would keep all the baking pans, like bread pans. Kirsten pointed toward the shelf. "These pans that you see on the shelf have been known to fly off."

The glow of twinkling light added to the spookiness as she disclosed the many unexplainable occurrences that happened after dark. The next stop was the soldier's quarters, and as I entered the room, I noticed a stale smell of burnt ambers. Lights seemed dim in this space. Jude and I sat on a bench across from the wood stove. Kirsten continued explaining her ghostly encounters and the activities of this particular room.

As we were leaving, we felt a shift in the energy in the room. It had seemed very warm when we walked in, however; when we left it began to feel chilly. Kirsten shut the door. Jude and I looked at each at each other. That very moment Jude turned around. "Kirsten, the lights just turned off in the soldiers' quarters."

Kirsten smiled. "That is a common occurrence."

I almost jumped out of my skin. I grabbed Jude's arm. "It's okay, Katie," she said, reassuring me nothing could harm us.

We made our way to the dungeon, down a wet spiral staircase with a smell of the past. At the bottom of the stairs were tombs of the past, Kirsten explain that the first room had lots of ghost activity. It had been a bedroom for a colonel and included a library, and kitchen. All lights were on for display. The last room was also lit. When we walked in the wine cellar, it was very cool, like being in a walk-in freezer. Kirsten reminded us this was her least favorite room. I asked why, and Kirsten said, "The last guy to work this shift got locked in and never did another shift since."

We acknowledged there definitely was a presence in this room.

We left, talking and keeping very close to one another. When Jude felt something and looked back to the room, instantaneously the light turned off. "Kirsten, the light turned off in the wine cellar." Both Kirsten and I stopped in our tracks. Kirsten shrugged her shoulders. "Not an uncommon occurrence, but I really hate when the ghosts do that!"

Once we made our way up that old staircase, Kirsten concluded her tour and thanked us for being great tourists and making her job easier. We left Kingston, heading south toward to Montreal.

♥   ♥   ♥

After a sleepless night, I was still feeling spooked from our ghost tour. I was also concerned about a dream I had about Jude telling me I wasn't from the fairy realm after all.

In the dream I was very angry at her. This unnerved me because of the dream's vivid, realistic nature.

Once we hit the road, Cassidy cruised at top speed toward Montreal, with lists of things to do! As we got closer and closer, my mind was racing, thinking about the things we had to do before leaving: paint and sublet, pack everything up, clean…

By the time we had hit the outskirts of town, I had worked myself into quite the tizzy. As I was silently obsessing, my mood got darker and darker. Sensing a shift in my energy, Jude said, "Katie, what is the matter?"

She turned to me, waiting for a response.

"Well, I really don't know," I said, shifting in my seat.

Jude refused to believe me. She commented, "So why do you still struggle with yourself?"

"I don't know!" I was squirming by this time.

"Really, Katie, what are you not telling me?" she asked, sensing my bullshit.

"Okay, what are we doing?" This was a perfect bullshit question.

"Well, I seem to remember that you came out here to go to school, and possibly start a business with me." She stared at me.

"I don't know," I said in a whisper.

"Okay, that is a start," replied Jude

"Let me decide what is good for me!" I said, barking at Jude.

"Katie, what is the real truth? Why do you seem so upset and what do you think we have been doing on this journey?" she asked in a concerning voice.

"I have no immediate plans for my future," I said, feeling defeated once again in all my endeavors.

Frustration mounted as I tried to find our appropriate exit into Montreal mayhem. "Katie, what have we just spent the past few weeks discussing? If you believe, you will achieve. You have been shown many situations where relying on your belief system has worked to your advantage. But you truly have to believe in yourself as well. Do you? Do you believe in yourself, Katie?" Jude asked as I frantically tried to find any form of landmark I could recognize.

As I contemplated her questions, I heard a soft "no" echoing through me, answering Jude's question. I responded, "No, I don't

Jude. Somewhere along the line I gave up and have never had anyone push me to demonstrate the strength I hold within."

Saddened by this piece of information, Jude sighed and looked out the window, "Look, kid, we all have pasts. It's how we choose to accept them that shapes us today. You can either allow previous patterns to mold you or say 'I am going to rise above this' and change your story. Now having said that, where are we heading? Come on, Katie, use your intuition. Don't think, feel!" Even more enraged, I began swirling around Montreal, taking random turns and exits.

"The way I see it, Katie, you can either choose to stay in an unhealthy mindset and buy into what everybody told you or you can start believing in yourself and recreate new opinions of your own. Personally I don't understand what you are holding onto!"

As I continued my chaotic driving around Montreal, I struggled with Jude's questions. "You know, Jude, I don't even know anymore. I am so tired of playing this internal game with myself; I just want to believe I can achieve my potential and truly feel it." Finishing my sentence, I looked around my surroundings; miraculously I had driven Cassidy right into our familiar neighborhood without any thought process.

Wowzers! Jude had been right! The instant I stopped stressing about finding the apartment and tapped into my intuition, the solution seemed to manifest itself before me.

I contemplated this new moment of enlightenment. I truly could do whatever I put my mind to if I believed in myself! True understanding dawned on me and I looked over at Jude. "Okay, Jude, I understand what you are saying. I want to believe in myself more than anything."

Smiling, Jude answered, "Well, Katie, start now and don't ever stop. The only person who can ever get in your way is you, remember that." And with that I began maneuvering Cassidy toward the apartment. The storm was over and I had resolved to believe in myself, for the moment.

♥   ♥   ♥

My spirits heightened, Jude and I put on soul town funk music and grooved to Stevie Wonder. As our energy levels rose, Jude began

174

yelling out the window, "Are you happy, Montreal?" on the busy street. No one bothered to even look at us.

After driving another block, we noticed an outdoor pub, then Jude again yelled out the window, "Are you happy, Montreal?" A table full of young people yelled back "Yes, come have a drink!"

"Jude, what do you think?" Her eyes told the story of mischievous behavior, and I parked Cassidy without second-guessing myself.

After formal introductions Jude and I disclosed we were traveling writers looking for information to articulate in a book. Eager for their ten seconds of fame, the boys told us their versions of Montreal and its grandeur. "Yeah, there is all the great bars and they even stay open till three p.m."

"Nah, dudes it's not that, it's the outdoor taverns on a summer day."

"No way, our churches and heritage sites are amazing, so old and full of history."

As the boys excitedly spoke about their hometown, I loved watching their expressions. They were passionate and full of pride. I secretly hoped they maintained that optimistic attitude throughout their lives.

Once our conversation regarding Montreal had simmered down, the boy in the pink shirt Mike, sparked a conversation about politics. During our discussion, he mentioned his absolute dislike for our American neighbors. Six months prior I would have agreed, bar none, but now I felt differently. Instead of agreeing with his statement, I challenged him on his belief, having just spent three weeks in the states. My original biased opinion toward the American people had made a complete turn around. Contrary to what my family and friends said about their ignorance, I found Americans to be not only intelligent but kind and generous as well.

When I heard Mike's harsh expressions that afternoon, I demanded to know why he carried such hostility toward them. As I challenged Mike in the pink shirt about his viewpoints, he looked very surprised. Not being used to anyone challenging his thoughts, he cocked his head toward me. "You want to know why I have such opinions."

Nodding my head, I encouraged him to continue. Temporarily silenced, Mike didn't know how to react. As though searching his mind for the answer, he inhaled and slowly began speaking. "I just don't like them. They all listen to an idiot president and follow whatever he says. They don't have any thoughts of their own and are ignorant!"

Amazed by such judgmental statements, I understood this judgment. I had held the same opinion at one time, so I proceeded to challenged him further. "Oh, I don't know about that. I just returned from the U.S. and I found them to be some of the most warm, inviting people I had ever met. Also, the majority of Americans I met were smart and highly educated. Have you ever actually spent any time in the U.S.?"

Taking a long drag of his cigarette, Mike responded, "Yes, I have family down in Florida with whom I visit every year. Trust me; I am creating this opinion on personal experiences."

Still not satisfied with his response, I pressed on. "And where exactly did you meet the Americans you are basing your decision on?"

Looking very sheepish, Mike paused before answering. "Well, most of the Americans I met were in the bars and nightclubs."

Nodding my head, I replied, "Then wouldn't it be safe to say that you are generating your opinion from a fairly small percentage of the population—that in fact, your opinion is only truly applicable to individuals you have met in a drinking situation?"

Sensing that he had been humbled, Mike slowly nodded his head. I went on to express my own personal judgments and inform him that mine had been created from other people. As our discussion on Americans morphed into the subject of useful degree choices, I silently gave myself a pat on the back.

In the past I would have been exceptionally feeble in a political debate. Not ever holding any personal opinions or convictions, I always allowed everyone else's voice be louder than mine. Since I had learned about the importance of speaking my mind, I had discovered there were many issues I held strong opinions on. Now I had courage to articulate my viewpoints. As I watched Mike throughout our discussion, it felt wonderful to have a guy actually listen to me and my opinions. In the past I would never debate or argue with men for fear of appearing stupid.

Jude always says "Interesting people are all around us. When we are real they come to us!"

This concept does work, and now I understand it.

♥   ♥   ♥

Leaving the pub, we made our way to Cassidy to get back to the apartment. I felt wonderful, confident, and excited to have decided to move once again.

Finding a parking spot close to our apartment, Jude and I unpacked our suitcases and wearily headed upstairs. Jude asked if we should put the satellite radio in the glove compartment. I shook my head no.

We posted on Craig's List, subletting our apartment for rent. Once we entered the apartment, the energy didn't feel right. I opened the windows to let fresh air into our "Amityville horror" apartment.

We had arrived back on June 20, 2007; had five days to sublet the apartment, paint, clean. Jude was very confident it would all work out. Friday was spent racing around the apartment, packing all our personal belongings into apple boxes. Around 3 p.m. I received a phone call from a girl named Melissa. She was enquiring about subletting the apartment. Thrilled that we had a potential renter, I made arrangements for Melissa to come by at seven thirty that evening.

We cleaned the fridge and stove; got boxes to give away items we no longer wanted. Taking a break, Jude and I sat on the living room floor. Jude's cell phone began to ring.

Jude grabbed for it. "Hello, this is Jude; I will send Katie down to let you in."

Grabbing my front door key, I headed back down to the lobby to let her in.

Melissa was a lady in her early twenties, and I recognized her immediately as I walked into the front lobby. Wearing a big smile, she introduced herself and apologized for being late.

♥   ♥   ♥

Melissa

Holy parallel universes, Batman!

Meeting Melissa felt like the most epic time traveling adventure I had ever embarked upon. Allow me to further your knowledge on the subject...

Melissa was a young, vibrant woman in her mid-twenties searching to create her own identity. It just so happened that her search had brought her to Montreal, specifically to our apartment that late June. Melissa was the first caller to respond to our online advertisement for the sublet. From the moment she walked into our world, I could sense she truly wanted to discover her true identity.

After falling in love with the place, Melissa sat down for some peppermint tea and a heart-to-heart chat. While Jude asked her deep questions, Melissa demonstrated qualities very similar to mine:

❖ Unsure of her own power
❖ Indecisive
❖ Actively exploring spirituality
❖ Confused
❖ Allowing others to make her decisions

Melissa spent forty-five minutes in the apartment disclosing her life path and family issues that shaped her into the person she was. She explained that she had recently begun her spiritual exploration and said that meeting us had been a serendipitous affirmation providing great hope. Despite Melissa's instinct to rent the place, she also possessed a strong intellectual side that held her back. Touching Melissa on the arm, Jude suggested that she call us in the morning with her final decision. Sure enough, the following day Melissa called expressing her great disappointment that she would be unable to accept the place. She had discussed the situation with her parents and they instilled fear into her regarding legal matters. Hanging up the phone, I felt empathy for Melissa's situation. I too had allowed external sources to dictate my decisions, thoughts, and opinions. Having spent months learning to stand in my own power, I could easily identify with a young woman's struggle to find her inner strength and belief system. Melissa served as a wonderful affirmation that I wasn't alone in my quest to assert my individual identity and personal value system. I also learned that I could not make anyone believe in spirituality if they did not want to. Melissa was her own person, and I had to detach from the situation and allow her life path to take over (even if she was going against her vibes!).

♥   ♥   ♥

After hanging up the phone with Melissa, I suggested we go for breakfast to recharge our batteries. Several hours later our tummies were full and I walked over to the internet café to re-post on Craig's List and felt confident about our apartment being subleted. Life is funny, especially when it comes to direction I needed to take. The universe answered by that afternoon. A lady named Ingrid was moving to Montreal due to a new job she was taking.

"Jude, we might have found a new renter. I am going to phone right now." Going crazy with excitement, I said, "I can't find my cell phone, Jude, have you seen it?"

"I plugged it in to recharge" she said, raising her voice.

"Where?" I asked.

"Katie, on your nightstand," she said, raising her voice once again.

I found my cell phone finally and dialed Ingrid's phone number. It … rang once … rang twice … rang a third time, and then a woman's voice answered and I left a message.

I checked the clock and saw it was 1:00 p.m. I decided that now we just had to wait. "Let's watch a movie. How about *The Heartbreakers*?" I asked Jude. She nodded her head with approval.

While we were watching the movie, Ingrid phoned, and based on the description I gave her, she took the apartment. I came out of the bedroom with my arms up high, screeching "We got new renters. Yeah, ooh," prancing around like a little pony.

That evening Jude and I prepared the entire apartment for painting, taping around windows and baseboards. I have to say that the one job we acquired was painting, so the job of painting our apartment was a cinch!

car stealing

As Jude and I were packing up our life possessions at the apartment, Cass was waiting patiently three blocks away. The morning prior to our departure, I awoke remembering that I needed to move her in order to avoid a city parking ticket. While I was walking the few short blocks to her, a strong unsettling feeling came over my body.

Approaching Miss Cassidy, I knew something was amiss. Sure enough, upon further investigation I realized that Cass had been robbed. The satellite radio, Jude's backpack, including all of our new contacts, camera, and fairy books all had been taken from our humble van-home. Feeling very violated, I walked back to the apartment to share the bad news with Jude.

Now writing this, I find the entire fiasco very intriguing. Jude and I traveled thousands of miles across North American cities, including New York, Miami, and Detroit. And did we have any problems with theft or robberies? Absolutely none!

Our Montreal robbing served as yet another affirmation that indeed we were not meant to be staying in the multicultural city. Although I accepted the ill fate of our possessions, I still shake my fist at the crook running around in Jude's sneakers AND reading my fairy book. May the sparkle critters of the forest come and bite your toes, you bugger!

♥   ♥   ♥

Two days later we accomplished the task of packing the apartment, and I say we should go into the house-painting business; we would be millionaires!

Monday morning we handed Ingrid the keys in the lobby and made our way out of Amityville Horror.

After unloading a bunch of Yukon winter clothing to relieve Cassidy's weight load, we headed down to Rue Notre Dame to have a cup of coffee.

After several minutes of discussion, I suddenly was hit an inspiration to call my grandmother. In the past our relationship had been growing more and more distant, but since revaluating my life,

I realized that she was a vital person I wanted in my world. Dialing her number, I reached my Cobble Hill grandma upon the third ring. Checking in with Kate, I informed her that I was writing a novel and that I was leaving Montreal. Her response was amazing, completely devoid of judgment. Instead of questioning why I was again leaving another city, she simply stated her support and encouraged me to continue writing. So very refreshing! Kate and I chatted for ten minutes, and then she exclaimed it was time for her to head off to bed. Hanging up, I smiled knowing that I was rebuilding essential bridges in my life.

♥   ♥   ♥

Although all of our belongings had fit quite nicely into Cassidy's interior, Jude and I were challenged with one slight problem: placing the bench seat and two bucket seats appropriately into the back. Overly optimistic, I had initially shrugged off the problem, stating that we could easily maneuver the seats to our liking. WRONG!

As I surveyed the scenario within Cassidy, I had to laugh. It looked as though a bomb had exploded within the inner cavity. "I guess we will just sleep in our seats" had been Jude's comical response as she assessed the situation.

Later the evening we found ourselves outside an intermediate care facility on the outskirts of Montreal. As the sun set, we witnessed such a magical view around us: a flock of honking geese flew by as the pink and oranges created a breathtaking background. While we enjoyed the view, Jude had played a instrumental meditation tape that made it sound as though the ocean waves were crashing into the van.

Looking out at the geese, Jude reflected upon our current situation. "You know, Katie, it has been such a wild adventure so far and I have to say, I think you have finally comprehended the lessons and tools I have shown you over these past few months. Now that your past is released, we can start the new stage of truly discovering who you are. Trust me, Katie, this is the fun part!" Peering out at the stars, I nodded wistfully and imagined what the future had in store.

Six hours later Jude and I both awoke feeling like a pair of overextended pretzels in the van. Our grandiose plan of keeping the bucket seats and bench had turned into a nightmare. As we had attempted to squish ourselves among our many suitcases and boxes, waving the white flag of surrender, I finally gave up the dream.

"You know what, little buddy? I think we are going to have to dump those seats somewhere in the middle of Montreal. Our epic plan of placing boxes around the seats isn't going to fly."

Agreeing, Jude sat up and wiped her sleepy eyes, "All right, Katie, you lead the way. Let's try to be sneaky about it." As quietly as humanly possible, I pulled Cassidy out of the space and headed toward the downtown neighborhoods of Montreal. After ten minutes of sneaky driving, Jude pointed to a pile of garbage outside of a duplex. "Let's just leave them here," she hissed as I pushed on the brakes.

Like skillfully trained cat burglars, we dumped the evidence on the side of the road. Arriving back to our original nesting spot, we quickly rearranged our bed. Grabbing my pillow, I conked out immediately.

♥   ♥   ♥

Sweltering heat greeted us the following morning as we opened our eyes and greeted the day. Grabbing the road map, we planned our next move, to find Lily Dale, New York. This was the mother ship compared to "Cassadega, Florida." It was another spiritual community that we wanted to investigate. Tapping with her index finger, Jude pointed to Lily Dale; it was approximately four hours directly below Niagara-on-the-Lake. Making an executive decision, Jude and I decided to head south into New York state, then farther west toward Arizona.

As I pulled Cassidy away from the intermediate care facility nesting spot, I realized that we were attempting to leave downtown Montreal, again at rush hour, and it was 32 degrees Celsius in the shade. Frank Sinatra's song "My Way" piped into my mind as we crept our way toward the freeway.

Two and a half hours later, Jude and I finally reached the city limits of Montreal. When we hit a cruising speed of 110 kilometers per hour, warm air hit our faces, taking a slight edge off the summer heat. Reaching over, Jude tuned into the hit radio station and cranked our favorite song "Rock Star." As we were singing on the top of our lungs, the new journey had begun.

♥   ♥   ♥

At suppertime we arrived in Niagara-on-the-Lake, just in time to observe a brilliant sunset. Pulling into the parking lot, Jude and I prepared for an evening stroll around the lake. Sensing a opportunity for closure, I rummaged around my boxes to uncovered letters and notes from my past. Jude had suggested releasing old energy by burning past memories and reminders. A few minutes later, I retrieved a huge stack of sentimental papers and placed them firmly under my arm. *Enough holding onto the past,* I said to myself.

Jude and I made our way toward the scenic hike. Several minutes along our trek, I noticed some huge boulders poking out of the water. Upon closer inspection, I gestured to Jude that I wanted to conduct my energy-releasing procedure down below. Nodding, Jude plunked herself down upon a flat boulder and assisted as I clambered down to a nearby boulder.

After expressing my gratitude for my past memories and memorabilia, I ignited the pile of papers and watched as they burned down into ashes. *What a perfect moment,* I thought to myself as I felt another chapter of my spiritual growth nearing a close. I breathed a great sigh of relief. As I clambered back onto the main path, I felt as though a phenomenal amount of weight had miraculously lifted from my chest.

As we drifted back toward Cassidy, Jude reminded me about the ear-coning procedure we had been planning on doing throughout our journey. I was constantly asking Jude to repeat herself due to my inability to hear. (Little did I know I actually had incredible hearing; I just choose to hear certain things.) Reaching into the back of Cassidy's interior, I located the wax candles we had bought earlier.

The whole procedure lasted around fifteen minutes, and I was amazed by the amount of wax that came out of my ears. Super gross too! Let this be a lesson: ensure you clear your ears out every year!

After we had fully cleansed our ears of junk and jazz, we sat in Cassidy, trying to decide where to go from here. As Jude stepped out to stretch her legs, a dark red van pulled up right in front of her. A middle aged fellow with a handle bar mustache called out a greeting, " Evening ladies." Jude responded, "Good evening, sir." And so began their conversation. It turned out that Roy, the man with the moustache, worked for the town of Niagara-on-the-Lake and was shutting down the park for the night. He informed Jude that two guys on his crew had observed our entire ear-coning procedure, assuming that we were shooting heroine. Laughing at the idea of us shooting heroine in Cassidy, Jude soon set the record straight for Roy.

Upon hearing about our ear-coning procedure, Roy threw his head back and chuckled. "I knew you girls didn't seem the type to shooting heroine in the neighborhood park!" he exclaimed while shaking his head. "It's truly amazing that idea popped into those boys' minds. I will inform them the latter is true. You ladies have a great, safe trip and enjoy our beautiful community, Niagara-on-the-Lake." Roy pulled away, leaving a smile on Jude's face.

Ten minutes later Jude and I were determining where to bunk down for the night when from behind we could here *boom, boom, boom*. This sound rolled right beside us. Two young guys stepped out of a car, chattering away if they were the only ones in the parking lot. Another vehicle arrived shortly thereafter with another group of guys; they hopped out and came over to the car parked next to us. One of the guys noticed our license plate was from the Yukon. Curiosity got the best of them and a tall guy with shaggy brown hair inquired if we had a home up north.

"Actually, we don't have a home right now," I stated as the guys turned their attention toward us. Jude commented, "That's right, boys, it's been quite an adventure. We have been all throughout all of Canada and the U.S. living in this here minivan."

Fascinated by our tale, a tall dark-haired guy in the passenger seat leaned forward, requesting more information. "So, what exactly do you girls do?"

Jude responded, "Basically, this is about Katie's spiritual journey and all the particular lessons and tools she has picked up along the way."

"I have wanted to do something like that for a really long time." His eyes lit up as he spoke. "Tell us more abut your journey." With that I started disclosing the incredible truths I had discovered about myself as well as within others. Still feeling really self-conscious and unsure of myself, I paused, wondering if what I was saying sounded even remotely interesting.

Sensing my tension, Jude stepped up to the plate. "Basically, boys, we have been traveling around and Katie has been an observer of life and I have been along for the ride. Anyone can pick up life lessons if they are willing to take the risk and be active participants in their destiny." As she continued on her teachings, I watched as the boys gathered around Cassidy, hungering for more information.

"Remember, boys, always listen to your heart, not your head. Throughout your life your heart will never lead you astray from your true destiny." While the boys nodded their agreement, one fellow piped up. "I disagree with that statement. I have always gone with my head. Following your heart does nothing but cause problems." A hush fell over the crowd as he finished his statement. Shaking her head slightly, Jude answered, "Well, I'm sorry you feel that way. It has been my experience that our heart is our true guidance." Coldly the boy violently shook his head and disagreed.

Shivers cruised up my spin as I watched his reaction to Jude's words. I wondered what acts he was capable of doing because of his cold nature. It has been my experience that when you think with your head instead of feeling with your heart, the choices you make are not satisfying to your soul's passion. A few minutes later, Jude gave me the silent code, "Let's go," through eye contact and proceeded to climb back into Cassidy. Bidding the young guys good night, we commenced our nightly ritual of locating a camping spot for Miss Cassidy.

As we drove away, I contemplated the situation I had just witnessed. Throughout my teenage years, I had always felt intimidated by guys my age, mainly due to lack of understanding. As a little girl, I had been ridiculed by boys, and I had carried those feelings of hurt through my teenage experiences.

Now, finally, at the age of twenty-six, I saw the other side of young men; not hurtful creatures but indeed fellow individuals pondering the same questions I did—exploring the same truths, experiencing the same heartbreaks, learning life lessons. Everyday I was discovering new lessons, exposing prior judgments, and biases. The fact that I could share my new found path with a groovy teacher made my enlightenment that much sweeter.

Thirty minutes later we had found a spot under a dark elm tree right beside the cemetery.

"Now don't get spooked here, Katie. There is nothing to be scared of, just some trees and wind."

The minute I turned the lights out, my imagination had taken over. The rustling of the bushes transformed into evil spirits stalking us, and trees tapping on the roof became skeletons sitting on the van. After a half an hour of my self-induced fears, I couldn't handle it anymore. Rearranging some boxes, I hopped in the driver's seat and moved Cassidy to a "safer" place. The funny thing was that I could create the "safer" place in my mind, not at a geographical location. Unawake of this at the time, I drove the dark streets of Niagara-on-the-Lake till I found a "safer" place. Quietly muttering in the back, Jude tried to sleep as I once again parked Cassidy. "Ah, much better," I said, checking out the new place. Then I snuggled down into the floral comforter and fell asleep contented with my new location.

♥   ♥   ♥

Nearing the border crossing the following morning, I once again felt my anxiety kicking in. Jude looked over at me and reminded me to remain calm. Approaching the intimidating border crossing, I mentally prepared myself for the onslaught of questions. A woman guard looked down at us and requested our IDs. Upon quick inspection she wordlessly handed them back to us and motioned Cassidy through. Releasing the deep breath I had been holding, I felt my heart resume its normal pace as we drove into New York state. Looking back, I think it's pretty silly the anxiety I would put my body through while dealing with authorities, especially that day, when the crossing guard didn't ask any questions of me whatsoever and simply motioned us through.

Jude placed her hand on my arm. "See, Katie. That wasn't so bad now, was it? You have to remember to relax while going through those type of procedures. Trust me, there is nothing to fear. For someone who had no fears, I most certainly am seeing several fears surface since we have embarked on this journey."

Biting my tongue, I fought back a determined response. Due to many years of fighting with my mother, I had grown extremely accustomed to defending my viewpoints and opinions. The habit had continued throughout my adult life, and I instantly grew into a defensive devil whenever Jude would point out a personality flaw. I was slowly training myself that Jude wasn't my mother, but it truly was difficult not to react to her words with anger and defiance.

♥   ♥   ♥

Five hours southwest of the border, we had reached the community of Lily Dale. Beautiful fountains and flower gardens greeted us as we slowly pulled into the neighborhood. Brightly colored homes and yards were scattered around a spectacular lake in the middle of town.

After we parked Cassidy in a dusty parking lot, Jude and I roamed around the town. A gray tabby joined our venture and trailed behind us for several blocks as though it was our own personal tour guide of Lily Dale. During our wonderings we came across the "Enchanted Forest," a nature trail complete with a reflection stump that hikers could sit upon and contemplate life. Intrigued by the description, Jude and I headed into the forest. We followed the wood chips trail into the lush surrounding woods. About ten minutes down the trail, we came across the reflection stump, which was essentially an old tree that had fallen to the ground.

Upon Jude's encouragement, I made my way over to the gnarly stump and climbed aboard. Silently meditating for several moments, I felt roots from the bottoms of my feet digging deep into the moist dirt below. A sensation of inner peace and tranquility came over as I visualized fairies and gnomes dancing around my aura.

Coming back into conscious state, I made my way back down the trail to find Jude. Together we wondered back toward the end of the nature trail. Long willowy grass kissed our faces as we trekked through a field of nearby hay. A low rustle from the leaves overhead created the sound of magic percussion instruments brought over from faraway lands. I closed my eyes as I looked up toward the sunshine and felt the healing rays beam down upon the top of my head.

Ah, this place most certainly has positive healing energy, I thought to myself as I emerged back into the village. The following hour, Jude and I wandered around investigating the uniquely decorated homes throughout Lilly Dale; there were many creative artistic gnomes and bird fountains, but my attention focused on the angel house. With a wrap-around porch and a white exterior, the angel house was exquisite. It had silver orbs scattered throughout the gardens and wind chimes that rang beautifully with each summer breeze. I stood in awe of the house and imagined what the interior must look like. Several minutes after staring at the whimsical home, I turned to Jude, indicating my desire to continue our tour.

♥   ♥   ♥

The character homes along our path were all numbered one to fifty, which I found completely adorable. Reaching the main spiritual church, to the left I noticed a nearby circular park that included a gazebo. The gazebo was open and had seating capacity for fifteen people. Intrigued by the gazebo, I wandered over and sat on the old weathered benches. Strong smells of fire and smoke encompassed the area as I tapped into the energy. From what I had gathered, the public would have drumming sessions as well as a smokehouse. The smokehouse concept was to purify of all evil spirits and energies that had attached themselves to your essence.

While I sat imagining the procedures of purification, a blast of cool air drifted across the park and into the gazebo. Slightly alarmed by the chilly draft, I stood up and headed over to Jude. She had found herself in front of an old sign that had been resurrected in memory of a family whose house had been destroyed in a fire.

The two little girls who had lived in the house had been strong believers in fairies and hence the community had created a fairy garden specifically in their memory.

Once we had finished reading abut the unfortunate fire, Jude pointed toward a white lattice archway that served as the entrance into their fairy garden. "Maybe you should pop in and check it out?" she suggested. Quickly nodding, I agreed and started walking closer to the entrance. Tall, dark spruce trees framed the trail as I gradually moved deeper into the woods. Every twenty feet I would come across a miniature fairy display created by local families within the communities. Some were mermaids, some silver fairies, and others had pet unicorns. I continued my walk in enchantment, breathing the earthy scents of the forest that grounded my spirit. After whispering my two greatest wishes into the magical wish box, I resurfaced into daylight through a small clearing in the forest.

Feeling very relaxed and calm from my forest fairies visit, I located Jude, who was waiting patiently for me. Continuing on our journey of exploration, we returned to the main park in town overlooking the lake. As we meandered through the brilliant rose gardens, we sat down on a nearby white bench.

Again I felt a cool draft surrounding us, which was strange because the day itself was very warm. Jude confirmed what I had been thinking about. "I have a feeling we are in the presence of a spirit, Katie." As the goose bumps on my arms increased their intensity, remembering that spirits couldn't harm us, I tried my best to put on my brave face. Since having been exposed to several ghostly encounters on our trip, I was slowly getting comfortable with the idea of the spirit realm. Though I had always known that it existed, I hadn't truly experienced the unique encounters until the past few months.

A few minutes ticked by; Jude and I decided to leave the village. Its main spiritual programs and courses were starting in a few days and we didn't feel like waiting around. Locating Miss Cassidy, we hit the road and located the closest Tim Horton's for a well-deserved coffee and treat break.

♥   ♥   ♥

Tummies full of freshly baked treats, we determined what route we were going to take toward Arizona. After much discussion we decided to use our intuition to guide us. While I sat in the coffee shop, I mentioned to Jude how little about myself I truly knew. I had created so many different masks and layers for myself that now I honestly couldn't define myself.

Jude nodded in understanding. "This is very common when people are recreating themselves. They discover that many of the personality traits or behaviors they have are due to past experiences. In order to learn more about yourself, you'll need to start a list of positive attributes, get a notebook. It sounds kind of strange, but write down anything from the color pink to Scooby Doo cartoons, whatever works for you." Excited about starting a list of my new self without judgment and lies, I pulled out my green-and-blue notepad. After five minutes the list I had written look like this:

1. color pink, animals, being a girl
2. Aveda hair products, talks with Jude
3. outdoors, fresh air, silence, kids
4. chocolate chip cookies, clean environments
5. sunshine, scuba diving

It felt great to have my words written down on paper. This way I could reflect back whenever I was feeling lost or unsure of my personal opinions. After brushing our teeth in a local gas station, we said good night and turned out Cassidy's interior lighting.

♥   ♥   ♥

The following morning we awoke feeling invigorated from a great sleep. We cruised to find a country bumpkin restaurant. Jude noticed an old country family restaurant and turned Cassidy in the parking lot.

It was your typical country restaurant, complete with a red roof and rooster memorabilia. Taking a seat into the old wooden booths, we greeted our friendly server as she approached. Ordering oatmeal and eggs, we sat back in the old booths and took in the surroundings.

After fifteen minutes of silence, Sally, our waitress approached the table with our breakfast.

"Hope you enjoy it," she expressed before heading back toward the swinging kitchen doors. Looking down, my initial excitement over my healthy oatmeal breakfast quickly turned into a wrinkled-up nose. Examining my oatmeal it was quite watery, like soup, not oatmeal. Jude glanced over from her over-easy eggs and said, "Well, you can always send it back, Katie." Despite my starving hunger, I knew Jude was right. Sheepishly flagging Sally down, I informed her that the oatmeal was super watery and not cooked. "Oh right away," Sally replied and headed back toward the kitchen.

Several minutes later, Sally interrupted my thoughts as she placed a new bowl of oatmeal in front of me. "Ah, much better," I responded as I peered down into my bowl. Thick, creamy, just how oatmeal should be!

During our breakfast Jude had noticed a couple of ladies had sat behind us wearing T-shirts that had a slogan "I walked for Breast Cancer—2007." Jude excused herself from the table and made her way to the washroom. A few minutes later, Jude stopped at the ladies' table, and struck up a conversation. The ladies invited Jude to sit down and I joined them. We introduced ourselves and they did the same. The lady who sat next to me was Teresa and next to Jude was Faye.

Jude perked up when she heard what they did and how much fundraising did for your spirit. Faye was the coordinator of a seniors' facility, whereas Teresa is a preschool teacher and nun. They both shared their passions about what they did for employment and community service work. I was in awe when witnessing women in true conversation without their egos present.

I was pretty quiet, enjoying the conversation, when Teresa reached out and touched my hand with hers. She looked into my eyes and stated, "Well, I think what the two of you are doing is fantastic."

I was completely in awe of her kind and gentle nature; there was not one ounce of judgment as she instantly accepted me the way I was. Minutes flew by as Jude and I sat at their table and discussed many topics from nearby campsites to the ways in which Faye asserted herself. During our conversation I felt completely calm with these beautiful women.

Due to their strong religious backgrounds, they both exuded a quiet peace about them that was entirely unfamiliar to me. Growing up in an atheist environment, I had never been exposed to individuals with strong belief systems. Patience, non-judgment, and acceptance were all virtues I was unaware of, though I knew I wanted to possess them.

Watching Faye and Teresa that morning, I knew truly wanted to possess the qualities they had ingrained deeply into their souls.

In the past I had always shunned religion, assuming it was not for me, and remained resistant to those who did express religious beliefs. Having spent many months with Jude and now witnessing these fabulous spirits, my narrow-minded opinion was being opened into new awareness. If religion had provided such beautiful qualities in these strong women, could it not do the same thing for me?

At the time my ego was still bothered by the admitting that I needed teaching, so Jude had taken on the task of explaining.

"Having a belief system is the most essential aspect of being a spiritual being. Without it, your entire essence will lose its meaning and your existence becomes a quest to locate your inner truths. Many of the problems today are stemmed from individuals not having a belief system and hence living a life without passion, without meaning."

Jude, 2007

♥   ♥   ♥

That late June morning, Jude and I spent two hours with these women while they ate their breakfast and disclosed their opinions and beliefs. As we got up to leave, Faye and Teresa gave me the most heartfelt hugs, completely unfolding me their arms. I stepped into Cassidy in quite an altered mindset. Gratitude toward the universe swelled up inside me as I acknowledged the beautiful women who had been placed on my path.

My lesson that morning was that there were indeed individuals with strong religious backgrounds who were incredibly good people. Years of judgments and assumptions had led to my extremely negative opinion of religious individuals, but all that was changing as I traveled deeper down my path.

♥   ♥   ♥

So about four days later, I had hit the most horrifying night of the entire trip. Jude and I had pulled into yet another rest area for the night just outside of Illinois.. I had taken a magical stroll with pink hazy clouds of sparkling fireflies and finally felt inner peace and tranquility. Seemingly at ease and at peace, I gently strolled back to Cassidy to check out a movie on our new acquired laptop from Derek. As I approached the van, I suddenly felt a shift in my headspace and felt feelings of anger and irritability.

I began fumbling through the boxes for the brush to pull through my knotted excuse of hair. I asked Jude where it was and she responded by challenging me to use my intuition to locate it among the boxes. Not being in a great mood for a challenge, I ignored her and continued my search for the hair brush. My anger and frustration began bubbling even more to the point that it was uncontrollable. I barked out blame at Jude and my anger was fueled when she didn't respond to my accusatory words.

Hostile words flew out of my mouth, and before I knew it, I had claimed words fueled with hatred and spite directed at the one person who was such a positive influence in my life. Rage flew through me and I frightened myself with the knowledge that I possessed such deep anger issues I had been unaware of. Why would I push this great opportunity away?

♥   ♥   ♥

The next morning the reality of the prior night sunk in as I reflected upon my emotions and how my misguided anger was fired at someone I deeply cared for. It really scared me; that morning was one I will never forget. Entirely through my own doing, I managed to manifest the most horrible headache ever as the consequences of my behaviors were sinking in. My insides churned and swished around as we debated on the logistics of getting back to the coast. It felt similar to the entire divorce procedure after the fatal quarrel that pushes one to the edge.

As Jude spoke, her feelings of disgust radiated. "Since we embarked on this journey, I have always told you to use your words with integrity and respect. Last night, you showed me the real side of you—the side that is so dark you have hidden it away from everything. But you can only conceal such anger for so long until it resurfaces, but quite frankly, I have a beautiful family who all love and adore me. I do not need to be traveling around with some spoiled middle-class girl who is throwing vindictive and hateful words toward me. All I know is that I want to head west and then take it from there."

As my heart sank into the deepest, darkest obis I had ever witnessed, I continued driving, lost in a jumble of self-deprecating words. Blame shot up as I tried to pin my behavior on someone else. After the most horrendous inner battle, I decided I needed to call my parents and attempt to resolve these questions that I realized had spawned my anger. The call went completely unexpectedly.

Finding the nearby fast food restaurant, I pulled Cassidy over and began dialing my parents' phone number. Hearing the familiar British accent of my father, I barked that I wanted to talk to Mom. My entire body quivered as I prepared myself for whatever was going to fly out of my mouth.

My mom's voice resonated over the phone lines as she picked up and launched into her explanation. "Before you say anything, sweetheart, I love you" Unaware of my deeper sadness surrounding my mother's love, I started crying. For my entire life, I never thought my mother loved me. Because of her cold demeanor and selfish attitude, I had grown up feeling unwanted.

Almost incomprehensible, through tears I managed to stutter, "Why did you have me, Mom? You didn't even want children." Hurt and anger poured over the telephone as I remembered my deep hurt. Exhaling, my mother explained that she had been curious and thought it would be interesting experience. I retorted by expressing that children are not an experience; they are human beings with feelings. Uncontrollable sorrow came from my core as I listened to her explain what love meant to her.

As she began detailing our family history of depression, her excuses were driving me crazy. As I listened I suddenly felt Jude's hands pulling my hair back out of my face into a ponytail. My sobs continued as Jude massaged my shoulders. Even in my dark hours, after I had said horrific words and spewed hatred, Jude still demonstrated qualities of unconditional love. Her actions of strength shone through as I quivered in a ball on the green grass. Concluding the conversation with my mom, I disclosed that I needed to hear her express her love toward me much more. Hanging up, I felt fairly calm as I sat in silence and wiped the tears from my eyes.

♥   ♥   ♥

In the meantime Jude had called her son Aaron and was enlightening him about our latest adventures. Mid-conversation she handed the phone over to me. Awkwardly I answered, "Hi, Aaron, how are you?" Hearing Aaron's deep, grounding voice instantly shook me out of my dark funk and back into reality. It was very magical to feel my mood shift so quickly from despair to hope in a matter of ten seconds.

As Jude hung up the phone, she looked over at me. "No matter how deep and dark you feel, there is always someone that cares about you in this world. Remember, Katie, you can't always do things on your own, and you need to learn to ask for help."

For years I had created a fake persona of one who had the perfect relationship with her parents and was happy all the time and easygoing. My false identity had finally caught up with me as I realized I had been living in delusion for many, many years. Harsh reality had kicked in I acknowledged the unhealthy situation I had created for myself through my relationship, unhealthy lack of self-confidence, and suppression of my true feelings.

Determined to deal with my anger issues, I silently resolved to do whatever it took in order to eliminate them. I had learned so many truths from Jude, and I refused to throw all of my wondrous beliefs to the wayside due to my previous denial of anger.

♥   ♥   ♥

As the state of Indiana seemed to cruise past us as a blur from the speedy interstate highway, it had been two days since the hairbrush incident and my mood had shifted drastically. Since I had spoken to my parents, particularly my mother, my spirits had lightened because I had the courage to express my feelings.

Despite my lighter spirits, I still hadn't mustered enough courage from within to inquire if Jude was staying true to her plans of returning to the coast. My fear of abandonment soon revealed itself as I soon realized how deeply I wanted Jude around and not to leave. While driving through a small rural town of Indiana, I finally mustered enough courage and jokingly stated, "No matter what happens, I still think our journey would make a phenomenal story," referring to our adventures and my spiritual lessons about the universe. Slowly Jude turned toward me. "Who said we can't," she stated, still as cool as a cucumber despite the fiery temperatures.

Hope, dreams, excitement all came over me like a tidal wave splashing over a fresh sandy shore. As I excitedly turned my head toward Jude, she shrugged her shoulders and said "What? Never say never, kiddo. Life can change so drastically from one day to the next, and don't get too far ahead of yourself."

As we continued toward Kansas, renewed hope regarding the future shone through me as I took a big gulp of cool water.

Later that smoggy evening, we drove through a small town by the name of Greensburg. Devastation and destruction radiated out of the soil as we surveyed the scene. Several months prior to our arrival, Greensburg had been hit with a massive hurricane which had destroyed most of the town. Epic piles of rubble and dirt were all that remained of a once vibrant town. A lone Blue Cross tent stood in the centre of town as though to reconfirm the loss and ruin the town had experienced. Again, the true severity of our rapidly self-depleting planet was shown to me. I silently sent out a prayer for all who had been impacted in the town.

Later that smoggy evening, Jude parked Miss Cassidy at a small rest area in rural Kansas. When we turned off the headlights, the night sky became alive with stars. Bright twinkling lights shone down upon us as we lay in Cassidy. As I stared out of the windows, I thought about how tiny I truly was within the grand scope of the universe. I often found it so easy to get caught up in the trails and tribulations of my own reality. It's rather comical to think about, because at the end of the day, I am essentially just another animal trying to survive. Wondering where I fit in the great pecking order, I drifted off to sleep.

Five hours later I was awoken to a deafening sound of a freight train right outside the van. Fearful that Cassidy was about to be flattened by a freight train, I leapt toward Jude for protection. Looking back, I have to laugh at a tiny lady wearing her floral pajamas. What could she do, stop an entire train with her bare hands? Instinctively I had cowered behind Jude for protection.

Upon reflection I think it was a huge lesson for me in terms of my trust toward her despite our arguments. Deep in my subconscious, I knew that Jude deeply cared for me and I returned the feelings. My instinctive reaction to cower near Jude was an affirmation demonstrating my deep trust in her.

Laughing, Jude sat up. "Don't worry Katie," she yelled over the blasting sound of the freight train. "It's not going to hit us! Just try to go back to sleep."

Easier said than done. I rolled over and said, "Good night." That's all I remember.

♥   ♥   ♥

The midnight train to Kansas ensured that Jude and I slept approximately four hours between the two of us. We awoke that morning to an extremely clammy and overheated van. Glancing quickly at the thermostat, I realized that it was 30 degrees Celsius at 8:26 a.m.

"She's going to be a hot one," I exclaimed as we rolled down the windows, trying to circulate the stuffy air out of Cassidy.

Hearing a grumble from my tummy, Jude suggested we find a restaurant. Entering a small town north of Greensburg, we spotted a terracotta Mexican-style bistro. "Looks good to me," she stated as we pulled into the driveway. The intense rays of the sun were now shining at full power and we quickly raced to locate some shade.

Entering the restaurant, I soon felt like a tourist, standing out like a sore thumb. Directly in front of us sat a group of four men all wearing farmers clothing. Giving us the once over, they watched us as we located a table. "Good morning, ladies," one of the men called out as he nodded his head in our direction.

Nodding back, we returned the greeting.

Glancing over at their half-eaten meals, Jude inquired what the best meal on the menu was. An older man with white hair and coveralls responded, "Well, since you asked I would have to say the pecan pancakes. They are absolutely delicious." With that he walked his plate over to our table to show us the meal. *What service,* I thought to myself.

As the man stood at our table introducing himself as Garland, our new farmer friend began explaining to us the severity of the latest tornado that had twisted town. Midway through the conversation, a Mexican woman approached us to take our order. Jude opted for the pecan pancakes and I remained Plain Jane with my two eggs scrambled and toast. Once the waitress had departed, Garland resumed his chattering with us. "Yup, we've met lots of Canadians rolling through our town over the years. Most of 'em doesn't know anything about twisters, but I can say this: they've been hitting pretty hard," he said, concluding his lesson about tornadoes. Garland shuffled back to his table to finish his breakfast.

While we waited for our breakfast to arrive, I focused my attention upon the television screen above Jude's head. It was an episode of *USA Today* featuring an interview with a very famous blonde celebrity. She had recently been set free from jail and was discussing her altered perspective on life. Intrigued, I pointed the screen out to Jude and we both tuned in.

As I was watching the TV show with the blonde, a realization dawned upon me. There are so many of us out there who have never been put in a situation where we must reevaluate our lives. Why must we wait till we hit rock bottom to truly find ourselves? Or to seek inner peace? Why not start before any of that poop starts and have a better understanding of our wants for unconditional love and understanding.

As I watched this woman make claims of finding God and changing her life around, I began pondering the idea: Why can't people find the meaning of life before they begin all these self-destructive behaviors, especially those who are looked upon as role models? It's amazing what one uncovers when forced to sit still and reflect on one's life patterns and imprints.

When I told my close friends about the spiritual mission I was embarking upon, many of them replied with the response, "I couldn't stand spending that much time with myself." That statement alone should get people wondering, why? What is it about self-reflection and inner discovery that frightens others so greatly?

As the blonde chattered on, I had a light bulb moment. Adrenaline surged through me as I thought about her words. No matter what social class, upbringing, and race we are born into, we all have the option to choose how to live our lives and be positive role models to younger generations.

Enlightened from a light bulb moment, I wolfed down my scrambled eggs and began brainstorming potential business ventures involving women's empowerment. Seeing the blonde served as an affirmation that indeed women in their mid-twenties are lost and need to learn about themselves. As the goose bumps multiplied, I knew I needed to communicate my struggles to the rest of women my age. Often during my life, I had felt alone and misunderstood when struggling through personal issues. Now seeing this celebrity discussing her parallel conflicts, my entire essence lit up with excitement. Jude sat back from her pecan pancakes and smiled. "Well, looks like you've discovered something that truly makes you passionate, now, haven't you?"

Nodding my head, I began frantically scribbling down notes in my journal.

As we left Kansas, it was growing hotter and New Mexico hit us with a vengeance. We stopped for a couple of hours to cool off at a truck stop. We lounged in the upper level of the mini-mall, where truck drivers showered and watched television. We left there at dusk and continued on our journey. Although it was growing darker, the heat didn't let up. There was no wind.

Around 8:00 p.m. we decided to head out further toward our final destination of Sedona, Arizona. Refreshed from our afternoon head soaks, we climbed back into Cassidy, ready for more adventures.

Red clay colored by atmosphere
Temperatures that drop to chills at dark,
So creatures great and small
Can explore the territories once ruled
Predominantly by their ancestors of Darwin

♥   ♥   ♥

The following is an excerpt from my journal dated July 4, 2007.

Good morning. We now find ourselves in the heart of the most incredible energy vortex in the Sedona desert of Arizona (the middle of the planet).

Arriving last night down a windy mountain path was incredible as we took in the mass clusters of stars and energy, which were flowing freely through the atmosphere. Still learning about fear and containing it, I struggled last night as I allowed my creative imagination to take over as the energy vibes and foreign sounds were introduced to me. What is it about nighttime that makes me and my fears magnified times five million? It's unbelievable to realize how close I have become with Jude. Last night as I was whimpering, a simple rub on the back soothed my anxiety. Pretty cool!

Looking back upon our adventures thus far, I realize many people don't get our relationship at first, but once they realize the depth of it, there seems to be a slight hint of jealousy. It is a very magical experience to have a true friend, no matter what age, race, gender, and cultural background—someone who believes in you and has no underlying motives or ambitions.

♥   ♥   ♥

Indeed Sedona truly was magical. After a rather restless slumber, I awoke with feelings similar to those I had down in the Everglades National Park: extreme primal energies.

Glancing outside Cassidy's windows, I saw a jet black raven peering in from a telephone wire. "Caw, caw, caw," he called out in a morning greeting as though he was personally welcoming us to the Sedona desert. Magical vibes radiated as we made our way toward the main town center, on a quest for morning coffee.

We saw Spanish-style buildings and cobblestone roads. Finding a vibrant coffee shop, Jude and I stood in line awaiting our morning java. After a five-minute line, we were armed with our coffees and headed out onto the patio. The view from the patio was breathtaking: jagged rock formations created the backdrop as the sun beamed its healing rays across the blue sky. Vibrant purple flowers were scattered throughout the mountainsides and there was a hint of sweetness in the air.

Jude and I spent two hours simply vegetating on the patio and performing our daily tarot/angel readings. As Jude began discussing the many diverse animals and birds found within the desert, I felt a weird sensation come over my body. It was similar to the feelings I got when I didn't eat or was overwhelmed. Suddenly my attention span disappeared and I felt lightheaded. Stopping mid-sentence, Jude glanced over at me and shook her head. "You are probably starving right now, girl. You need to start paying attention to your body."

Awkwardly I allowed Jude to guide me through the cobblestone streets, searching for a restaurant. "Katie, I truly can't understand how you don't correlate between your body and your mind. You need to stop thinking with your mind and listen to your body. You need to eat to fuel your body and you right now. It's your mind screaming 'feed me.'"

Feeling embarrassed by my physical meltdown, I sunk into the cushy seats of the diner and ordered a huge breakfast.

Jude continued with her conversation. "Look, Katie, there's nothing you have to be embarrassed about. I am just making you aware of your own body. In order to be a healthy human being, you must focus on the four elements within:

- mental: mechanics for the body, mindfulness
- emotional: feelings from the heart
- physical: looking after the vessel; water, vitamins, food, and exercise
- spiritual: vibes directing (sensation)

"Now you have done all the aspects except for physical. If you intend on being a mother in the future, you definitely need to sort your own body out first. Don't worry; we will get to the bottom of this issue."

With that the waitress presented us our oversized meals. Within fifteen minutes I had digesting my food, my health returned instantly, giving color to my face. As Jude and I walked down the street, the intense rays of the sun baked our skin. Sensing it was too warm for a hike, Jude and I decided to leave Sedona and headed north toward the Grand Canyon.

♥   ♥   ♥

While we slowly wandered back in the direction of Cassidy, a slight beeping sound echoed in the background. A few paces later, the beeping grew to a loud honking car alarm. Jude looked over at me, silently inquiring if it was Cassidy, but I immediately shook my head. "Nah, it's not Cassidy, must be somebody else's vehicle."

About five minutes later, we arrived back at the original block where we had parked Cassidy. By this time the honking was ear-shattering and did appear to be coming from Cassidy's direction.

Feeling extremely foolish, I hurriedly approached the green minivan; indeed it was our vehicle making the entire racket. As I fumbled for the car keys, I frantically pushed the red panic button to end the noise pollution. No luck. Obnoxious honking still continued. Just as I was reaching to pull my hair out, Jude grabbed the car keys and diffused the situation. The honking ceased and tranquility returned again to the sunny streets of Sedona. "Nice work!" I called out to Jude while my nerves were being brought back to earth. Just then an old man poked his head out of a shop. "Ah, you ladies were the culprits behind the honking minivan. I was wondering what was going on. It was like that for at least five minutes."

Stopping in front of his store, we noticed freezing cool air streaming from within. Drawn by the appeal of air conditioning, we wandered in and allowed the old man to launch into his whole marketing speech about the Sedona desert. Picking up a brochure with a pink jeep on the cover, he proceeded to enlighten us about different tours of the desert we could experience while zipping around in a pink SUV.

Sensing my increasing boredom level, Jude cut the gentleman off. "You know, Al..." When she was in mid-sentence, Cassidy's alarm went off again, blaring loudly as ever. "We've got to be going," Jude called out from behind her shoulder as we attempted to stop Cassidy's crazy alarm system. As mentioned earlier, Cassidy seemed to possess magical qualities within her electric devices. She could sense particular energies and informed us when we need to stay or depart certain areas. Looking at Cassidy, I stated the obvious. "Well, it looks as though our decision has been made. Let's roll out of here." I was still feeling weak from the heat; Jude offered to drive north toward the Grande Canyon. By this point the temperature had hit 37 degrees Celsius and was holding strong. Despite the cold towel wrapped around my body, I still felt weak as we retreated away from Sedona and its incredible energy forces.

♥   ♥   ♥

Thirty minutes down the road, Cassidy began making all sorts of groans every time Jude turned a corner. Determining that Cassidy needed a break, Jude pulled into a nearby rest area in search of shade. Unsuccessful in the shade department, she parked Cassidy,

"No such luck!" Jude settled on a parking spot so even Cassidy could cool off.

We climbed out and walked over to the washrooms to get the towels wet again. We found a small shady area where I still felt woozy and lightheaded. Eyeing me, Jude expressed her opinion. "Don't allow your mind to take over, Katie. This is simple a task of mind over matter. Go beyond your mind, don't let panic set in."

Slowly nodding, I focused on visualizing swimming through a sparkling ocean, completely refreshed and cool. While I fixated on my visualization, Jude began chatting with a nearby girl who was standing under the tall trees for shade. "You are looking rather hot there," Jude expressed as the red-haired girl wobbled slightly. Within the blink of an eye, the little girl had fallen over, fainting from the heat. Out of the crowd, her father emerged asking what had happened. Jude explained to him the situation followed by a suggestion that she needed more water.

After the little girl came back to consciousness, I began thinking about what I had witnessed. My mind started racing. As I allowed paranoid thoughts of fainting and public embarrassment to wash over me, "mind over mater" echoed through as I considered Jude's earlier words of overcoming unpleasant situations. Sensing my distraught mental state, Jude walked over to me and gestured toward the parking lot. "Come on, kiddo. I think Cassidy has cooled off enough." Gingerly I stood on my feet and shuffled slowly toward the parking lot.

As the sun burned down, again I was reminded about global warming. I was smack dab in the middle of experiencing the effects of our sad state of affairs. Sweat beaded from every inch of my body as I crawled back to the van. Glimpses of the food chain popped into my mind as I contemplated how similar to an animal I felt at that moment. During such intense heat, the only topic plaguing my mind was survival.

Gone were the worries of the future and past or obsessive thoughts of old self-destructive behaviors. Water, shelter, and maintaining a cool body temperature were the only issues that mattered when driving in such intense heat spells. Humbled by the insignificance of my position in comparison to Mother Nature, I sat in silent reflection of the elements as Jude drove us farther down the windy Arizona highway.

♥   ♥   ♥

Forty-five minutes later, we found ourselves driving through Flagstaff, the capital city of Arizona. As the heat intensified into the mid-afternoon, I decided that I didn't want to travel toward the

Grande Canyon in such a weak physical condition. Pointing to a nearby motel, Jude turned left off the main highway and found a slightly shady patch to park under.

Fifteen minutes later we were lounging by the pool in complete bliss. It's incredible how quickly circumstances can shift and change if you are willing to keep an open mind. One minute I was cruising down the Arizona desert, suffering from heat exhaustion, and in the next moment I was happily floating in a pool, calm and refreshed.

Doesn't the universe work in wondrous ways?

Another teaching from Jude was the following:

"In order to live in a six-sensory life, you must be able to live outside the box, Katie. Every time you put constraints on a particular situation, you are working against natural flow of the universe. You must be able to allow events to take place when they are meant to take place. The more you allow universal laws to guide your life, the more satisfied you will feel."

♥   ♥   ♥

Here is another journal entry from my visit in the Flagstaff motel.

Ah, another affirmation! We were chilling off by the pool and I felt drawn to a woman swimming alone. I began chatting with her, and it turned out that she needed some warm words and a reality check in her life. It was beautiful to see such vulnerability as I witnessed the openness of a complete stranger discussing her issues. So magical. If I can do this every day for the rest of my life, I will be a happy camper in my endeavors and stronger in my belief and dreams. I am going to write this amazing tale of mentorship and tell people how belief in myself is the most important gift I have even given myself.

Upon reflection I realize I was still trying to make other people understand me. I still hadn't grasped the concept that it didn't matter what anyone thought about my actions or how they judged them. The only opinion that mattered was my own. This was yet another tragic example of searching outward instead of inward for acceptance.

The following morning Jude and I awoke feeling suffocated and clammy. At some point during the night the air conditioning had kicked off, creating a stuffy, smelly atmosphere. Since we had been living in Cassidy for nearly a month, we had grown accustomed to plenty of fresh air at nighttime. Despite the fact that we slept on a lumpy futon mattress, our sleeping outdoors was great in comparison to the few times we splurged on motel rooms. Stale air and trapped energy didn't seem to agree with us.

Over the past few days, Jude had begun a new awareness in me. It was a check she did every morning with my feelings and sensations or vibes.

Journal excerpt, July 5

What is going on? So I woke up this morning with feelings I couldn't identify. Try as I might, something was amiss. Jude encouraged me to explore deeper, and I realized that despite my efforts to set and create boundaries with my parents, they are still resorting back to previous thought patterns of minimizing their emotions and remaining uncommunicative. Also my frustration lies within myself for allowing this malarkey to have gone on for as long as it has. Sorrow rushed over me as I reflected upon my life, family, loved ones, and that a woman I have known such a short amount of time knows more of my essence and what I stand for than my family does. How did this come about? Even discussing it now, I feel a lightness as the issue becomes smaller and my feelings of anger and sadness ooze out of my body and I look forward to another day of freedom and clarity. Please send us where we are meant to be. So far the morning has consisted of rescuing a ladybug and sending her back!

♥   ♥   ♥

Taking one final dip, I headed toward Cassidy and prepared to set off into the sweltering heat. Driving through Flagstaff, Jude and I decided to stop and explore the town. Setting foot out into the new surroundings, I was instantly charmed by the cute setting; bright colorful mystic shops lined the streets as we decided on a coffee shop.

The first step was a spiritual store where I instantly felt a connection with a twelve-year-old girl who was looking at fairy figurines.

As we contemplated which fairy was the most magical, I felt myself zooming back to being twelve years old again, when wondrous discoveries were found in the most simplistic forms. Moving beyond my awkward barriers of human interactions, I kept chatting with her, and it felt fabulous to relate with her.

After departing the store, I asked Jude if I seemed awkward. "I just don't know how to behave around younger girls. I always get self-conscious."

Jude smiled and responded, "Just be yourself, Katie. Kids can sense your nervousness, but once communication happens between both parties, then it is human qualities that soften the moment and you will automatically relax. Please take a breath. It will calm you down. Remember yourself at twelve years of age and trust me, interaction will be memorable."

When I understood the information given, we continued our investigation of what the main street offered. Gentle music drifted out onto the street, beckoning passersby to stop in for a visit.

♥   ♥   ♥

KELLY

Ah, Kelly. Thinking about him brings a smile across my face. His radiant spirit and kind heart shone similar to the bright stars within the Arizona desert. While Jude and I roamed the streets of Flagstaff, Arizona, we were drawn toward a spiritual shop called Sacred Rites. Soul-soothing flute sounds drifted out, beckoning pedestrians to sneak a peek within. As Jude asked about his musical talents, Kelly disclosed he had known his entire life he was meant to share the gift of music. His father had come to him in a dream, holding up a flute symbolizing his desire for his son to continue the musical tradition within the family. Kelly's natural ability was undeniably a true gift from the universe. Further along in their conversation, Kelly mentioned a recent video he had viewed from the United Nations Conference in Rio de Janeiro. An incredibly conscious girl from Vancouver was speaking about her opinions of everything from cancerous salmon to impoverished children, Kelly offered to show us the video clip and eagerly we agreed.

As the passionate twelve-year-old spoke her angry truth to global politicians, I could feel the emotions in my body. Unable to hold back any longer, I allowed my tears to flow as I truly felt touched by her speech. In the past I would never have shown my sorrow, fearing public embarrassment. Now I simply don't give a rat's ass! By crying in public, I was allowing others to feel comfortable to do the same.

Kelly spotted my tears and instantly gave me a fantastic, comforting bear hug. What an unbelievable lesson this was: I showed my true emotions and a stranger accepted them with compassion and love. Too cool!

As we left the store, I sent out a universal thank you for having been sent to Kelly. He served as another example of a beautiful spirit using his gifts to instill peace and serenity during such scary, unpredictable times.

♥   ♥   ♥

As Jude and I emerged from Sacred Rites, our coffee cravings could not be denied any longer. Spotting a funky coffee shop across the street, we darted through bicycle traffic and entered the old store. The aroma of dark, roasted beans and freshly baked treats greeted us as we took our place in the long winding line. Once we had acquired our two beverages (plus one tasty brownie!) we began sniffing out a table to sit at. The place was packed and Jude and I soon discovered that a table was simply out of the question.

Using her creative imagination, Jude grabbed a nearby stool and transformed it into our very own personal coffee table. As we started people-watching, a woman behind us cleared her throat.

"Excuse me, ladies. I'm terribly sorry. I was so involved in my taxes I didn't notice you didn't have a spot to sit at. Please, you are more than welcome to join me."

With that the attractive red-haired lady shifted her colossal pile of paperwork off the table and into her briefcase. Upon informal introduction, we learned that she was originally from Scotland and currently lived in Flagstaff. A writer, Kathy went on to explain that her father and little sister were out visiting from Scotland and were having several issues with the sweltering heat. "You know, it's not normally like this. These past few years temperatures have been soaring to new highs." While Kathy started shaking her head, an older man and teenaged girl walked through the front door. "Oh, Dad, over here." Kathy waved and motioned for the duo to approach the table. With a mischievous twinkle in his eyes, the older gentleman advanced toward our table.

In a fabulously thick Scottish accent, he introduced himself as William and his daughter Felicity. "Well, I don't know about you ladies, but I most certainly can't stand this heat."

After explaining we came from Canada, his wise old eyes widened.

"Well, then you girls know exactly what I'm talking about! Scotland never receives such crazy weather." Instantly William felt like a comfortable old sweater with his fatherly demeanor and kind spirit.

Within five minutes Jude had nicknamed him Billy, and the two commenced a discussion pertaining to old Scots living in the Canadian prairies. Looking across the table, I noticed Felicity sitting quietly, observing the conversation. Watching her, I automatically was reminded about myself at her age. Being raised an only child, I had often found myself at a table of adults, bored beyond comprehension. Leaping to conclusions, I assumed that Felicity felt the same boredom and I proceeded to chat with her. It turned out she had spotted an adorable puppy outside but was too shy to approach the owners. I agreed to go with her, and we both kneeled down and petted the adorable chocolate lab puppy. For the second time in one morning, I had connected with teenaged girls who reminded me of getting back to basics.

Thirty minutes later, after promising us a home in Scotland, Billy, Kathy, and Felicity prepared to leave. Jude swore on her morning coffee, agreeing to go visit Billy on his Scottish soil.

Invigorated from our magical visit in Flagstaff, Jude and I wandered around for an additional hour before deciding to head toward the great Grand Canyon. Along the drive north of Flagstaff, I could sense a microscopic shift in my energy. Unsure of the reason why, I continued driving and ignored the nagging feeling. Desert heat enveloped us as I witnessed scorching hot energy vibrating off the pavement.

"They sure were a nice family," Jude disclosed with her usual foot out the passenger window.

Nodding in agreement, I interjected my opinion. "Yeah, they certainly were and the daughter Felicity reminded me a lot of myself at her age."

Curious about my statement, Jude glanced over in my direction. "Oh really? How so?"

I responded, "Well, when I was growing up I often was placed in scenarios where I was surrounded by adults and often grew very bored by their discussions. Watching Felicity today brought me back to those days."

Jude shook her head slightly and responded, "There you go again, Katie; you are creating assumptions based on your own personal experiences. How do you know she was bored? Due to the fact that she has an older father, she is bound to be extremely accustomed to these circumstances. Not every little girl is similar to you."

Biting my lip, I knew Jude was right again. It had been customary for me to project my feelings on others, and I was barely aware I was doing it. As the desert heat intensified to 39 degrees Celsius, I resolved to pay attention on my personal projections upon others.

Around forty-five miles south of the Grand Canyon, Jude and I entered into the Wapiti National Mountain Range, spectacular canyons in the middle of nowhere. Ready for a break, I pulled Cassidy off the road and parked her in a dusty lot. Careful to avoid over exerting myself, I slowly walked over to the viewpoint. On the way to the vista, I saw that many local artisans and craft-makers had set up booths selling their latest and greatest creations. Silver jewelry, dream catchers, and semiprecious stones were all on display as Jude and I made our way through the assortment of vendors.

Reaching the very hot tent, we stopped to admire the intricate beadwork displayed. A girl eight years of age approached us and began explaining the different meanings behind each animal in the beaded jewelry.

"Hey, did you ladies know what? According to our folklore, the turtles are the most sacred symbols representing internal life. If you look on his back, you will see the swirling lines, indicating ancient wisdom."

As she disclosed this information, I could see Jude's eyes sparkling as she prepared her response. "Now that's some interesting information, little one. See, according to my folklore and beliefs, the spider is the most sacred symbol due to their ability to survive in any type of severe conditions. Throughout the ages, the spider has managed to endure, making her the symbol of internal life."

Watching both Jude and the little girl was interesting as they stated their different beliefs. "My name is Candice and my mom makes all of this jewelry," she proudly stated while running her fingers across the table.

Jude introduced us and told Candice that her mother made beautiful creations. As I watched the mother and daughter interact, I found it very heartwarming. They regarded one another as equals—as teammates in the game of life. Candice's mom had taught her about their ancestral heritage, and she was proudly sharing it with people she met. Sensing very radiant energy from the two, I suddenly resolved that I wanted to purchase a dream catcher from them. When I informed Candice of my plans, her eyes lit up and she led me toward the handcrafted inventions. After a few moments of agonizing over my decisions, I choose a black one with red, orange, and yellow star beads.

"I added the star beads," Candice explained, her bright brown eyes shining in the sun. Realizing I didn't have my wallet, I turned back and explained to the duo that I would return with money shortly.

Fifty meters away from Candice's booth was the phenomenal view of a deep, ancient canyon. Jude and I slowly climbed down the rocks and found ourselves standing on a steep cliff guarded by very flimsy fencing.

Out in front of us were gorgeous red clay formations that exuded old age and many wrinkle lines. *If only those rocks could speak,* I imagined as I breathed in the silent vibrations emanating from the earth. *I know they would have so many words of wisdom to share.* Contemplating the advice ancient Arizona rocks would provide, I cocked my head to one side and prepared for answers.

"Helloooooooooo" was the response I received. Turning my head to the right, I saw Jude yelling out greetings into the canyon. "Is anybody out thererererererer."

Smiling, I decided to fellow suit: "Echooooooooooo."

The sound resonated across the canyon and beyond. As the sound faded across the desert, I felt woozy and decided to wobble my way over to a nearby shelter for shade. Concerned, Jude followed in my tracks and gave me her hat. "Let's move out of this heat, kiddo!" As I tried to visualize cool breezes flowing through me, we gradually found our way back to Cassidy through the canvas tents and artisan displays. Weakly grabbing my purse, I started back to Candice's booth to purchase the magical dream catcher.

"You sure you want to walk back, Katie? I can go if you want."

Ever stubborn and bullheaded, I responded that I didn't need any help and continued trekking into the scorching heat. After what seemed like a million hours, finally I approached Candice's booth.

"I hope you enjoy it and have a great drive out toward the canyon."

Admiring my new purchase, I thanked her for enlightening our day with such insightful wisdom and warmth. Trudging back to the van, I tried to prevent my mind from controlling my body.

♥   ♥   ♥

As the heat intensified, hot moisture beads dropped off my brow. I slipped into animal mode, taking tiny steps to maintain my depleting energy levels. Survival mode popped into my mind while I dug deep into myself and charged forward, understanding how the prehistoric dinosaurs must have felt. I reached Cassidy ready to re-hydrate and take a seat.

Hopping into the driver's seat, I stepped on the gas pedal and headed out into the long stretch of road. Hot air blasted through the open windows while we focused on staying positive. After ten minutes of driving, Jude and I stopped talking in feeble efforts to save energy.

Around suppertime, we arrived at the gates surrounding the Grand Canyon. Excited to experience one the world's greatest wonders, we grabbed an information map and headed into the park.

First stop was called Great Viewpoint, and it certainly was. Approaching the lookout, I felt speechless and truly absorbed the magnificent energy bouncing through the atmosphere. The huge canyon opened up in front of us and seemed to expand beyond imaginable horizons. Jude and I weaved our way through the many tourists and staff till we reached the end of the lookout.

A lone hawk floated above us as he serenely surveyed the scene below. Allowing myself a huge breath, I breathed in the incredible clean-smelling air in such glorious surroundings.

Standing alone, I felt entirely complete as I expressed my gratitude out toward the universe. Over the past few weeks, I had been so consumed with my own selfish behaviors I had neglecting to direct attention toward the higher energy source.

Making her way toward me, Jude nodded in the direction of the parking lot. "There's just so many people here, it makes it hard to truly appreciate the entire grandeur of the landscape."

As we returned to the car, I quickly darted into a nearby washroom and soaked my towel with cool water in order to keep cool. Jude had invented a unique system that involved a wet towel and baseball hat. I must admit on those hot desert days, I truly fell in love with the concept.

For the next hour we journeyed through the canyon, stopping at various lookouts along the way. Each view was increasingly spectacular as we traveled westward through the canyon. Throughout our explorations, the lone hawk still soared, adding a primal sensation to the experience.

Leaving the Grand Canyon, I felt sad. Despite the heat, our day had been so magical, from Sedona's vibrant energy source to the majestic grandeur of ancient rock formations.

Deep down I knew we had to move forward, but I still felt sorrow for leaving such pristine beauty.

♥   ♥   ♥

Later that evening Jude and I hit the Arizona road heading west. As we flew past bunches of tumbleweeds and prickly cactus, a light bulb sparkled, illuminating our visit to Niagara-on-the-Lake. It had felt glorious to release old memories by burning items near the lake. At that time, I had recalled old photo albums containing memories of Stephen. Wanting to cleanse myself of the old relationship, I had inquired if burning them would be appropriate.

Jude had contemplated the question, and then responded, "No, don't burn them, Katie. This was your old love. If I might make a suggestion, bury them in the desert. That way they will return back to the earth gradually, not as severe as burning them."

Understand her point, I had resolved to wait until the desert to release Stephen's memory. As we drove into a glorious sunset, I decided to stop the van. It was time.

Grabbing the old photo album of our travels and an old journal he had given me, I clambered down the embankment and started digging a hole in the sand. Reaching wet sand, I stopped my burrowing. Placing the album in the hole, I said a prayer expressing my desire to release Stephen from my mind and wish him happiness in the future. Just as I placed the last load of sand over the album, one lone bird flew over head away from the sunset.

Jude gave me a big hug while I truly felt a release from old ties. Having her there was so wonderful; knowing that I had a friend who supported my endeavors. As we drove toward California, my self-worth grew. I knew that I was truly an independent woman learning to be herself.

This is a poem I wrote on the Queen Charlotte Islands in September 2007 when I had finally resolved the finality of our relationship.

STEVEN

One lone path inseparable by nature,
Now a pitchfork with two separate travelers questing after different
missions
One has chosen that of gold and greed
In hopes that one day enough will be enough
The other, in search of universal truths
Hoping one day to spread wisdom to little ones
Eyes wide open to new ideas and concepts
Though no one's fault our paths have parted
And never will either wanderer
Head back to the well for one last drink
The charts have been drawn
Destiny made
And the heart that once beat as one
Now is two separate entities searching for their truth

Goodbye

♥   ♥   ♥

That morning we were found ourselves two hours east of
California. Starting Cassidy, I couldn't believe my eyes. At 8:43 a.m.
the temperature gauge read 34 degrees Celsius—34 degrees at eight
thirty in the morning!

Sighing heavily, I anticipated another heat-induced battle as we
headed forth on our journey.

Two hours down the road, the temperature had climbed to 43
degrees. Yikes! Barely able to concentrate on the road, I requested
Jude inform me the moment she saw any body of water whatsoever.
At that point, I was willing to take a puddle! Spotting a sign for a
nearby marina, I turned off the exit and attempted to locate the body
of water.

Twenty minutes later we still remained waterless. Desperate to
find water, I pulled over at a local hotel and offered to pay them for

their pool services. Shaking her head, the lady broke my heart. As I was on the verge of a meltdown, the lady behind the desk piped up. "We can't allow you to use the pool services, but there is a marina five minutes from here." Thrilled at this juicy piece of information, I encouraged her to continue.

"Well, you just follow the road back through town, hang a right and continue till you reach the marina. There will be a golf course on your left and fast food outlets on the right. Just keep following the road until you reach the marina. Have fun and try to stay cool."

After thanking her for this godsend, I zipped back to Cassidy and proceeded to drive in the direction of promised water. Fifteen minutes later Jude and I arrived at the fantastic marina. (It wasn't actually that fantastic, but at that point a puddle would have been classed as fantastic!)

Parking Cass in the shade, I quickly glimpsed up to check the temperature: Gadzooks! 46 degrees! I couldn't believe it! Never in all my days had I experienced anything like it. Slowly Jude and I made our way over to the swimming beach. Rows upon rows of motorboats all sat on the shore as their owners fumbled around trying to determine how to move them.

Stoked at the idea of cold water, Jude and I skipped down to the water's edge. Putting my big toe in, I felt the frigid coolness travel through my body. "Whoa Nelly, it's chilly," I announced to Jude, who was standing behind me. After about four seconds of contemplation, I submerged my inferno of a body underwater and felt my core temperature dropping. Retreating back to a lovely patch of shade, Jude and I stayed stationary all day, not daring to venture out in the epic heat wave.

The following is a journal entry I had written while under the shady trees of the Colorado River:

So we have hit the most insane heat. It was 46 degrees and hence we stopped our travels to stay by a riverside. I awoke this morning with feelings of sadness mixed in as an underlying theme. Last night

I buried the last memories of Stephen in the Arizona desert and blessed them as the sun set behind the horizon. It was such a magical moment and I am so grateful to have Jude to share it with. I wished him love and released any hold I had, and during the process a bird flew overhead. So cool. I truly do not want him to be held down by me, and I wish for his happiness. I know I did the right thing, but I do have feelings of sadness this morning and still do now. I swear it would be easier if we couldn't talk but could instead merely communicate through eyes and body language, which is essentially what we do anyway. It's awesome to feel that the universe has my back as we find ourselves in yet another perfect setting given the circumstances. I swear there is a little fellow behind the curtain watching over the journey, like in *The Wizard of Oz*.

I am also discovering that all my wishes come true, which is pretty spectacular. Earlier this afternoon I had wished to go on a boat ride, and sure enough, a man offered me a ride! Pretty cool.

As I mentioned, I was discovering that once I projected a specific thought process out into the atmosphere, it was miraculously delivered. I am by no means a scientist, but this knowledge was rather groundbreaking. Another discovery about universal studies was that once I had learned a particular skill or tool, the universe would inevitably test me on my competency. The boat ride was a perfect example of being completely congruent within myself and truly check in with my vibes prior to accepting offers.

During our day near the river, an older gentleman offered me a boat ride. Throwing my intuition aside, I hopped on without even a second to check out my vibes. Sure enough, as we zoomed around the river, I didn't feel quite right.

Several hours after the first boat ride, the same man offered a second ride. Once again ignoring my vibes, I hopped on and still felt off. True to form, at the end of the Seadoo ride, the man turned around and asked me to put sunscreen on his nose.

Flabbergasted by such a wacky suggestion, I managed to sputter out "I beg your pardon?" in hopes of evading the strange request. Unfortunately the man simply repeated his statement and I consented begrudgingly. Feeling mortified and embarrassed, I quickly returned to the safety of our towels. Unable to look Jude in the eyes, I fidgeted with the towel. Devoid of judgment, Jude inquired why I had gone on the Seadoo ride. "Because I really wanted to and I thought it would be fun," I responded, trying to defend my silly actions.

"And did you have fun?" she asked.

Shaking my head, I responded, "No, not really." Waving her arm, Jude gestured for me to continue. "Once we returned back to the shore, he asked me to put sunscreen on his nose, which made me feel really uncomfortable."

Jude followed up, "Then why didn't you say no, Katie?"

Raising my eyebrows, I responded, "I don't know. I felt bad because he had given me a ride and therefore I thought I needed to reciprocate."

Jude answered, "I can understand your desire to go for a boat ride, but had you trusted your vibes, you could have avoided the entire situation. Think about it. You really put yourself in danger. You are still so trusting of strangers, Katie; you need to realize that bad things can happen. I didn't want to tell you, but I was worried about you. There are certain things you must consider when accepting offers from complete strangers? Okay?"

Eyes full of care, she waited for my response. "I get that. I do. I will be more mindful of trusting strangers. Promise."

Upon reflection I realize my instant trust of complete strangers had stemmed from my desire for attention. If I felt I didn't receive enough attention from my parents, I would actively search outward for approval and acceptance. Instead of loving myself, I looked externally for others to give me what I thought I was missing.

♥   ♥   ♥

Similar to African animals on the Sahara, Jude and I rested all day at the watering hole, cooling ourselves down every twenty minutes. Around 6:30 that evening, the temperature had finally dropped to a tolerable 40 degrees. Braving the elements, we went out in search of supper.

Spotting a Mexican joint, we turned in and made a mad dash for the front door. Cool air conditioning greeted us as we made our way to the front counter. Suddenly I remembered I wasn't wearing any pants and grew very self-conscious. I sheepishly looked over at Jude. She nonchalantly shrugged her shoulders as if to say "Who cares?" Adopting her carefree attitude, I ordered my bean burritos and sat down, proud to be pant-less in public. Starving from heat-zapping energy, Jude and I wolfed down our Mexican meals effortlessly. Just then, the front door bell chimed and I looked up to see who was entering. Two large men with baseball caps breezed in and took a seat across from us. The older fellow with white hair sat across the aisle from us and began fanning himself,

"Sure is hotter than the hounds of hell out there," he drawled in a thick Texan accent.

Amused by his demeanor, I answered, "Yup, sure is. Me and my friend spent the entire day lounging by the Colorado River, not daring to drive in such heat."

Nodding, the old guy continued, "Ah, a river, you girls found a river. Tell me all about it."

Smiling, I disclosed how fantastically cold the water had been and talked about the shady willow trees that sheltered us from the sunshine. Several minutes later, his partner appeared with their burrito dinner. Through mouthfuls of taco and salsa, the man introduced himself as Joe, and his friend, Charlie.

Their lighthearted humor and goofy stories entertained us for more than an hour as Jude and I awaited the coolness of nightfall. Switching topics, Joe began a tale that included guns and shooting. Joe continued by stating that he had indeed shot a man several years back. Immediately I went into judgment as I created my own conclusions. Just as I was drawing a bad opinion of Joe, he mentioned the fact that he shot the man because he had been robbing old people. As quick as my judgments had flared up, they had been put back in their places.

Upon reflection I realize I used to judge very harshly and quickly. I would create instant impressions and cement them into my mind. As I was traveling with Jude, she was teaching me about acceptance and non-judgmental thinking. That night in the restaurant was a great lesson for me; I had been shown the other side of the story. Indeed

Joe had shot a man, BUT he had done it to protect old people. I was learning that life is definitely not the black-and-white portrait I had painted it as. No sirree Bob! It indeed consisted of a whole variety of colors from cherry red to emerald green.

Two hours after our magical meeting with the charming Texan truck drivers, Jude and I decided to venture into the great outdoors. Bidding the delightful Joe and Charlie adieu, we left satisfied after having met such jolly souls. Still hot enough to fry an egg on the pavement, the Arizona sun was definitely showing no mercy.

Being the warriors we were, we plodded forward through the desert into shimmering heat. Around 11:00 p.m. the atmosphere cooled off and we stopped at a dirty town to rest for the night. Leaving the doors open, I reflected on the day and all the wondrous lessons I was learning from simply living life. I could feel so many changes within my entire essence that at times I wondered who I was—not in a bad way, just an inquisitive way. I had lived my entire life allowing others to dictate to me who I was, what I liked, didn't like, etc.

Looking in the rear-view mirror, my green eyes stared back at me. The underlying hints of childhood sadness were slowly being replaced by vibrant hope for a new future—a future I created for myself. After we turned out the lights for bed, I gazed out into the Universe illuminated by bright twinkling stars. Finding the brightest one, I whispered that I wished Jude and I would write a fantastic book that educated other women about the life lessons I had been learning. The star winked back and goose bumps covered my overheated body. I guess the Universe truly was paying attention.

♥　　　　　♥　　　　　♥

California was cooler than Arizona, which made our drive westward effortless in comparison. Managing to avoid LA, we headed north through overcast clouds of San Francisco. Although we had bypassed LA, smog and pollution still filtered into Cassidy.

Taking a deep breath, I could feel tiny particles of chemical and toxic waste drift into my lungs. Shaking my head, I wondered how millions of people could inhabit such an unhealthy environment.

Given that both Jude and I are Vancouver Island girls, we couldn't wait till we could place our toes in to the Pacific Ocean. It was just past 3:00 p.m. when we finally caught our first waft of salty ocean air.

A half an hour later, Cassidy pulled into a sandy parking lot, preparing to say hello to the glorious waves. As I was running to the sea, my heart sank as I saw what was ahead. Orange foam covered the ocean's surface while plastic garbage plagued the sandy beach area. My visions of a beautiful west-coast scene were rapidly destroyed as I took in the polluted surroundings. In addition to witnessing the dirty scene, I felt heavy sadness that decided to land on top of my shoulders. Wandering down the beach, I quickly checked my vibes, who responded, "You feel as though you are a failure to your parents and ultimately yourself. As you approach closer to Victoria, you are feeling as though you have been a huge disappointment. You are also saddened by this realization that you don't want to see your parents. In the past, you looked forward to visiting home, but now you are realizing how much you have grown. Old friendships have been outgrown and you feel a disconnection with your hometown and ultimately your old self."

Agreeing with this information, I felt much better. Since learning that all my answers were located within, I adored that I could uncover my personal truths whenever I so desired. After several minutes of roaming around the polluted beach, Jude and I quickly grew fed up with the depressing landscape. Pulling away from the beach, we continued driving north.

♥   ♥   ♥

Approaching the surf town of Santa Cruz, I announced that I would enjoy a pit stop to cruise (pardon the pun!) and explore the boardwalk. Parking in the heart of downtown, Jude and I grabbed our sunglasses; out to explore what forms of trouble we could find.

After forty-five minutes of wandering, we found ourselves peering out at a crowded boardwalk complete with an adjacent amusement park and vendors. As we walked along the vibrant boardwalk, I couldn't help but notice how many people were perched with fishing poles in their arms. Far in the distance, a volleyball game was well underway while a large crowd cheered their support.

Noticing a flash in the sky, I focused my eyes and concentrated on the flying object. A flock of pelicans were leisurely cruising through the air, on the lookout for potential dinner. The moment they spotted an attractive fish, they would cease flight and drop rapidly down into the ocean, eagerly searching for supper. The entire process was very entertaining and kept us preoccupied for a few moments.

Watching the pellis plunge and soar, I imagined what life would be through the eyes of a bird. It must be incredible to fly effortlessly along the shoreline, playing with the wind and ocean. It also must be nice to simply focus on one task at a time and not obsess or concern yourself with future plans or destiny.

Ah, to be a pelican, I thought while admiring their agile method of hunting.

Pointing to the beach volleyball game, Jude suggested we check it out. Nodding in agreement, I followed her toward the sandy courts. Though the heat didn't compare to Arizona, I still felt energy drainage as we stood watching the game. After twenty minutes of watching the tanned, toned women exert their force on the courts, I suggested we continue our trek down the beach.

As Jude and I were walking toward the amusement park, I felt woozy lightheaded; identical to my feelings in Sedona, Arizona. Unable to conceal my sketchy symptoms from Jude, I stated that I wanted to find some food. Sighing, Jude responded, "Well, come on, kid. Let's get you some food."

Entering an over-stimulating arcade, I tried to relax. No such luck! Bright lights and screaming kids made relaxing impossible as I frantically searched for a pop machine. A loud whirring sound blasted behind me and I felt surges of adrenaline jolt through my body. Sensing my silent meltdown, Jude grabbed my elbow and led me out into fresh air.

"Seriously, Katie. You have got to pay attention to your inner body. You are a tall girl; you need to eat adequate amounts of nutrients and minerals to nourish yourself. Save yourself before anyone else. Just remember, you have lofty dreams of saving the world. Let's focus on getting you healthy before you quest off into the sunset with your sword blazing."

Humbled by the thought of my quest off into the sunset, I followed Jude as she directed me toward a neighboring Greek restaurant. At this point I had allowed my ego out of her box and she preceded tap-dancing on my nerves.

Whispering fears of public embarrassment and ridicule, I soon grew panicky and very scattered. Hanging onto the hard wooden counter, I weakly managed to squeak out an order of falafel and ginger ale. Seven minutes later, I glanced down at my empty plate of pita crumbs. Relief washed over me as my ego was forced back into her box. Essential minerals were absorbed into my body and my system felt as though it had just experienced a fill-up. As my energy level returned, we left the restaurant and headed toward the town. Jude talked more about my patterns.

"I've been thinking. I realize you need certain levels of energy to maintain your rapid metabolism. But there seems to be a sugar issue as well. Perhaps you have low blood sugar levels and need insulin to regulate yourself. I would suggest getting a blood test once we are back in Canada."

Mulling over the new piece of information, I hoped we would get to the bottom of my health issues rapidly.

The following is journal entry from July 10:

I have to say it's pretty scary having health issues. This process is painstakingly hard and I can understand why people don't embark on personal transformations all the time. Living in a van is testing me beyond my realms of even thinking and I am charging through, but I am also feeling that I really want to be in a little cottage surrounded by trees, writing the book.

Upon reflection I realize I was manifesting physical symptoms due to my suppression of emotions. In the past I had experienced similar symptoms of anxiety, but I had simply believed I had an anxiety disorder without recognizing underlying feelings they manifested into anxiety. Had I taken time to soul-search and be truly honest with myself, I would have discovered that anger and sadness were ever-present in my subconscious mind.

Unfortunately, in the past, whenever I inexperienced either anger or sadness, I would instantly shut it off for fear of getting angry. Years of unhealthy suppression led to physical symptoms manifesting themselves such as heart palpitations, fainting spells, or feelings of being overwhelmed.

But of course, I would feel overwhelmed, dear Watson. I was suppressing my true feelings for years; they were bound to eventually explode out of my body somehow. Other common symptoms of suppression of denial include:

1) Stomach ulcers
2) Weight fluctuation
3) Panic attacks
4) Heart murmur
5) Little to no attention span
6) Scattered or discombobulated thought process

Due to my wavering health conditions, Jude took over as lead driver through the Californian freeway. One hour north of San Francisco, Jude pulled off onto a state rest area. Surrounded by old growth trees, this was best area yet! Radiating off a West Coast vibe, the territory had a Vancouver Island feel about it. Burning cedar incense and playing our new CD courtesy of Kelly, I feel asleep feeling completely calm and relaxed. Ah the magic of the forest.

♥   ♥   ♥

By mid-afternoon the Californian countryside had transformed into the rugged coastline of Oregon. Steep cliffs and crashing waves were introduced as we cruised into the southern part of Oregon. Overhead a flock of gray seagulls drifted past, squawking their salute. My stomach started growling and I commenced scanning the small coastal villages for a diner.

"ORGANIC FARM FOODS AND HERBS" read a wooden sign out to the right.

"Interesting, very interesting," I expressed as we walked into the small diner, complete with cozy couches and a health food store in the back. A tall, lanky man in his forties appeared at our table and asked for our orders. Fresh gazpacho soup and veggie burgers were the selected items, and the man disappeared behind the counter to prepare our feast.

During the wait, I wandered around the store, investigating the nearby bookshelves. Spiritual enlightenment, natural foods, and yoga principles were all popular topics of the books. Fascinated with a Good Health article related to Kundalini yoga, I pulled it off the shelf and brought it over to our table. As I flipped through the pages, I happened to stop on a chapter discussing spiritual mentorship. Intrigued, I briefly scanned through the paragraphs.

"Often when a student is first starting out upon their spiritual path, they have one-on-one teachings from a mentor. During such time, they may struggle with feelings of lost identify and completely allowing the process to unfold. This process may last months as students are still become accustomed to their new perspective."

Agreeing with the passage, I passed the book over for Jude to read. While she was reading the excerpts, the tall gentleman arrived with our scrumptious-looking West Coast lunch. Since we had left Montreal, the restaurant food had been heavy and greasy. So you can imagine the glee I felt when fresh, clean soup made with organic ingredients arrived.

As I was digging in, my taste buds danced the jig on my tongue while my stomach sang songs of happiness. After licking the plate clean (seriously, I did), I wondered over to the health food store to check out their products.

A pleasant-looking woman stood behind the counter and expressed her desire to help. Remembering my recent troubles with blood sugar levels, I asked her if she knew any natural remedies. Wrinkling her nose, the woman pondered for a second and reached below the counter. Using all her arm muscle, she hoisted an epic-sized book onto the counter, introducing it as *The Natural Home Remedy Book*.

Locating the appropriate section, she cleared her throat and announced, "Yup, it's all in here and all you need for your sugar levels is chlorin nacinate, which we happen to have." Delighted there was a natural remedy for my condition, I purchased the pills as well as licorice treats. As I made my way out of the diner, my unsettling and anxious feeling returned.

Leaving the restaurant, Jude instantly recognized my symptoms. "Not feeling well, are you? You know, I can see when your energy levels get depleted. It often occurs when you are in a conversation with people for long periods of time when they are talking at you. Just remember, breath and relax. Don't hold your breath." Frustrated at myself for getting scketcharoo, I rolled down the window and let the cool air ground me.

♥   ♥   ♥

Coastline stretched for miles in front of us as we traveled north along the ocean. Massive rocks extended from the sea past the highway and created the feeling of primal days. Seagulls and cormorants flew by and allowed the blustery wind to carry them away beyond the horizon.

Nightfall came and we found ourselves in Coos Bay, a coastal fishing village that had a very touristy vibe. After munching on some slimy french fries, I turned on the computer to check out our e-mail account. Jude and I had received a message from Charlie, the charming Texan truck driver. He was checking in to see how life was going for the Canadian writers and what our book was going to be about. I responded back with the following reply:

"Hey! Charlie. Nice to hear from you. The book we are writing is about women's spirituality and their needs to learn about their own power. I'm really looking forward to writing it and promise to send you a copy. Take care, Katie and Judy."

Jude reread the message and looked over at me. "Katie, you do realize the book is going to be written from your perspective, don't you? Why did you write it expressing it is women in general?"

Growing instantly defensive, I replied, "I was just writing a broad statement. I fully intend on writing the book from my perceptive." Feeling tension mounting, I prepared for a conflict. Jude continued, "Katie, the only person you can write about is yourself. When you include other people, it sounds like judgment and that you are laying blame on others. Again, don't look externally; it's within you that the truth lies. Oh yeah, french fries late at night are horrendous on your digestion."

Angered by her words, I leapt out of the van and shouted, "Look, I do not need to hear you tell me how to write the book. I will write it just how I want to. And I will eat french fries whenever I want to."

And with that I stormed off for a walk to cool off my nerves. Upon reflection I realize there were several things going on that evening. For starters, I was revealing my ego in a book. My ego was trying desperately to protect my persona. For years I had been hiding behind a mask of false pride, and my ego hated the idea of me exposing my true self. Another issue was that I still viewed Jude as a mother figure. Though consciously I knew she wasn't my mother, subconsciously I was still resisting her words.

As I roamed around Coos Bay, I began asking myself why I had reacted in such a dramatic fashion. How could I turn from a calm, even demeanor to frightfully angry in the matter of three seconds? I realized that I still had residual anger within and needed to get a handle on it. Barking at Jude simply was not appropriate. Looking back, I feel very ashamed for the behavior I exhibited toward her.

Here was this woman, excited for new adventures, stuck in a van with me, having to be the victim of my bubbling anger spells. Tail between my legs, I returned to Miss Cassidy and Miss Jude and tried to fall asleep. Try as I might, my obsessive mind refused to shut off and I lay awake the majority of the night, worrying about minor issues. I still marvel at how I could create such mountains out of pebbles. If there was a trophy for overactive worriment manifestation for nothing, I would be queen bee!

♥   ♥   ♥

Morning breakfast was tense as we sat in silence; instead of admitting my wrongdoings, I maintained my icy disposition, attempting to make some sort of point. (Please don't ask me what!) Self-oppression continued through the morning as we drove toward Eugene, the capital city of Oregon.

At lunchtime Jude declared that she wanted to stop for a coffee and to check the computer for e-mail messages. As we neared the shop, I started feeling strange and off-kilter. Once we settled into the cozy chairs at the corner table, Jude booted up the computer. Curious to check my e-mail account, I anxiously waited while Jude conducted her business.

Several minutes later, she passed the laptop over to me with the Hotmail page open. Eagerly I opened the inbox and studied its contents. The old unopened e-mail from my parents sat staring me in the face. Feeling courageous, I clicked on the icon, nervously awaiting what I would find.

As I read their message, my heart sank. My mother's words were cold and formal as she asked official questions of me and my journey. Old hurt resurfaced as I felt her chilly demeanor through the computer wavelengths. *They still don't get me,* I told myself as I typed back a response explaining that I wouldn't be returning to the island to visit them.

I fought back tears while Jude sipped her coffee. Without even looking up, she spoke. "Katie, why are you allowing them to make you so upset? It is only hurting you."

Inner turmoil churned through my insides as I tried to defend my emotions. "I guess I really want them to understand and listen to me. I asked my mom to speak from the heart and disclose her feelings, not mundane items such as where they should send my mail. I just don't know if they are ever going to understand me at all."

Putting down her coffee cup, Jude began twirling her fingers in a circular motion.

"You see this, Katie? It's a tornado and I am going to use it as a visualization tool. Imagine that this tornado represents all different people from your past: Mom, Dad, Steven, Autumn. Now each of these individuals are in their own self-induced tornados of mayhem, full of gunk and debris swishing around. Every time you buy into their dramas, you are instantaneously thrown into their mayhem tornado. Each time you try to explain yourself or your dreams, you are giving them your power. Do you want to do that?"

Amused by the vivid images of crazy tornados whizzing around, I shook my head, smiling. "Most definitely not! I guess I am just so used to seeking exterior guidance and approval. It's a bad habit, yet I keep repeating it."

Jude looked straight at me. "Today is the day. You are living for you and no one else. No more worrying about what others think, feel, judge. It's their issues, not yours. You just keep your own eyes on your own fries." Brown eyes vivid with sincerity, she finished her chat with another sip of coffee.

♥   ♥   ♥

Eugene was the city of choice for dinner that evening. Repeating our days of Arizona, the temperature had skyrocketed to 35 degrees. Sticky and sweltering and desperate to seek cool, refreshing air conditioning, I stopped the van at the first restaurant we came into contact with. Tony's Pizzeria was buzzing with activity due to a local BMW owner's convention. We entered the slightly cool interior, and I noticed they had an individual washroom.

Having spent weeks as essentially a hobo, I had grown savvy about scoping out potential hair-washing sinks. Individual sinks were always best yet often very tricky to find. Eyes illuminated by the new prospect of clean hair, I hurriedly ordered us a pizza and darted outside to gather up the shampoo. Gleeful, I skipped back into the washroom and proceeded to wash the dirty road dust from my tangled rats' nests.

"Ah sweet clean hair," I expressed as I inhaled the glorious scents of squeaky clean hair. Hair washing had soon become a huge, brilliant luxury on the road, and tonight was no different.

Looking back, I see we truly were living such a radiantly simple life. There had been times when I didn't think I could continue living in Cassidy, but we did, and the more I accepted the circumstances, the easier life became. It felt great to be contented with a yummy breakfast and clean hair. I secretly hoped that my perspective in that sense never changed.

♥   ♥   ♥

While I had been excitedly washing my hair, Jude had made new friends from Calgary. A father and daughter had driven down to help their grandmother move as well as enjoy the beautiful Oregon state. As we received our fresh, hot vegetarian pizza, the new friends from Calgary expressed their true feelings. "Hey, we ordered ours way before these ladies," the man exclaimed while winking over at us.

Despite several offers of veggie pizza, they politely declined, inquiring jokingly how we could possibly eat pizza without meat. Swallowing that last piece of mushroom, I glanced around the room. A bright, colorful machine caught my eye as I focused my attention on the far corner. A Simpson's pinball machine sat patiently waiting for a challenger's professional touch.

Gesturing to Jude, I beelined straight toward the stimulating game. Placing my quarters in the slot, I got my best game face on and kept my eye on the ball. *Zing, ping, ding aling, aling!* Whirling sounds came out of the machine as Homer and Bart taunted. Three minutes later, I was drenched in sweat and defeat. Jude was next up to bat. As the game began, Jude knocked the pinball between Marge and Krusty the Clown, creating quite the frenzy. Minutes flew by as she continued to smack the silver balls into submission.

After Maggie claimed her last ball, Jude stepped back from the illuminated machine. Rubbing her hands together, she announced, "Yup, I did play a bit of pinball in my day." Impressed by the epic scoring, I realized Jude was more than just a pretty face. Climbing back into Miss Cassidy, we headed toward Salem, the witch capital of Oregon.

♥   ♥   ♥

It was just after 8:00 p.m. when we pulled into the picturesque town of Salem. Flowerpots and running sprinklers created a cozy feeling as the sun shone its radiant rays across the land. Finding a parking space, we hopped out to stretch our poor weary bodies.

Ladies, I must warn you. If you decide to embark upon a spiritual mission of a lifetime, please remember to stretch your bodies. Your issues many not span the entire nation of North America, but mine sure did, leaving my body to feel similar to a pretzel. OUCH!

Curious about potential ghost sightings, Jude and I walked around attempting to tap into foreign energies or forces. After ten minutes of no ghostly energies or encounters, Cassidy became the next destination. Jude piped up, "Oh, I have an idea. Why don't we look up haunted spots online?" Agreeing, I pulled out old Blue the laptop and booted him up.

Despite my earlier statement of "I am never checking my e-mail again," I automatically checked my Hotmail account. A new message from my parents appeared and curiosity got the best of this cat. Opening it, I started mentally preparing myself for another impersonal e-mail. As I was skimming over my mom's message, a tiny smile came over my lips. Though the message was very short, it had been written from the heart and I could feel it.

Instead of responding, I shut down my account and prepared to search for ghostly locations. Upon reflection I realize I had become so accustomed to reacting defiantly with my mother that even when she was making an attempt, I was pushing her away. Yet again this was another form of self-sabotaging behavior I had developed many, many years ago.

Luckily for me, Jude piped up her opinion regarding mother's e-mail.

"Katie? Aren't you going to respond to your mother's message? Truth be told, I could feel the sincerity in that one. I really could."

Sheepishly I turned to my right and sighed. "Yeah. You're right. It did sound different, didn't it?"

Jude responded, "Yes, it did. And by ignoring it and not answering, you are simply continuing the spiteful cycle. If you ever want to resolve issues between the two of you, you are going to have to start treating this relationship like two grown adults, not children."

Closing down the website search engine, I pulled up my Hotmail account and started typing a new message to my mom. Expressing my happiness about her willingness to start communicating honestly, I felt light years better. After I sent off the response to my mom, I looked over at Jude.

Smiling she said:

"And that is how you start mending bridges, Katie."

♥   ♥   ♥

Typing "ghost sightings in Salem" into search engine, we waited for helpful results.

"Oregon ghost sites" appeared on screen and we investigated further. A huge list emerged as ghost occurrences were placed in alphabetical order throughout the state. Like two kids in a British candy store, Jude and I poured over the listings.

Grabbing a pen, I began scribbling down various locations near Salem. "Hmm, a haunted city park and old mansion," Jude exclaimed as her eyes stopped at a town named Sheridan. Chills rushed up and down my arms as I reached for our trusty map. After a quick scan, I located Sheridan; it was only forty-five miles northwest of Salem. When I disclosed this information to Jude, we both looked at one another and nodded. When I rolled down the window, refreshing evening air hit my face, adding more anticipation to our ghost hunt.

One hour later dusk blanketed the tiny town of Sheridan as we pulled in. Redneck and gun-slinging vibes emitted from its city center as we slowly searched for the haunted house's street address.

Taking many misguided turns, we finally found City Centre Northwest, a street running vertically through town. Chills came over my body as I turned right onto the dimly lit street. Eerie vibes hit me while we drove farther down into the dark, spooky night. One lone dog barked, creating an ominous feeling. Reaching a fork in the road, we opted to head right onto an old gravel road. Bumps and jolts did nothing but intensify the anxiety of my already frantic nerves.

Noticing my energy shift, Jude reminded me, "Katie, we are all made up of energy. Luckily for you, your body has an abundance. If you don't release it into the universe, it stays in your body and can eventually make you sick. Just remember the tactic I showed you."

Placing her palms upwards toward the night sky, Jude displayed her method of removing residual energy. Mimicking her action, I placed my palms upwards, visualizing all the nervous vines flowing straight out of my hands into the atmosphere. Instantly my entire body cooled off and I felt surprisingly refreshed. Cassidy approached a steep hill and her high beams illuminated the surrounding forest.

Though feeling cooler, I still jittered as we slowly started climbing up the gravel hill. 'Round and 'round we drove until the sparkling city lights of Sheridan shone brightly below.

Since my childhood I had always been drawn to sparkly, bright lights, and my adult days were no different. As Cassidy neared the top of the hill, I turned back to thoroughly absorb the view.

I marveled about how many people were down below, living in their homes full of sparkly lights. I wondered if they knew they had sparkly lights on top of their homes that grabbed my attention. Among my random thoughts were the following: How many people were eating dinner, talking about taxes, or watering a plant? There were so many different lives all living so closely together yet isolated at the same time. I wondered if they ever thought about spirituality and universal truths that I had been questing after. It is often so easy to feel alone, yet the moment you begin speaking of your hardships, it is as though a secret brotherhood of man emerges from hidden caves, expressing their similar tales of life's challenges.

Just a random thought from the mind of Katie Sutherland!

'Kay, back to the ghost hunt.

Reaching the tip of the hill, Jude and I soon discovered that the haunted mansion was not located up there. Disappointed (and a little relieved!), I turned Cass around and headed back toward Sheridan city limits.

Resolving that we would conduct a daylight search the following morning, I pulled Cass out onto the freeway, searching for a home.

Ten miles along the road, we caught sight of a country road. Swerving Cass to the left, I journeyed down the road many miles until I found a roadside turn-off. Turing off the engine, I surveyed our home surroundings for the night.

Brilliant stars winked down from a crystal-clear sky, and long wispy fields of grass whispered gently in the wind. After we performed our nightly duties, Jude slid open her side door to allow fresh air to flow through our bedroom. Glancing over to the left, I felt the cool oxygen hit my cheek. As I drifted off, I felt complete and as though I truly was an essential part of the universe.

♥ ♥ ♥

Bright and early the next morn, Jude awoke expressing her undeniable need to use the ladies room. Unfortunately the farmer's hayfield didn't offer a ladies' restroom, so we quickly rearranged our boxes and sped off toward town.

Returning to the strange little town, I recalled the local gas station in the heart of downtown. Noticing that we were running low on the gasoline front, I pulled up to the pump while Jude scuttled off to find the washroom. One minute later she returned shaking her head. Sensing a shift in her energy, I cocked my head as though silently asking if everything was all right. Not saying a word, she sat down in the passenger seat. Quickly I had the attendant fill up the oil.

Even as I write this, I realize how selfish I was being. Our most important mission that morning was finding a washroom, and within twenty minutes I was already distracted, consumed by my own agenda.

When I inquired about a tasty breakfast joint, the attendant pointed in the direction of Willimina, a town thirteen miles west. Stepping on the gas, we drove toward Willimina in a jiffy.

Breakfast went well as we were under scrutiny from the local gossip table. After they expressed their undying love of Canada, we were off the hook and free to leave.

Still wanting to locate the haunted house, I drove east, backtracking toward Sheridan.

Jude looked over at me and said, "Still want to go on a ghost hunt?"

Excited, I responded, "Yeah, I thought it would be cool to try and find it in the daylight."

Nodding her head, Jude stuck her toes out the window and resumed daydreaming.

I did the same, and before long we were back in Sheridan, locating City Centre Northwest. I turned off the main road and resumed our initial search for the haunted home.

The address scribbled on the scrap paper read "#197 City Centre northwest." Peeking out the window, I attempted to discover where we were. A newer duplex with a red rose bush displayed the number eighty-five outside its door, so we traveled a few blocks up. As we approached Number 197, it appeared to be a fairly new home with little to no damage. My visions of broken windows and millions of resident cats were shattered as we parked Cass across the street. Refusing to give up on our ghost hunt, we descended from Cassidy and stood at the white picket fence.

A red-and-white sign hung in the yard, indicating that the house was on the market. Raising our eyebrows, we ventured closer. Looking around the neighborhood, Jude declared, "Well, we could be prospective house hunters now, couldn't we?" Catching her sneaky drift, I agreed, "Oh absolutely. I have been simply dying to check this place out."

Determined to scope out the property, we opened the creaky gate and entered the front yard. Neither of us felt any form of spirit, so we moved closer to the house. Ensuring no one was watching, Jude and I snuck to the right and began walking along the parameter of the house.

Sneaking a peek inside, I saw an empty room with white walls. There was no sign of ghouls or ghosts whatsoever. Sensing no strange energies or vibes, we carried on to the overgrown backyard. Noticing the large back door, Jude and I approached it and looked in. A long empty hallway stretched out in front of us with white-and-black checkered linoleum. Still not sensing any peculiar vibes, Jude and I headed back toward Cassarama. A feeling of defeat came over me as I climbed back into our van-home.

"Well, so much for that spooky house," I said, feeling rather dejected.

"Never say never," Jude replied and rolled down her window. Determined to get to the bottom of the haunted house mystery, Jude searched the neighborhood for a local town dweller. She muttered, "There's got to be someone who knows about these sorts of things." Jude spotted a middle-aged man mowing the lawn.

"Aha," she said. "Watch this!"

Leaning her head out the window, she called out a morning greeting to the gentleman. Pausing mid-push, the man glanced up from his morning grass-cutting duties.

"Ur, yes, good morning, can I help you with something?" He called out from his front lawn.

"As a matter of fact, you can!" Jude called out.

Winking over at me, she continued. "See we are travel writers and are compiling a novel on haunted sites. According to our research, there happens to be a haunted house on this very street. Do you happen to know anything about it?"

Slowly shaking his head, the mustached man responded, "No, ma'am. Not to my knowledge. We moved here three years ago from Georgia and not once have I heard about a haunted house. Perhaps the Smiths across the street could be of more assistance. They have been living in this particular neighborhood for twenty-three years." With that he turned around and resumed his lawn-mowing duties.

Sighing heavily, Jude said, "Well, I don't know. It seems to me as though this ghost hunt has hit another brick wall."

Nodding, I remembered her advice regarding forced situations.

"As a sixth-sensory person, you have to pay attention to energy shifts and teensy, tiny clues. If a situation doesn't seem to be working, you must not force it. Instead, accept that it isn't meant to be and adjust your plans as best you can. The universe works in wondrous ways but in order to accept its messages, you must be flexible and open."

As though reading my mind, Jude looked toward the highway and stated, "Well, I guess it wasn't meant to be. Let's hit the road."

Taking a sharp left turn, I swerved Cassidy back onto the open road. Turning on the satellite radio to rock and roll classics, we cranked out Don Henley and sped west in the direction of the gorgeous Oregon coastline.

♥   ♥   ♥

Touristy coastal towns were found all along our travels up the #101 North. Lunchtime found us in a little fishing village that used its primary industry to lure people in (pardon the pun!). Unable to resist the temptation of greasy, grimy fish and chips, I subtlety walked into the local restaurant, hoping Jude would catch the hint.

Once we were inside, an extraordinarily distracted lady gestured to the empty restaurant. Assuming she meant "seat yourselves," we chose a table near the front doors and awaited her arrival.

During the ten-minute wait for our coffee and water request, I looked around the café. With its high ceilings and oceanfront view, it had tons of potential, but I didn't believe the owners thought so. Cracked walls and cobwebbed corners were just two examples of neglect the beautiful old building was receiving.

Such a shame, I thought. *So many beautiful places with tons of potential yet the owners don't want to put the time in.* Even as I write this sentence, I realize why this particular situation saddens me. I myself was similar to the old building. I had potential to shine and sparkle, but I needed somebody to invest proper time to help me restore my old foundation, which had major cracks in it. It is my belief that we all have the ability to shine from within, but it takes patience and a support system for us to create belief in ourselves. I had been neglecting my foundation of beliefs for so many years that I had forgotten my true potential. It took the kindness, compassion, and strength of Jude to recognize this potential and educate about the skills of recreation. All it takes is one person to believe in you to create a ripple effect. Having spent several months with Jude, I know her chosen words of truth and kindness had deeply impacted and positively changed countless people's lives. She has the most incredible ability to remind people of their inner sparkle that never truly dies.

♥   ♥   ♥

Our waitress finally presented us with our beverages and began walking away without taking our lunchtime requests. Hearing my tummy rumbling, I piped up. "Ah, I think we are ready to order." Seeming almost annoyed at my request, she slowly made her way back to our table.

Raising her eyebrows in expectance, she waited for us to begin. Clearing her throat, Jude requested a new coffee and clam chowder. Satisfied with my lukewarm water, I simply ordered fish and chips with extra pickles.

Giving us a strange look, the lady wandered over to the cash machine. *Strange folks on the coast,* I thought to myself. *Must have something to do with too much sea water.* Snickering to myself, I continued looking around the restaurant. Jude broke my silent investigation. "Hey, Katie. How come you never eat chowder soup?" Puzzled by her question, I gave her my well-rehearsed response. "Well, I just never truly enjoyed heavy foods and I find they stay in my stomach for a long time."

Unconvinced, Jude looked at me. "I don't think it's that at all. I think you are paranoid about fatty foods and have persuaded yourself never to eat them." DUH! Foiled again! Secret number 5,803 revealed. Despite my well-rehearsed lines, I still couldn't fool this lady.

Clenching my jaw, I responded, "I suppose you could be right. FINE! You are right. I think chowder is fattening Okay? You win." My defensive side flared up as I had flashbacks of arguing with my mother.

Rolling her eyes, Jude shot back, "Look, Katie. I am not saying this to win a particular argument. You have to stop assuming I am arguing with you. I was simply trying to make a point. You need certain fats in your diet, so don't be so fearful of them. And please, stop regarding me as your mom. I am the complete opposite."

Biting my thumbnail, I stubbornly listened to her truthful words. Unable to find an appropriate rebuttal, I shut my pie hole, admitting defeat. While I began stewing over Jude's comments, our meals miraculously arrived.

Scanning our table, the waitress visibly twitched as she realized she had forgotten Jude's coffee from twenty minutes prior. Scampering off, she frantically poured another cup of Joe and raced back. Firm and stern, Jude thanked her. We enjoyed our fishy meal and waited patiently for our bill.

After ten minutes, I flagged the waitress down (with both arms) and indicated our desire to pay. Sheepishly she brought the bill over, explaining that she had initially lost it in the cash machine. Shaking my head, I had to admit I was finally seeing what Jude was so frustrated with: the service industry on a whole was a calamity of epic proportions. Leaving a minimal tip behind, we scooted out into the sunny outdoors.

♥   ♥   ♥

Service Industry

There were great lessons learned on this topic. Having spent many years as a waitress, it was interesting to be on the opposite side of the table. Due to our cravings for peanut butter and toast, Jude and I spent a majority of our time in restaurants, victims of brutal deteriorating customer service. Forgotten knifes, unsanitary conditions, and snarling servers were all aspects of our North American dining experience. As the service began dwindling, I watched Jude's warm disposition fade and her slowly lose patience.

As a young woman who hadn't been taught assertion, I initially didn't understand Jude's frustrations. In the past I would simply ignore mistakes, not wanting to come across as a pain or as being a cheeky bugger. And what did this wimpy behavior do for me? Absolutely nothing!

I would continue to get terrible service, eat cold mashed potatoes, and feel bad about remaining silent. Doesn't sound like an ideal situation, does it? NOPE!

Observing Jude, I eventually came to accept it was a sign of self-confidence to demand quality service. *Hmm,* I thought to myself.

Self-confidence = great service

Low-confidence = cold mashed potatoes

Slowly I put it together and imitated Jude's behavior. And, wonder of wonders, servers responded immediately to my confidence.

"Just remember, Katie. The fact that you are in your twenties doesn't mean you aren't entitled to great service. Everyone should be treated as equals in restaurants regardless of how old they are."

Equality, what a concept! Upon reflection I realize Jude's words were true. Women in their twenties were not standing up for themselves yet dined out more than any other age category. That means a lot of cold mashed potatoes served to miserable diners. We as women need to remember to stand up for our hot meals and feel worthy of great service.

A secret I learned about equality is that you have to believe you are equal in order for it to work.

♥   ♥   ♥

Souvenir shops and coffee kiosks lined the highway as we cruised from coastal town to coastal town. Mid-afternoon marked standard coffee time, so when I spotted Martha's Java Stop, we stopped. A beautiful white gazebo covered in summer flowers and sunflowers offered weary travelers sanctuary from their journeys.

The moment I set foot outside Cassidy, I could feel an energy shift in my body. *Oh here we go again,* I thought to myself as we neared the counter. Unsure of where my shift came from, I decided to ignore it instead of talk about it. Jude and I grabbed two coffees (and a scrumptious cinnamon bun) and retreated to the tranquil garden gazebo.

As Jude started discussing my eating habits, my old buddy, anger, flared up to attack. "Why do you always talk to me like you know everything?" I declared, adrenaline surging through my body.

Jude, weary from arguing, sighed. "Katie, I don't think I know everything, not in the least. When I speak it's from the heart and I am mentioning health concerns. I have noticed you have this switch inside you that seems to go on the instant anyone tells you a suggestion. Don't be so defensive."

Feeling defensive, I barked back, "I am not defensive. I am simply telling you how I feel." With that I crossed my arms, similar to a six-year-old, and challenged Jude with my eyes.

"Katie, I don't know how many times I have to tell you this. I am not your mother; please do not treat me like her!" After I sat for several minutes, reality splashed over me full of ice water. Jude truly wasn't my mother, and I was treating her terribly through my defensive words and immature behaviors.

Hanging my head in shame, I softly muttered, "Jude, I know I am treating you like my mom. I just am so used to arguing with her and being treated with no respect, you know?" Jude broke off a piece of cinnamon bun and contemplated the new information.

"Katie, I can understand where you are coming from. I really can. But you need to get a new story. Seriously! Your old one is boring and full of excuses. I don't want to hear anymore excuses coming from your lips."

I nodded and resumed my fixation on the garden gnomes that seemed to be watching our conversation.

Upon reflection I realize I just couldn't let go of my past behaviors. Though I was fully aware of my insane demeanor, I continued to bite the hand that fed me. Jude had proven to me countless times her kind heart and genuine compassion, yet I still rebuked her love.

♥   ♥   ♥

Astoria was the town we found ourselves at by 6:00 p.m. Bordering between Washington and Oregon, it was a fishing town that offered beautiful views of the west coast. Turning toward me, Jude made the suggestion of going for drinks in town. Pleased with her idea, I pulled Cassidy toward the main street. Nearing the central traffic light, I noticed that the old movie theater was showing *Shrek 3*. I had wanted to watch it since leaving Montreal and hadn't had the opportunity to. Raising my eyebrows at Jude, I asked, "Would you be into checking out *Shrek 3* instead of drinks?"

Waving her arms, Jude answered, "You know me, Katie. I'm easy. *Shrek 3* sounds great to me."

Parking Cassidy, we backtracked a block toward the movie theater. Despite its broken tiles and windows, the Astoria movie theater had a certain charm only ancient buildings possess.

Entering the theater, I suddenly became very conscious of the fact that I was wearing very short shorts. (Anyone remember the song?) Self-conscious, I began tugging on them, attempting to cover an extra inch on my thighs. Jude noticed my fidgeting and said, "Oh, Katie. Who gives a flying flip about your shorts? Don't even give it another thought. Honestly, kid, what am I going to do with you?"

I stopped fidgeting and turned my focus on finding the perfect movie seats. Due to its ancient nature, the theater had old-school seating that held particular aromas from 1974. Holding my breath, I pointed to two pink velour seats two rows from the back. Jude and I took a seat and waited for the magical fairytale to unfold.

As I took a sip of water, I heard the most adorable giggle drifting up from three rows below me. Cranking my neck forward, I saw three little ones all dressed up in medieval costumes: such a heartwarming view even for myself, the Grinch!

As the movie unfolded, the gorgeous giggles continued from the three children. Though Jude and I loved the movie, their laughter was absolutely the highlight of the evening. Hearing such pure, simply joy from a child reminded me to lighten up. I had been living in my head for so long that I had created a fabulously dark rain cloud over myself as well as all whom I made contact with. The doom-and-gloom side of my personality would often take over and erase all memories of warmth. Hearing glorious, brilliant giggles brought me back to an awareness that no matter what happens, we always have a choice of how to behave; we can either chose to think the worst and project that into the universe OR lighten up, giggle, and remember we all have beautiful inner children within.

That evening spirits were high as we located a rest area for the night. As I turned off the lights, I peered into the overcast night sky and listened to the coastal waves crashing beside us.

♥   ♥   ♥

Breakfast that morning was magical. After driving back into Astoria, we had sniffed out Pigs in a Blanket, a family restaurant that had a very cozy feel. Surveying our table of coffee, pecan pancakes, and Spanish omelet, I silently gave thanks for having such an abundance of food and warmth in my life.

Jude was just finishing her second mouthful of pecan pancakes when an older gentleman across the aisle turned his head in our direction. Noticing his glance, Jude winked at me,

"Hey, Katie! It looks like someone is trying to check out our breakfast. I wonder of he is planning on ordering pancakes 'cause they are really tasty!"

A huge grin spread across the old man's face and he responded, "All right, ladies! You caught me! I was checking out your pancakes and thinking how I wished I had ordered them instead of my liver and toast!"

Laughing, Jude offered a taste of her breakfast to our new neighbor. Shaking his head from side to side, he replied, "No, thank you. But you can tell me where you are from?" At this point his wife looked up from her coffee and smiled.

"You will have to excuse Bob. He is extremely friendly. Please tell him to behave himself and perhaps the fourth time he will listen!"

Enchanted by the friendly couple, Jude began explaining where we were from and what we had been up to. "So essentially this is a spiritual journey for Miss Katie, and I have been mentoring her along the way." Charmed with Jude's words, the man extended his arms.

"Well, Judy and Katie, it is very nice to meet you. My name is Bob and this is my wife Shirley." Indicating we should join them, Shirley shifted over to make room. Jude slid in next to the couple and started asking them about themselves. As they spoke, she reached out and touched their arms as a form of connection. I remained at our original table, feeling socially awkward.

Since I can remember, I have been nervous around strangers, even those who are warm and friendly. I have always been awkward with touching, even though I love touch; I grew up feeling alienated from this action. Tuning into their conversation, I overheard Shirley warn Bob, "Oh Bob, it looks like we have a toucher on our hands!" The table exploded with laughter.

As Jude effortlessly conversed with the charming couple, I uncomfortably doodled by myself. Bob noticed me sitting alone and patted the seat beside him. "Hey, Katie, come on over. I promise I won't bite!" Giving me a reassuring smile, he waited. Truly touched by such a kind offer, I immediately gravitated to the space he had created for me. We spent the next thirty minutes with the couple, who disclosed stories from their past. Bob was a pastor, and he and Shirley had spent many years living in a small coastal community of Washington.

As their eyes sparkled and danced, I knew I was witnessing true love. Even as I write this, I am feeling very moved. Their unconditional love for one another was so beautiful and pure. Their rock-solid foundation was apparent as they spoke about their beliefs and the importance of family. As I sat in the coffee shop, I recalled the feeling of unconditional acceptance and non-judgment. They laughed and giggled with one another as though they were still teenagers. Pure magic!

Eventually Bob looked at his watch and declared that they needed to head out toward their California home. Stretching out his enormous arms, he enfolded me with the most incredible bear hug I had ever felt. It was so fantastic. Shirley and Bob passed us their business card and told us to keep in touch. Promising we would, we watched as they went on their way. Meeting Shirley and Bob showed me the type of person I wanted to be:

❖ Kind
❖ Patient
❖ Loving
❖ Unconditional

Departing from the restaurant, I was filled with hope of who I would one day become.

♥   ♥   ♥

The following is a journal excerpt from that morning:

Good morning. I awoke with feelings of sorrow and acceptance regarding the release of my past. I will always love my parents, but right now I need to let go of my past and move forward. Since embarking upon this adventure, the people along the way have been magnificent. We just met a couple name Bob and Shirley. He was a pastor and they were also clowns. It was incredible to hear about how they devoted their lives to helping others. Bob spoke of being very human as a pastor and said that he found many pastors very impersonal and cold. It has meant so much for me to witness the silent heroes all across North America. They ask nothing in return other than people's lives be inspired and enriched. I recall a time when I would sit with my friends and complain about the inaction and laziness of the world. I now know that I myself was part of the issues. Instead of taking action, I was sitting around judging others for their personal choices, their chosen destinies. Now I have chosen to only speak for myself and speak my mind—dig deep till I find my truth within. No mater how ugly it may be, it's a part of me. My wish is that I can share this magical transformation with others so they can experience the same for themselves. I am surrounded with beauty and love that I am slowly learning to appreciate and recognize.

Upon reflection I realize I was writing about magical heroes when in reality I didn't realize the most magical one was sitting beside me. I spoke of gratitude and appreciation, but honestly I still couldn't see past my nose. Ah denial!

♥   ♥   ♥

Later that day we pulled into a small town to recharge the computer. Noticing a yellow coffee shop, Jude grabbed her Bucky's cup and walked in. Large ceilings and First Nations creative art gave the shop a real West Coast feeling. A pretty young woman behind the counter smiled at us as Jude approached her. Ordering a cappuccino, Jude complimented the girl on her smile. Instantly the girl's aura shifted and she sparkled.

"It's never the big, grandiose things Katie. No, it is the small, little things we can do every day to connect with others."

Jude, 2007

While I checked my e-mail, a gentleman at the next table started flirting with Jude. "Hi there. You look like you keep yourself in great shape."

Flashing his pearly whites, he awaited her swoons. Unfazed by his complimenting nature, Jude laughed and walked over to him. Giving him a playful tap on the shoulder, she responded, "Oh please! I know fellows like you! I bet you are trouble, aren't you?" Flabbergasted that his compliments didn't work, the man resorted to speaking truthfully and providing Jude with respect. Yet again, I observed another lesson Jude was showing me. "Remember, kiddo, most likely men are after one thing. They will say many things to get what they want. If you call them on their bullpoop, you are forcing them to be real. And trust me, you want a real, honest man, not one who wins you over with false words and empty compliments."

After a while Jude returned to our table and an older lady appeared. Introducing herself as the owner, she began inquiring about our story. Remaining silent, Jude gave me the floor. Though I was nervous, I managed to open my mouth and say, "Err, well. We have been traveling around, writing a book."

Interested, the woman leaned forward. "And what's your book about?"

As she waited for a response, I dove in, "Well it's basically about my inner struggles as a twenty-six-year-old female and recognizing unhealthy choices and behaviors. Basically, I am learning about being accountable for my own actions." Heart racing, I stopped talking. I held my breath and waited for her reaction.

The older woman nodded her understanding and replied, "That sounds like a great idea. I know I have lived through many difficult struggles, many I have brought upon myself."

She continued by speaking about her daughter, who held similar issues. In awe, I sat back to truly absorb what I had witnessed. I had dug deep, expressed my true feelings, and a stranger had accepted my words! Sheer magic!

♥   ♥   ♥

As we continued on our path through the Olympic Park, our conversation topic shifted to sex. As Cassidy soared around dips and corners, we giggled about various sexual experiences.

Growing up, I hadn't had a female role model to explain the basics of sex. This inexperience carried through into my adult years, and

I came across as very prudish to my girl friends. While they had openly discussed their sexual encounters, I had always remained silent, feeling embarrassed about disclosing my sexual blunders.

Meeting Jude, I learned of the importance of discussing sex with another female. As our conversation grew increasingly heated, Jude suddenly yelled out, "That's it! I'm calling Quinn!" Quinn was an old friend from Jude's days in the fishing lodge business. Her and Quinn shared a connection that stemmed from a past life. And with that, I pulled over to the nearest rest stop.

Dialing the ten-digit Vancouver phone number, Jude waited to hear Quinn's deep voice. The fourth ring is when he finally picked up. As Jude briefly spoke with Quinn, it was fun to watch her get nervous and excited. Although she constantly reminded me not to put her on a pedestal, I often did. Having said that, it was wonderful to watch her reaction.

Hanging up the telephone, she let out a big scream. "Ah what was I thinking?"

Giggling, I responded, "You were living in the moment!" Watching her brown eyes sparkle, I thought about how cool it was to see the connection Jude had with her inner child.

Once the initial excitement of the phone call died down, we checked out our surroundings, a 360-degree view of a crystal-clear lake surrounded by dramatic mountain peaks. Green alpine forest framed the lake as the nighttime creatures began their nightly musical. Quiet darkness created the feeling of security and we both decided to stay there for the evening.

As I feel asleep that night, thoughts of confronting my parents plagued me. I knew it was an inevitable encounter, but I still didn't feel 100 percent courageous. Due to many years of caring what others thought, I was still desperately trying to grasp the concept of self-love above all others.

Upon reflection I realize I still craved external attention and praise even though it should have come from within. Looking at my fear of confronting my parents, I realized there were two underlying reasons for this:

1) My fear of conflict: As mentioned earlier, due to my low self-esteem, I would always back away from conflict. The idea of someone being angry at me was frightening, and I lived many years avoiding confrontational settings.
2) My need for attention and love: Another reason I feared confronting my parents was because I felt that they would stop loving me if I told them the truth about how I felt towards their relationship.

♥   ♥   ♥

Pink and orange sky radiated through the mountains the next morning. Neighboring frogs croaked outside, and the odd truck would cruise by, reminding us we were still on the highway. Playing our morning game of repacking Cassidy, my spirits felt light.

A quick check of the trusty, rusty map and we decided to venture out toward the San Juan Islands, a string of scenic islands that were spread along the Washington Coast. Sunshine at our backs and blue skies ahead, the day promised good vibes and picturesque settings. Sailing closer to Vancouver Island, a.k.a. closer to my parents, I started dreading the thought of having to go back. I felt as though I had experienced so much growth, yet seeing them still intimidated me. Trying to ignore my conflicting thoughts, I turned up the soul town music channel and lost myself in Michael Jackson's killer beats.

♥   ♥   ♥

By nightfall we found ourselves in the grand city of Anacortes. Eager for a walk in the great outdoors, we stopped by a nearby coffee shop. Stretching our old bones, we began walking toward the ocean. Sea breezes and gulls greeted us as we strolled along the water. Walking, I started feeling antsy.

Observing my motions, Jude looked over and said, "Katie. You need to meditate to discover what is bothering you. You have been carrying something all day." Agreeing with her advice, I found a patch of grass and assumed the position. Inhaling deeply, I allowed my subconscious to show me symbols: a dragon tied in knots, plenty of dead ends, and Pac-Man was the vision within my third eye.

When I relayed the images to Jude, she questioned me, encouraging deeper answers. "So dead ends, eh? What do you think that means?"

Keeping my eyes closed, I responded, "Well, it means I have hit another dead end in my life path. I need to try a new route."

Opening my eyes, I had my answer. Although I had already known about the dead ends, my meditation served as an affirmation. Pressing further, Jude continued, "So what do you think the new life involves?"

Pondering for a minute, I answered, "Starting fresh for myself, not anyone else. I have been shown throughout this entire trip all the dysfunctional patterns I have created in the past. Now is my opportunity to turn over a new leaf." Satisfied with my response, Jude announced, "Well madam, looks like my work here is done."

That evening we rented an inspirational movie about mentorship. This story was of an eleven-year-old girl from a rough neighborhood who had the amazing gift of spelling words. She needed a challenge.

Enter Mister Russell, a teacher who accepted nothing but brilliance from her. As the movie rolled forward, it dawned on me why Jude had been adamant that we watch this specific show.

Throughout our entire journeys across the North American continent, Jude had continually repeated, "Katie, you need a challenge. Not once in your life have you truly been shown how far you can go. Now you have met me and I refuse to back down. I want you to show the world your inner strength."

Watching a stunning sunset over the marina, Jude and I had an emotional chat that evening. "So you know, Katie. I have been trying to figure out when you walked out on yourself. You have such inner strength, but somewhere along the line you stopped fighting for yourself."

Instantly I remembered my short-lived rowing career when I was eighteen. There had been a citywide rowing competition and I was entered as a rookie. The day of the competition, I was a bundle of nervous energy. Prior to the race, I had eaten a handful of apricots, and one hour later I sat awaiting the bell to start the race. For the next eight minutes, I pulled harder than I ever had in my lifetime. Winning by the skin of my teeth, I hurriedly raced to the washroom. Nerves combined with dried fruit apparently didn't agree with my tummy and I threw up the apricots. Seeing how hard I had pushed my body really frightened me and I had internalized that experience. Soon after, I stopped my rowing career altogether.

Upon reflection I realize this moment stayed with me, so when Jude inquired about walking out on me, that moment popped up into my conscious mind. As I described my old rowing experience to Jude, she nodded her head. "So that would be the day, my dear, you walked away from yourself. Now what I want to know is, was there a role model or anyone who pushed you to challenge your limits? A teacher? A coach? Anybody?"

Scanning my memory bank, I came up blank. "Nope, not that I can remember."

Jude accepted my words and continued. "Well, girl. You have met me and I know you have strength in you that needs to be harnessed and challenged. I want you to go back to that eighteen-year-old girl who rowed with her entire essence. You have to go back to her because you walked away from her eight years ago. That was the real Katie. This person you have created these past eight years is not the real you at all. When you gave up on yourself, you began masking your true identity with false characteristics. Buying into what everyone told you, you believed you were fragile and easily broken. Instead of harnessing your inner warrior, you let her go and took the easy way out. Well, girl, it's time to bring her back."

Tears in her eyes, Jude looked at me with unconditional love shining. Staring back at Jude, I was speechless. Even as I write this, *speechless* isn't even the tip of the iceberg of how I felt.

Upon reflection I realize that though I know my mom and dad truly loved me, Jude's unconditional love was deep. Despite my insanely horrendous behavior throughout our journey, she still cared for me at a depth I couldn't even comprehend. Seeing her eyes full of hope shining at me, I truly saw what I spent my entire life looking for: a female role model who loved me and challenged me to be the greatest person I could be. I will never forget that night. Through unconditional love that was the night that Jude showed me who I truly was and how important it was to get her—myself—back.

Upon reflection I realize Jude had asked me about coaches, teachers, or friends who had challenged me. Being honest, I am sure there were women who had demonstrated an interest in my personal growth. But I had scared them off through my defensive, defiant attitude. In the past I had viewed all older women as my mother; therefore, I showed them little to no respect, sadly, I realize, as I think about it, for the only person I was hurting was me. Cheesy cliché, I realize, but true! Self-sabotage, I soon learned, was stemmed from my poor self-esteem.

Falling asleep that night, I felt more empowered than I had in many, many years. And this wasn't false pride or vanity empowerment. No, this was true empowerment that came from the belief in oneself. Expressing my gratitude to the universe, I blew a kiss outside and drifted off.

♥   ♥   ♥

That morning I awoke to a glorious sunshine shining down upon the marina. Due to my desire to locate "the perfect spot" to write the book, I had been consulting ancient runes to gather information. As I shook the purple velvet bag, I grabbed three wooden morsels and threw them on the bed. According to the old fortune-telling method, Jude and I were meant to travel to Kelowna, British Columbia.

Set on traveling toward the interior of British Columbia, I felt relief because I had a plan. Although Jude always spoke about projecting to far into the future, I was still clinging to my old habits of control. The uncertainty of not having a game plan was definitely a tactic I wasn't accustomed to.

Due to this habit of control, I often tried to make Jude plan as a way of making me feel better about the future. Her response was always the same: "I am in the moment, Katie. I can't even talk about the future, because it isn't here yet. In order to get to tomorrow, you have to stay in today. Truly, I have no plans besides from what I am

251

doing in this very moment. When you project too far into the future, you stifle the universe from working its magic. By putting too many constraints on your future, you don't allow for serendipitous events to take place. Remember Katie, STAY IN THE MOMENT!"

Nearing the Washington state / British Columbia border, my usual panicky vibes became activated. Noon had brought with it many, many travelers at the border, which simply added more fuel to my increasing fire. For a half an hour, we sat in Cassidy as the line crept excruciatingly slowly. Noting my jitters, Jude pushed the windows down and took a deep breath of fresh air.

"Can you smell that, Katie? Beautiful oxygen. Now take a few breaths and calm yourself down. There is absolutely nothing to fear about crossing the border."

Taking in a big gulp, I felt myself relax marginally as Cassidy approached closer to the guard. Once we became the next car up to bat, my nerves flared up and my body went into freak-out mode. With my entire body quivering on the inside, I drove Cassidy up to the window.

The guard looked down at us and barked to see our identification, including birth certificates. Instantly my hands turned to butter as I clumsily handed over our IDs. Peering down his nose at me, the guard said, "No birth certificate?"

Stuttering, I answered, "Nonononono, sir, I don't." As he began asking about our travels, I anxiously answered his questions, obviously nervous and verging on being neurotic. After what seemed like an eternity, he flagged us through, warning me to be sure I had my birth certificate for the next visit. Exhaling deeply, I stepped on the gas and sped on.

Shaking her head for the millionth time, Jude said, "Katie, I honestly don't understand why you enjoy getting yourself all worked up for nothing. Do you have any idea how harmful stress is on your soul?" Sheepishly I nodded and continued driving, cursing myself for allowing my mind to control my behaviors.

Cruising along the Canadian freeway, it felt good to be on home turf. I still was holding onto feelings of anger toward my parents, but

I also had resolved that I wasn't going to see them this particular day. After discussing things over with Jude, I came to the conclusion I didn't have to see them upon my arrival to the coast.

The conclusion of this discussion led to an incredible feeling of relief, illustrating that it was indeed the right decision for the time being. Halfway to Vancouver, Jude turned the music down. "Katie, I know you have wanted to go for a reading for quite some time. Why don't we head into Vancouver and see Crystal? I really feel you need an affirmation that you are doing the right thing by writing this book." Patting me on the arm, Jude continued, "I know you do. Its fine, I am not offended that you want to consult another psychic, honestly. It doesn't bother me. We can head toward Granville Island for a quick visit before we head to the Okanagan."

♥   ♥   ♥

Crystal had been conducting psychic readings in Granville Island for many years and was highly respected in the psychic community. Back in November Jude had taken me to see her. The reading had been 100 percent accurate and had manifested itself before my very eyes. Spotting a Vancouver city center exit, I quickly turned right and headed into weekend traffic.

Driving into Vancouver, my entire body tensed up and I quickly became Miss Irritably 2007. Speeding through traffic lights and honking freely, I had magically metamorphosed myself into an aggressive city driver. Wailing on the horn, I yelled over to Jude, "I don't know what it wrong with me, but since arriving in Vancouver I am super irritable and cranky."

Turning to me, Jude replied, "You don't say. I really hadn't noticed! Seriously though, you are obviously picking up on all the negative energy flying around here. Also, you still have old memories of living in Vancouver, so you are reactivating old emotions."

Made sense.

One hour and ten honks later, I pulled into the brilliant marina of Granville Island. Colorful boats and touristy shops all created the perfect ambience on a Saturday afternoon. Strolling toward Crystals studio, I felt grounded as ocean smells surrounded us. Trudging up the staircase to her studio, I crossed my fingers in hopes that we

253

would see her that afternoon. Resolving that if it was meant to be we would, I waited for Jude in the front landing.

Looking up, I saw Crystal standing patiently behind the counter. She was a French lady with a long history of being a very intuitive psychic. Within her studio she had created a fantastic energy. It was very grounding and calm. After she greeted Crystal, Jude sat down on the cozy couches and began reading an article. Rather hesitantly, I walked up to Crystal to inquire about potential readings. Nodding her head, Crystal explained that she had two openings for later that afternoon.

Excited, I wrote down our names and informed Jude we had an hour to stroll around the outdoor marketplace. As I stepped out into the sunny day, all my early frustrations from the drive melted away as magnificent instrumental music radiated through the atmosphere.

Intrigued by the melodic sound waves, Jude and I crossed the street over to an open courtyard. A trio of musicians were performing as little tots danced and swayed to their vibes. *Ah summer concerts,* I thought to myself as we took a seat at a wooden bench. A feeling of peace came over me as Jude and I grooved to the funky beats of the Australian dijarido. The magical music soothed my soul as the sun comforted my nagging doubts.

For the next twenty minutes, all thoughts of negatron or sorrow were erased while I remained in the moment, acknowledging the gift of music provided by the universe. As three o'clock rolled around, we leisurely made our way over to Crystal's studio. Climbing the stairs, I got butterflies in my tummy from nerves. Like I felt around the authorities, whenever I had intuitive readings done, I also got a nervous sensation.

As Crystal cleansed my aura with sage and a lone eagle feather, I inhaled and waited for the messages she had to disclose.

Upon reflection I realize I was still nervous due to my old pattern of lying. If there's one thing about great psychics, it's that they can sniff out a lie from miles away. In the past I always felt exposed whenever readings were involved.

Crystal sat across the table from me and asked that I draw twenty-six cards from her deck. Anxious to begin, I quickly grabbed the cards and gave them to her. With her long, pointed fingers, Crystal overturned the cards and interpreted their meanings.

Her message from the universe was the following:

- ❖ I was on the right track and should keep on my path.
- ❖ Surround myself with positive people
- ❖ All of my dreams were coming true.
- ❖ There would be feelings of loss during the following six months.

Looking up, Crystal indicated that her reading was complete. Reaching into her antique wooden cabinet, she pulled out a small package and presented it to me. "This is but a humble gift, but I feel I need to give it to you. It is a belly rock and it is used when you can't sleep. You may need this in the future." Pausing, she glanced over at me. "Do you have any questions about your reading or words I have said?"

Nodding, I responded, "Yes actually. Do you have any advice on detaching?"

Though Jude had told me five million times, I wanted another affirmation to get through my thick skull. Eyes twinkling, Crystal responded, "Yes. You must remind yourself that in order to live in the moment, you must release any holds from the past. Just imagine yourself letting go of any imaginary rope. That helps with the art of detachment."

Accepting her words, I put the belly rock in my pocket and headed into the lobby. Smiling up from her magazine, Jude acknowledged my presence as I sat down upon the couch. Feelings of excitement and hope were beaming through me while I waited for Jude's reading.

My dreams really are coming true, I marveled to myself. After my initial excitement of the positive reading simmered down, I began thinking about how differently Crystal had treated me in comparison to my visit in November.

Upon reflection I realize that in November I was still lying and telling manipulative lies. As an intuitive, Crystal had picked up on my deception right away and had been rather distant and cold. Since Jude had been mentoring me and making me accountable for my actions, Crystal had noticed Jude's work and responded by showing more respect.

While I waited in the lobby, Jude connected with Crystal for her reading. As a highly intuitive woman, Jude had few whom she could speak with at her depth. Crystal was one of the women who were at Jude's depth, and they understood one another. Although I longed to be at that depth, I knew I had much work to do prior to arriving at that wisdom.

Resurfacing twenty minutes later, Jude looked teary-eyes from her session.

Feeling the need to get out of the big city, we decided to grab a quick bite to eat and then head toward the Okanagan. After eating our standard meal of colossal nachos, Jude and I bounced out of the city.

♥   ♥   ♥

Over the course of the evening, our roadside scenery changed from electric lights of the Lions Gate bridge to pink fluffy clouds scattered across green pastures. The farther from Vancouver Cassidy took us, the higher our spirits. Two hours out of Vancouver, Jude's silence had broken and she discussed topics she had never revealed. While I listened to her insightful knowledge acquired from many years on this plane, I felt truly blessed to be on this journey of universal enlightenment with such an incredible woman.

The more she spoke about her sadness for the state of the earth and mankind, the more I wondered who Jude truly was. She still remained an enigma to me, and her ability to demonstrate others depths was incredible. By far her spiritual teachings and understandings were the most profound life lessons I had ever learned during this lifetime.

Before we could say Scooby Doo, nightfall had crept over the serene countryside and I pulled Cass over at a tiny rest area. Upon further investigation I discovered a nearby stream, which provided us with a magnificent soundtrack to lure us into slumber land. Snuggling down under the covers, I wished my mighty wish upon the brightest sparkly star overhead and locked our car doors. Closing my eyes, I wondered what the next day would bring.

♥   ♥   ♥

Waking up to big transport trucks whizzing by, Jude and I packed our bedroom and hopped into our designated seats. Our breakfast that morning consisted of yummy eats and delightful neighbors. As I watched Jude interact with the family beside us, I marveled at how effortlessly she could connect with strangers.

Her simple words of "Just be real, Katie, speak from your heart and you will never go wrong" was the advice she repeated whenever I asked about her people skills. By midmorning, the temperature had heated up to 32 degrees and I was experiencing Arizona desert flashbacks.

My tolerance for the heat was increasingly lessening and it only stirred up suppressed emotions I had been holding onto. By 2:00 p.m. that afternoon, my hunger got the best of me and we pulled into a small town just south of Kelowna. Along the main town center, I noticed an Indian diner and made a beeline in its direction. My blood levels seemed to take a dive and I allowed my brain to manifest feelings of weakness. Blue and orange minimalist decor greeted us as we marched through the threshold. Simple Buddhist symbols and pictures were mounted on the wall, giving the restaurant a very Eastern feeling.

As I dug into my pad Thai, Jude began chatting with the waitress about her travels overseas. She had been living in a monastery for several weeks and had fallen in love with the culture. Upon her return to Canada, she had decided to keep the spirit alive by opening an Indian restaurant. Sarah went on to discuss how the men monks seemed much friendlier than the female monks, which sparked some interest from Jude. Challenging the girl on her opinions, Jude inquired, "Did you spend any time with the females?"

Hesitantly Sarah responded, "Err, no, actually I didn't. The men were always the ones approaching me and I found the woman rather standoffish. But now that I think about it, I didn't really make an effort to connect with women." Nodding Jude proceeded to educate Sarah on the women's perspectives that she had read about. As Sara and Jude conversed, I noticed how easily Sarah had accepted Jude's honest demeanor. Although Jude had caught her on an assumption, Sarah had not sprung to the defense; in fact she acknowledged the new wisdom.

♥   ♥   ♥

As Jude and I left the Indian restaurant, we headed to the closest lake to cool off. When we arrived at the beach, Jude's phone rang and she answered. After she answered, she proceeded to walk straight into the lake, holding her phone on her shoulder. Sensing it was Quinn, I suddenly felt twinges of jealousy; ridiculous I realize, but jealousy all the same.

As Jude chatted on the phone, I sat sulking on my towel, allowing my thoughts to drift away into self-pity. Upon reflection I realize my feelings of jealousy actually stemmed from my fear of abandonment. I was still scared Jude was going to leave me, though I knew deep down it was an irrational thought. When Jude had finished her conversation with Quinn, she returned to the towels and checked in.

Acting like a spoiled child, I sulked and answered I was doing fine and continued my doodling. Jude shook her head. "Seriously, Katie. What is bothering you?"

Due to my embarrassment of my feelings, I made up an excuse of feeling vulnerable.

"Vulnerable?!" Jude had exclaimed. "I don't buy it for a minute! Look, kid. I am not going to leave you for Quinn." As I tried to deny such feelings, she continued, "Trust me. I know you are fearful I am going to leave you but trust me I'm not." Silently nodding, I heard her words and absorbed them. I was acting extremely ridiculous and I knew it. I had allowed my own insecurities to filter into our friendship and was creating a heavy vibe. Moral of the story? Stay firm in your own shoes!

QUESTION: Who won this inner battle?

DARE: I DARE YOU TO CHECK IN WITH YOUR EGO'S MOTIVES'.
WHERE DOES IT LIE?

Later on that very night came the next of my series of personal meltdown. Go team me!

So, after Jude and I watched the latest student wizard solve mysteries, Harry Potters latest flick we located a spot where we could sleep for the night. Feeling unsettled and restless, I struggled to fall asleep. Sensing my inner battles, Jude started poking at me in an attempt to get me to speak truthfully. As I still maintained my stubborn nature, it took a two-hour session in order to get to the root of my issues. The following journal entry outlines my thoughts the next morning:

Good grief, Charlie Brown. Just when I thought I was out of the clearing, another invasion of the third kind. Seriously exhausting. It often feels as though I am never going to rise above all my issues surrounding me and that there is no light. I hate feeling like that. It is consuming, like the world is closing in on me. Pretty heavy stuff , but I want to release all this self-doubt. I can't believe how much I have inside me, it's insane. So, yeah, I have to say I am pretty much exhausted with this process. It's mentally, psychically, emotionally very tiring as I spend day after day being humbled till I am reduced to humble pie and try my new assertions on the world. (Writing this now, I know that the reason my process was so long and overdrawn was due to my own stubborn nature toward growth. Instead of accepting new knowledge and moving forward, I would let it fester for days and slowly build up. My unwillingness to let go of past behaviors led to an agonizing process. Moral of the story: DON'T

HOLD ON TO UNHEALTHY PATTERNS!) Personal growth feels like learning to walk again, wobbling. It's strange, foreign, exciting–all swirled into one human body. I still can't comprehend how one human body can contain so many mixed emotions within such a seemingly small cavity. Pretty crazy!

So as you can see, I was still processing and learning every day (which, by the way, I am still doing to this very moment).

♥   ♥   ♥

Gloria

Mid-July Jude and I decided to nest down in Vernon to take a crack at the book. We had managed to find a local park overlooking a lake. The park came with an electrical outlet, which meant we could use our computer (as well as our trusty toaster!) and wash in public facilities. The local park soon became our home as we set up shop under the band shelter. Morning after morning we would make our breakfast and plug away at the epic manuscript.

Due to the town's small population base, Jude and I stood out to many locals who roamed past the band shelter on their daily walks. One local in particular was extremely intrigued by our presence.

Gloria was an older woman in her sixties who had been on her spiritual path for several years. Having retired from her position as school counselor, Gloria had been enjoying the free life for six months. Instantly I saw a correlation between this woman and my father. Being from a classroom setting, they were accustomed to treating their children like students. Growing up, I was constantly grounded for speaking my mind, and eventually I stopped expressing my opinion. Years of suppression led to my final complacency. Instead of staying firm in my personal belief, I morphed into the perfect daughter, one who forgot about herself along the way. Forcing myself into the typical mold of going back to school, I ignored my true creative side by suppressing it with silent parental pressures.

HAVE YOU OPPRESSED YOURSELF?

♥ ♥ ♥

Mom and Dad

Having spent many wasted hours placing the blame on them for my issues, I feel it's time to flip the seemingly one-sided coin over. Throughout my path of self-discovery, I unraveled many truths about my old patterns and how I developed them. Obviously much behavior learned was stemmed from mirroring my parents. Saying that, again it is time for me to put on my big-girl underpants and grow some accountability. My parents learned many of their behaviors from their parents and hence copied what they saw. It truly is a vicious cycle until someone decides to work against the grain. For years I found it easy to use the excuse "My family has a past history of bad nerves" instead of choosing to fight for my health.

During the past year of discovery, I have learned that indeed I can take action for my own destiny by shifting my mindset. Instead of slipping into "poor me, poor me" syndrome, I chose to control my mind and thoughts.

I've said it once; I will say it another million times: you truly can do anything you put your mind to.

If you believe you will achieve!

If you believe all the excuses and issues that are handed to you on a silver platter, PLEASE be my guest!

Buy into a life that mirrors and imitates those negative influences around you. On the other side, you can choose to say NO THANKS. I think I will create my own opinions, my own truth and destiny. The choice is yours and yours alone.

After working through the many issues I had with my parents, I finally mustered enough courage to call them to have a true heart-to-heart in the middle of the summer. With my heart pounding, I dialed their number while my imagination drummed out the worst-case scenarios.

Reaching the answering machine, I left a message, feeling completely unresolved. Forty-five minutes later, my phone rang and peace of mind was mine for the taking. From the moment my mother's voice sounded over the wires, I stepped aside and allowed my emotions to do the talking. Miraculously she listened. Honestly, truly, cross my heart and hope to die, she listened. And she even agreed with many of the issues I discussed. It was incredible to have a conversation with my mother openly and honestly as though we were equals. My initial anxiety melted away as I felt that she was finally working at understanding my feelings.

As our heart-to-heart came to a close, Mom passed the phone over to my dad for his turn. Again I disclosed emotions I had kept inside for many years and opinions that had remained dormant dragons. Dad's reaction was similar to Mom's in that he treated me as an equal, not the little girl they had seen me as in the past.

Although it felt strange to be speaking so candidly with my parents, it also felt wonderfully freeing. All previous resentment and anger were releasing as I spoke my truth. Hanging up the phone that night, I felt many emotions churning:

- Relief
- Strength
- Courage
- Independence

Although we have many more discussions to have in the future, I know our relationship has forever been changed. Speaking from the depth of my heart demonstrated to my parents that I was worthy of their respect as an equal. Due to this opening, I know our relationship will continue to evolve at an emotional depth that will teach my family to love one another at an unconditional level.

IS YOUR FAMILY SILENT?
ARE YOU USING YOUR WORDS?

♥   ♥   ♥

During the week that we stayed in Vernon, I was silently stewing over the fact that we still had no fixed address. Growing increasingly frustrated, I started focusing my negative suppression on Jude. This went on for several days until the final showdown at an unsuspecting Vernon coffee shop.

As Jude challenged me on my behaviors, I told her to leave me alone and said that I didn't want to be around her. The instant I said it, I regretted it, but it was too late. She was out the door and I felt about the size of an ameba. That evening Jude expressed her feelings firmly and I was devastated. Due to our closeness, her words really affected me and would get right to my core.

The next day the tension continued. Finally, when I yelled at her that I couldn't continue any further, Jude shouted that she knew I was noncommittal and I always gave up. Silently stewing for a few minutes, I stormed over to her table and told her I was not a quitter. By this point my adrenaline was surging through my body. As Jude challenged me on my ability to take care of myself, I got even more angry.

In a funk, I started driving toward Kelowna to check my blood test results. Now this was when we hit a marker. Somewhere between Vernon and Kelowna, I switched on and suddenly everything became clearer to me than ever before. I realized how deeply ingrained the act of giving up was in my family. Till this point I truly hadn't recognized this pattern; it was really scary to see.

As I began truly, deeply understanding what Jude was saying, the most uncontrollable tears came flowing from my core. Inner shifts were indescribable as acceptance, peace, and love were being incorporated into my essence. Constraints and expectations seemed magically erased as I understood that the only expectations I was going to live for were ones I created.

Though this was an extraordinary day of clarity for me, my final eruption was yet to come. The one great thing I can say about meltdowns is the calmness after the storm. Once the chaotic debris has settled, the land is covered with new potential for growth and hope.

♥   ♥   ♥

We are all created equal. Somewhere along the way, man has been told that we are individuals, different and alien from one another. I beg to differ. My journeys through British Columbia brought many people, all who demonstrated aspects of my personality I was unaware of. They were all different shapes and sizes, but all had more similarities than differences, which indeed is the human existence. When given time to understand and notice, you realize we truly are all made of the same desires, fears, and dreams. You just have to look into your soul to view them in a different context. I have outlined several earth angels I met who served as wonderful reflections of myself.

Brent

Oh Brent. Brent was another Vernon local who seemed to gravitate toward Jude. One afternoon he had wheeled himself over to her picnic bench and struck up a conversation. As it turned out, Brent had been in a terrible car accident and had been a paraplegic for thirty-two years. During their interaction, Brent warned Jude he had very little short-term memory and wouldn't remember her in future meetings.

Denying his statement, Jude challenged Brent by reminding him he did have untouched memory reserves he could tap into at any time.

The following day Brent wheeled past Jude and looked up at her with glimmers of recognition upon his face. Smiling, she tapped him lightly on the arm and said, "I knew you would remember. You just had to make a point of it."

Returning her smile, Brent responded, "Since my accident, my life has been so mundane. Never any changes or is exciting."

Peering around the park, Jude responded, "Well, Mr. Brent, you seem to be out in the earth every single day. Perhaps you could pick up some local garbage around this park."

Acknowledging her words, Brent wheeled off toward the nearest coffee shop.

Two days later I noticed a flash of light zooming around the park. Upon further inspection, I realized it was Brent picking up fallen tree branches from the grass.

Silently cheering, I beamed at the enlightening lesson Brent had received. Jude had shown him that despite his disability he was still a vital part of his community.

A very heartwarming lesson to witness, I must say!

WHAT DO YOU THINK?
STILL FEEL LIKE COMPLAINING ABOUT LIFE?

♥   ♥   ♥

Jack and Diane

During our travels within the Okanagan, Jude and I spent many evenings meeting diverse travelers. One particular evening, we were staying at a strip mall parking lot in Kelowna. Fluffing my pillow for the night, I heard a man's voice inquire about our license plate.

"The old Klondike, eh? What brings you two ladies from the Yukon down to the Okanagan Valley?" Looking over my shoulder, I noticed an older couple pushing a shopping cart toward an older gray truck. When I explained our travels to the older couple, they stopped unloading their groceries and gave us their full attention. Jack and Diane began informing us that their son, Jack Jr., had Down's syndrome.

As the minutes ticked by, Jack and Diane spoke of the injustices they had experienced due to Jack Jr.'s disability. Prejudice and non-understanding seemed to be common occurrences for families with disabled children, and this couple was no different. Years of injustice had angered Jack, and his feelings became ignited during their discussion. While Jack continued venting his frustrations, I grew increasingly nervous and unsure of how to respond to him. After twenty minutes I finally retreated to Cassidy and sat down to ground myself. Unknown to me, whenever intense emotions were expressed, I would hold my breath, which caused a complete lack of oxygen to my brain. This worked wonders for scattering my concentration, I must say!

Eventually Jack stopped his angry venting and Diane began asking about our book. Looking her straight in the eyes, I openly communicated my year of personal growth and spirituality. Although I still felt intimidated at disclosing such personal information, I was learning to speak honestly, straight from the heart. Upon reflection I realize Jack and Diane were a marvelous example of complete unconditional love. They had raised a son with a disability and had faced many trials and tribulations during their endeavors. Listening to the sacrifices and undying commitment they had to their son

266

served as beautiful inspiration. Diane's eyes shone proudly as she discussed Jack Jr.'s talents and unique abilities, demonstrating that unconditional love comes in all shapes and sizes.

This interaction served as a wakeup call. Seeing their fierce commitment to their son, I thought about the different types of parents. Some will fight tooth and nail, pushing their children to brilliance; other parents allow their children to freefall, struggling to discover their true passions.

WHAT TYPE OF PARENTS WOULD YOU CHOOSE?

♥   ♥   ♥

The beginning of August brought with it several meltdowns, all self-induced. After my twelfth meltdown in a row, I determined that I needed to be alone. Repeating old patterns of running from my issues, I dropped Jude off at her son's and headed out into the woods to continue writing. Upon reflection I realize I was taking a serious step back on my path of spiritual growth. Jude had often explained how easy it was to resort back to old behaviors if I didn't actively take initiative for my own growth. Did I listen? Nope! In one ear and out the other, I'm afraid to report!

Dropping Jude off in Grande Prairie, I cruised solo to seek a quiet, non-distracting campground where I could write the book. Funny thing about my constant quest to locate a place without distractions was that I created them for myself! Anyway, back to the tale.

Despite my past background in outdoor pursuits, my campfire tactics were extremely pathetic and I managed to project "ridiculous city girl" across the entire campground. Thanks to my friendly neighbors at campsite number twenty-eight, I managed to cook a hotdog before pushing off to bed.

My second day at the campsite, I noticed a gang of kids playing on the swings. Unable to resist the distraction, I jumped out of Cassidy and headed over to introduce myself. Even in the middle of nowhere, I was still capable of creating all sorts of distractions for myself.

Introductions turned into a game of catch with an adorable little girl called Cassie. After an epic over-the-shoulder catch, Cassie invited me over to meet her mother. Agreeing, I put down my glove and sauntered over to their yellow-and-white trailer.

Sitting down inside, a blond woman stuck out her hand as a greeting. Her name was Sherrie and she looked about my age. Over coffee we soon found out we had many similarities.

Over the next week I spent my evenings with Sherrie and her little ones, Randal and Cassie. During my visits, I got to witness firsthand what it would be like to be a single mama. Holy moly! I had thought.
And I felt that personal growth was energy-consuming. Needless to say, I ate some very humble pie!

Watching Sherrie, I felt many parallels between us. She had a big heart, extreme caretaking qualities, and worrywart tendencies. On the flip side, she allowed herself to be spread so thin that she left no time for her own wellness. I realized that I easily could be in Sherrie's situation. As we discussed Sherrie's issues and dysfunctional relationships further, I struggled not to interfere with her life path. Her tales sounded exactly like mine, and I knew where she was coming from. Remembering Jude's teachings of detachment, I stopped my caretaking and sat back. Miraculously I felt an enormous weight being lifted as I didn't personally take on Sherrie's issues. What a magic skill detachment is!

Sherrie taught me many things about myself I hadn't noticed in the past. Her kind spirit was slowly being crushed through others taking advantage of her. It was not until I had met Sherrie that I truly came to understand what I had looked like during my caretaking days: tired, burned out, and completely scattered.

♥   ♥   ♥

Elsie

Elise was a safety officer on an oil rig site,
and I met her late one evening. After our formal introductions, Elise inquired what I was doing in the middle of nowhere. I responded by explaining about my book. Interested by the mention of spirituality, Elsie dug deeper. Once I had given my brief synopsis of the book, she proceeded to indulge in the horrible details from her past. Past physical abuse had led her too many dead ends involving drugs and alcohol.

As she described her personal path through hypnosis, I began feeling insignificant. Who was I to write this book about personal hardship when I had never been a part of such awful experiences? During my inner contemplation, Elsie reached over and handed me two magnetic beads. Proclaiming them as a gift, she insisted that I have them. This was her way of passing her energy over to me.

Upon my arrival back to Grande Prairie, I recounted my meeting Elsie with Jude. As we debriefed, Jude reminded me that although I had not been a victim of physical abuse, I had been one of emotional stifling, which could lead to the same symptoms. Elsie had served as a messenger to inform me that as a woman she held on way too long to unhealthy patterns, which was exactly what I had been doing.

♥   ♥   ♥

Radium Hot Springs

Magical, effervescent, uplifting: words that barely touch on the essence of the Radium Hot Springs. Nested away in the spectacular Rocky Mountains, Radium Hot Springs provided visitors with an ultimate relaxing experience through its warm, inviting pools.

Nearing the end of our voyage, Jude and I decided to unwind with a soak and massage at the pristine location.

After a long decision process, Jude opted for a cranial massage, which is essentially a scalp massage that releases blockages and tensions from your brain. Jude emerged from her session glowing and radiating warmth. The sheer vision of seeing Jude after her cranial was enough for me to switch my session. As the massage therapist worked his strong hands over my scalp, I could feel my over analytical mind releasing its obsessive thoughts. Upon the completion of the massage, I slunk back into the warm springs and closed my eyes. Glancing around, I saw natural surroundings, warmth, and tranquility: all of the important aspects any animal from earth needed for a truly content existence.

During my cranial, Jude met a wonderful principal from Grande Prairie, Alberta. During their discussion, the principal, Derek, had informed Jude about the increasing issues they were finding with teenage girls.

Jude had explained the concept of the book we were writing and how it related to young females learning to be accountable for their actions.

Enthused at the idea, Derek disclosed it as exactly what young girls needed to learn to stand on their own two feet and not rely on men for their futures.

"It is as though they don't even think about the future. Or the girls simply assume that once they find a man everything will be magically transformed. It doesn't work that way."

Hearing Derek's words served as a wonderful affirmation that Jude and I were on the right track.

Two hours later we met a woman who served as yet another serendipitous affirmation. This lady was seated directly across from us as we were diligently working on the book. Looking from Jude to me, the middle-aged woman asked what we were doing. Sensing it was my duty to respond, I explained it was a tell-all story about my personal growth and discovery. I continued by discussing how young females weren't taking responsibility for their own destinies. Raising her eyebrows, she questioned how a twenty-six-year-old could have enough issues to write a book about hardships.

Biting my tongue, I responded back that all females, no matter what age, have issues; it's just a matter of discussing them out in the open.

Accepting my words, the woman pressed on for more information. As I disclosed that Jude was my mentor who taught about self-esteem and belief systems, the woman seemed skeptical.

Intimidated by Jude's presence, she turned to me and said, "And what are Jude's qualifications to be teaching about women's esteem?" Amazed at her cowardly nature, I struggled to find the words to explain Jude. "Well, Jude is a female just like anyone else and has lived through many different circumstances and situations. Due to her life experiences, Jude has chosen to pass her knowledge down to younger females in hopes that they make positive choices for themselves."

As I prepared to continue, I could physically fell Jude's blood boiling.

Unable to contain her anger, Jude looked up from her typing and responded, "I personally don't feel you need a degree in order to be a teacher. Young females are long overdue for a wake-up call. I just watched you and your daughter interact and I have to tell you, it wasn't a great scene. She showed you absolutely no respect. None. And why? Probably because you have no control over her!"

Flabbergasted by Jude's honest words, the woman sheepishly nodded and preoccupied herself with the two nearby dogs. Eventually she grew bored with us and went off toward the parking lot, tail between her legs.

Meeting that woman served as a wonderful affirmation that women of all ages and sizes truly did need to learn self-esteem and assertion. Because of her intellectual nature, this woman refused to understand how Jude could teach about personal growth and transformation. It saddened me to realize her judgments toward post-secondary education. According to her belief, individuals needed a degree in order to teach and enlighten people about universal truths.

Having spent many moons with Jude and her wisdom, my judgments had been eliminated regarding post-secondary knowledge. Life skills and spirituality lessons weren't acquired in a classroom stetting. No, ma'am. They were an out-in-the-field experience that I got to practice every day. Self-esteem and belief in oneself came from this school of hard knocks and were applied through real life situations. You can read all you want about self-enlightenment, but until you live, breathe, and exude it, it simply won't be absorbed into your core.

♥   ♥   ♥

Kindness

"Kindness is the language which the deaf can hear and the blind can see."
–Mark Twain

Throughout the entire journey, and to this day, Twain's words ring true as I contemplate the many random acts of sheer kindness I witnessed from strangers and newfound friends. Ironically enough, I had originally planned on creating a kindness campaign prior to our voyage to Montreal. The reality was something completely different.

From Vancouver, Canada to Cassadega, Florida, strangers acknowledged my personal journey and reciprocated with gifts straight from the heart. Gifts of kindness came in different shapes and sizes, from many different walks of life. Derek was charitable and helpful with his offerings. During our short-lived time in Montreal, he would invite us to lunch and provide information on city life. His ultimate offering was to give us our cuddly computer, Blue, which has remained a loyal travel companion during our journey and book-writing marathons.

Down in Florida, our new found friend named Stan opened up his home to offer our smelly, sand-ridden bodies a bed and a shower. Stan's kind offer meant more to me than any money or material wealth ever could. His generosity served to show me that warmth and love come in many different forms.

Another beautiful gift of kindness was shown in the incredible spirits we met in the most random spots. Faye and Teresa, the two earth angels we met in New York state, demonstrated unconditional acceptance as they sat and listened to Jude discuss my spiritual journey. The look of pure serenity and tranquility upon their faces was calming, as I felt comfortable showing vulnerability.

Traveling further south in Arizona, we stumbled across Kelly, a man with an incredible gift of music. After a deep conversation about global issues, Kelly showed us a touching video that brought many emotions. As I allowed tears of sorrow for the earth to flow, Kelly looked up at me with compassion, giving me the gift of acceptance.
In addition to Kelly's warm demeanor and kindness, he gave us a copy of his CD, which was composed of the most melodic flute music I had ever heard. His gesture was so simple yet touched my heart deeply.

A hop, skip, and a jump into the state of Oregon and we encountered a glorious couple by the name of Bob and Shirley. Their zest for life and deep religious faith radiated from their souls. Inviting us over to their breakfast table, Bob and Shirley gave us the beautiful gift of words and truth. During our breakfast, Bob explained that in addition to him being a pastor, he and Shirley were clowns who spread love to children in small, isolated communities. Essentially they showed me how dedicating one's life to helping and healing humanity created incredible satisfaction and childlike glee. This was information I already knew but still needed to witness for myself. Ah! Stubborn Capricorn!

Upon reflection I realize the entire journey was essentially the most miraculous endeavor of kindness I had been oblivious to. The woman seated in the passenger seat had demonstrated the most profound lesson regarding unconditional love.

Through thick and thin, fear and enlightenment, Jude shone through like a ray of hope. During my darkest times, her honesty and compassion pulled me through and brought inspiration into a seemingly void vessel. To this day I am rather unsure how this type of kindness fell upon me, but this I promise: I fully intend on informing everyone of the magic one woman's belief brought into my world.

Needless to say, I have lived through a journey of many painful, silly days. It was the light of warmth, love, and words that pulled me through those days that seemed never-ending. Just when I would lose faith in myself, beautiful spirits and silent heroes would fall upon my path, spreading hope with their gentle gestures of kindness.

♥   ♥   ♥

Living in the Van

Seeing as how Cassidy was such an integral part of our experience, it is only appropriate that I discuss the relationship we had.

From the first day we left Vancouver, I had terrible attitude toward the entire scenario of sleeping in the van. After all, I had already played the role of tree-planting hippy; I was ready to move onto more glamorous roles, right?

WRONG! I have since learned it doesn't matter two toots where you live when you don't feel good about yourself inside, but you couldn't have told that to me at the time.

Anyway, during the North American journey, there were many times when I took my anger about myself out on Cassidy. Instead of admitting that I was unhappy inside, I projected outward toward my beloved minivan. All she ever did was love me and create freedom within my life, yet I still took my frustrations out on her. Many times I would flail my arms in the air and yell, "I can't do this anymore, Jude; I can't live in a van." Reading between the lines, what I honestly meant was "I can't live with myself right now! I can't bear to look at my deeply ingrained issues anymore." However, my old pattern of escapism didn't work this time. After I would have these meltdowns in the middle of nowhere—and I mean nowhere—I had absolutely no option but to get back into Cassidy, a.k.a. deal with my issues.

As I now reflect, I realize Cassidy was simply a projection of how much I couldn't stand the internal issues I had manifested over many years. Poor beautiful 1996 minivan. It wasn't her fault I couldn't stand myself. I do have to admit she handled my meltdowns magnificently, not breaking down once throughout our entire quest.

♥   ♥   ♥

Our British Columbia summer adventures led us to many places I never would have dreamed of exploring. In the many obscure places we visited, I was still visiting strange dark places within my soul. Though I had felt my past issues were resolved, I still possessed self-doubt and self-sabotaging qualities. That's the sneaky thing about old self-destructive patterns: they are often so deep inside your core from years of denial that they are like cement to move. In fact, the only natural disaster that could remove such blockages was a volcano. And that is exactly what was rumbling inside me. So began the tale of Mount Katie and her final eruption that cleared the path for a brighter destiny.

Similar to ancient volcanoes, I had been stewing in negative lava for several days. Bubbles and rumbles levitated through my soul as I suppressed my emotions. It was only a matter of time till my mounting negative vibes blast out upon the world.

Pressure mounted as I allowed self-destructive thoughts to layer on top of one another:

- You can't do this anymore!
- Jude is going to leave anyway, so why not push her away before she leaves?
- You aren't really going to write an entire book; you never finish anything you start.

Like platelets of the earth, evil thoughts compiled, creating the perfect setting for an explosion of colossal proportions. The day of the eruption was all quiet on the western front. I had been silently stewing as the pressure built to intolerable levels. After Jude and I ate supper in a small northern town, I felt a dark shift in me as though a permanent rain cloud had fixated itself over my soul.

Unable to contain my piping hot lava, I let out a quick toot, exclaiming that I was going to stay up all evening to complete the book. Staring at me in disbelief, Jude shook her head and stated that it would be impossible to finish in one evening. That was all Mount Katie needed to hear in order to unleash the dormant dragon. Words of contempt, anger, and impatience exploded out of my mouth, oozing negativity into the universe.

Sparks of red-hot lava spread everywhere as I exhaled the bubbling pressure from within. The words flowed down from the peak, eliminating all living creatures in sight.

From the moment I allowed my eruption to explode, I realized the aftermath of my behaviour. Demolition and destruction had ruined our entire atmosphere and Jude had retaliated. Claiming that she could no longer watch me sabotage myself, she explained that she was off my path and wanted to be dropped off at her son's place in

Grande Prairie. Instant remorse and regret flowed over my body as I heard her firm words. By allowing an internal volcano to build into an explosion of negative dust particles, I had wished away the storm that could cool the inferno.

It was in that moment I hit rock bottom. Silently surveying the destruction I had manifested, I frightened myself. How did I allow this to happen? It was in that moment in time that I truly understood how much self-hatred I held for myself. Due to a complete lack of self-love, I had created a self-destructive monster within that took no prisoners and left landscapes full of isolation and sorrow.

After the volcanic explosion had settled across the atmosphere, the true reality of my behavior settled in.

Jude was leaving.

Sleeping a total of three minutes that night, I awoke with feelings of dark regret. As we drove toward Grande Prairie, I felt completely devoid of energy and vigor. Volcano Katie had charged forward and taken all the life force from within. After two hours of stony silence, Jude inquired about my mental state. Exposing my vulnerable belly, I informed her of my feelings of remorse, regret and all other emotions volcanoes feel after their catastrophic event.

Jude looked over with concern and bewilderment and expressed her sadness about my feelings of low self-worth. She went on to state that she would give me one last chance to collect myself and rebuild. The shaky foundation within me shifted to solid hope filled my core. The floodgates to my soul opened as I started the cleansing process.

Tears of joy. Tears of release. Tears of sorrow, inspiration, and hope.

Pure, clean water flowed from my body as I purified all toxins from within.

After the flood had washed away all my sorrows and self-doubt, I stood on the side of the highway allowing rays of sunshine to refuel my empty tank.

Hope filtered into my soul like oxygen to a dying man. Breathing it through my pores, I felt a quiet strength take over my entire essence. Armed with inspiration from Jude and other mentors, I visualized the person I wanted to become: calm, serene, deep, compassionate, and accepting. The tears from earlier flowed effortlessly into a sparkling lake of hope—hope for a bright, positive future that consisted of inner peace and tranquility.

My inner dreams of inspiring and helping women appeared clearer than ever as though my tears had removed all murkiness from their manifestation. Visions of sharing my insights with other women appeared in my mind's eye full of bright vivid colors. Yellow, red, green, and blue all swirled together as I imagined the infinite possibilities that would emerge from my newfound belief in myself. Suddenly insurmountable roadblocks seemed lifted as
I understood the pure magic of self-belief and self-love. It has the power to heal even the darkest of dragons into powerful rays of hope and sunshine.

My dormant third eye blinked open and shared its foreseeing visions of the future. My subconscious showed me this scene: a glorious structure complied of stone, brick, and wood based on a lake sitting in a lush, green countryside. Romantic willow trees swayed gently in the wind as a haunting cry from a loon echoed across the land. The faint scent of spicy vanilla enfolds visitors, creating the undeniable sensation of home. Twinkling Christmas lights wrapped delicately around cedar posts illuminate the atmosphere, creating a tingling feeling inside. The resident pooch named Finnigan approaches all incoming visitors as though they were long-lost soul mates. Gentle flute music (courtesy of our new Arizona pal Kelly) drifts across the property, soothing visitors to their essence. Beneath the swaying willow trees awaits a red-and-white canoe eager to paddle to faraway, unexplored territories. Freshly-baked chocolate chip cookies sit upon the marble counter, daring passerbyes to resist their decadent nature.

A crackling fire warms chilly bones in a giant living room, complete with furniture fit for royalty. The high ceilings give the impression of eternal hope that has nowhere to go but upward.

And at the heart of the setting stands Jude and I marveling in the magical manifestation of our dreams. Eyes sparkling, we share a smile full of love and hope and a greeting to all who enter our self-awareness retreat.

Looking out across the unbelievable scenarios, I notice a soft ripple radiating across the lake. It starts out small and begins expanding across the crystal-clear water, creating quite the spectacular ripple effect.

Glowing with understanding, I reminisce on the wise words Jude had stated during the early stages of our friendship:

"Everything you do has a ripple effect no matter what the size. Events and acts of kindness are recognized and echoed throughout the universe on such a scale we can't even comprehend them. Don't ever feel as though your actions go unnoticed, no way. Indeed it is small actions of kindness and love that ever create the magical effects of changes upon people hearts."

♥   ♥   ♥

WINTER

The blustery blasts of snowfall bought with them inner contemplation as this flying spirit learned what life felt like on the ground, firmly planted. Eliminations of unnecessary wastes, materials, and relationships were made as I sat in winter hibernation.

Still young and naïve, I was questing after external missions. Save the world. Yes indeed, that is what I intended to do. Mistake 4837! Silly rabbit, you can't search externally for inner peace, now can you.

My spiritual belief and foundation began solidifying as my elemental teacher instructed me in ageless tactics of living a fulfilled life. Chilly dispositions were discovered as I plunged into the avalanche of my soul. Ice-cold frost had developed around my heart, making it impossible for my true love and inner beauty to shine for all to see. Grabbing the ever-essential tool of communication, I slowly began breaking off crystallized ice from my spirit through discussing issues from my past. Through a long and steady process, I was making way for the dawning of spring growth and regeneration.

SPRING

Rain showers poured down, bringing with them the ultimate soil for change. Blessed with a clear slate, I embarked on the process of planting new seeds in hope of a new crop of hope and bright future. Flowers of all colors of the rainbow were the expectation I had placed upon myself. I was changing and growing but still maintained the impatient nature of a spring chicken. Clucking my way through situations, I was learning to be honest and take responsibility for my actions. After all, I was the keeper of my soul and no one else, so could I truly point the blame at my old weed-invested garden? I think not!

My newly acquired green thumb as a spiritual being was practicing its skills through many, MANY attempts at growing that magnificent desert rose. Learning patience and kindness, I tenderly watered my new seedlings, speaking to them with thoughts of self-love and acceptance. Old negative thoughts were tossed aside as I learned the magical ingredient in any flourishing garden: love.

SUMMER

Summer months shone brightly, promising the hope of a future full of meaning and compassion. Rays of light beamed upon my world as my newly planted seeds were shyly peeking their new buds up from the spring's soil. Excited at the vision of hope, my new self shot forward, ready to take on the world and spread love. The impossible seemed surmountable now that I had armed myself with a rock-solid foundation, deeply rooted into the earth. Acknowledging my essential presence within our magnificent earth, I was filled with a purpose greater than myself. Embracing my newly acquired shell, I set out into the world ready to share my personal growth from an empty dirt patch to a fabulously moist garden filled with infinite possibilities.

The four seasons all molded into one another as I experienced the natural cycle as any being of the earth. Every day I was discovering new ways of perceiving the universe. Self-destructive patterns were being pulled out of my garden of paradise and I was learning how to grow new, healthy patterns. Old opinions and judgments were being tossed out as Jude opened my mind to viewing the world through a sixth-sensory perception. Reds came alive, emotions real, and flying was made possible through her teachings. As I write this, I am still in the ever-changing process called change, and though I love it, I also find it very difficult. There are many times when I automatically react to particular situations using my old dysfunctional habits. I have had to learn to be easy on myself and comprehend that spiritual growth is a lifelong process, one I get to practice every day. There's never a final ending. As long as I know I am doing the very best I can, I am charging forward, curious what next challenge destiny will throw in my path.

♥   ♥   ♥

Rather grumpily, I decided to patrol the entire neighborhood in search of enough spare change to purchase some bread from Wal-Mart.

As I warily walked around the North Vancouver streets desperately seeking salvation from my hunger, a bright light bulb shone within. Many souls lived everyday in such desolate situations. In that moment I had the opportunity to experience what it felt like to be truly homeless, completely dependant upon what the present moment brought to me. Block after block I marched, hoping for a glimpse of a toonie or better yet a vibrant blue five dollar bill full of possibilities. My heart sank further and further as my eyes scanned the penniless roads.

Just as defeat was settling in, I spotted it. A shiny, perfect 0.25 cent piece. Grabbing it with my icy hands, I felt a moment of true gratitude. Though it was only 0.25, at that moment it represented the difference between a growlie tummy and pumpkin seed butter sandwiches. Clutching the silver coin in my hand, I hastily made my way back to Cassidy (the green minivan a.k.a. home).

Upon reflection, I gained such an incredible universal lesson. Although I had no money to my name, I was still living in abundance. Even in the darkest of hours, toughest of times I knew that I had a belief within myself that all would be taken care of. I had a wonderful friend supporting me and that warmed my heart. Homeless people often do not have either of those essential aspects within their lives; an inner belief or strong support system. At the end of the day, I always knew deep down that the universe would never dish out what I couldn't handle, I was truly grateful.